Race after
Sartre

SUNY series, Philosophy and Race

Robert Bernasconi and T. Denean Sharpley-Whiting

Race after Sartre

Antiracism, Africana Existentialism, Postcolonialism

Edited by **Jonathan Judaken**

Published by State University of New York Press, Albany

© 2008 State University of New York Press, Albany

All rights reserved

Printed in the United States of America

No part of this book may be used or reproduced in any manner whatsoever without written permission. No part of this book may be stored in a retrieval system or transmitted in any form or by any means including electronic, electrostatic, magnetic tape, mechanical, photocopying, recording or otherwise without the prior permission in writing of the publisher.

For information, contact State University of New York Press, Albany, NY
www.sunypress.edu

Production by Ryan Morris
Marketing by Michael Campochiaro
This book was printed on acid-free, 50% recycled paper.

Library of Congress of Cataloging-in-Publication Data

Race after Sartre: Antiracism, Africana Existentialism, Postcolonialism / edited by Jonathan Judaken.
    p. cm.
Includes bibliographical references and index.
ISBN 978-0-7914-7547-8 (hardcover : alk. paper)
ISBN 978-0-7914-7548-5 (pbk. : alk. paper)
  1. Racism. 2. Phenomenological sociology. 3. Sociology—Philosophy. 4. Sartre, Jean-Paul, 1905-1980—Criticism and interpretation. I. Judaken, Jonathan, 1968–

HT1521 . R2333 2008
305.8—DC22

2007047993

To Mom and Dad
To Mark and Loren and David
To Jaynie
And to families everywhere emancipating themselves
from the bounds of "race"

Contents

Acknowledgments — ix

Introduction — 1

Part I: Sartre on Race and Racism

1. Sartre on Racism: From Existential Phenomenology to Globalization and "the New Racism" — 23
   Jonathan Judaken

2. Skin for Sale: Race and *The Respectful Prostitute* — 55
   Steve Martinot

3. The Persistence of Colonialism: Sartre, the Left, and Identity in Postcolonial France, 1970–1974 — 77
   Paige Arthur

Part II: Sartre and Antiracist Theory

4. Race: From Philosophy to History — 99
   Christian Delacampagne

5. Sartre and Levinas: Philosophers against Racism and Antisemitism — 113
   Robert Bernasconi

6. European Intellectuals and Colonial Difference: Césaire and Fanon beyond Sartre and Foucault — 129
   George Ciccariello-Maher

Part III: Sartre and Africana Existentialism

7. Sartre and Black Existentialism 157
   Lewis R. Gordon

8. Sartre and South African Apartheid 173
   Mabogo P. More

Part IV: Sartre and the Postcolonial Turn

9. Difference/Indifference: Sartre, Glissant, and the Race of Francophone Literature 193
   Richard H. Watts

10. Violence, Nonviolence: Sartre on Fanon 211
    Judith Butler

Contributors 233

Index 237

Acknowledgments

An edited volume is by its nature a collective enterprise. In this case, it germinated from a number of panels at the North American Sartre Society (NASS) that addressed the topic of race and racism in 2005. This was the year of Sartre's centennial, and I had already attended many conferences on his work. But the palpable excitement generated by discussions of Sartre and race made evident that this was an under-explored area of his work whose time had come. It became clear that a deeper interrogation of his oeuvre around this theme was warranted.

I shared my interest with Ronald Aronson whose enthusiasm and suggestions were formative for the project. We agreed that it would be important to have Lewis Gordon contribute. From my first contacts with him, his generosity of spirit and his electro-charged mind helped to propel the book forward, including his suggestions for additional contributors. My colleague and collaborator, Robert Bernasconi, quickly recognized the value of the enterprise and adopted it for the "Philosophy and Race" series. His support and stewardship have been exemplary.

I had already been working on the topic for some time in the course of completing my first book, *Jean-Paul Sartre and the Jewish Question: Anti-antisemitism and the Politics of the French Intellectual* (Lincoln and London: University of Nebraska Press, "Texts and Contexts," 2006). Both of these works owe much to Sander Gilman, the series editor at Nebraska, the doyen of the new Jewish cultural studies, and a vanguard contributor to critical race studies. The book on the Jewish Question would not have taken the form it did without his input and advice, and my own thinking about how racism functions has been much influenced by his work.

Just as the book was going to press, I sadly learned of the untimely death of Christian Delacampagne, a reader for my first book and a contributor to this volume. His chapter was surely one of the last things this erudite and prolific writer and magnanimous soul was able to pen. He will be missed.

My own contributions to the volume were aided by the pointed comments of Jennifer Geddes and Torbjörn Wandel, whose time and care with my prose has hopefully led to a clarity and distinctness in the presentation of Sartre's ideas that one hopes he would have embraced. This book has also benefited by the insightful suggestions of its two anonymous readers. The time to put it all together was made possible by the University of Memphis. It was completed during my tenure on a Center for Advanced Holocaust Studies Fellowship at the Center for Advanced Holocaust Studies (CAHS) at the United States Holocaust Memorial Museum (2006–2007), for which I am most grateful. Many hours were spent in that great chamber of reflection, the main reading room at the Library of Congress. That magnificent Renaissance revivalist structure and the wonderful librarians who so helpfully navigate it, made a fabulous environment for research and thinking, as did the CAHS.

The book is dedicated to my wife, my siblings, and my parents. All of we "southerners," whether in South Africa or Baton Rouge, were raised in an environment saturated by race thinking, which conditioned how and where we lived and thought and with whom we associated, such that it structured our place in the world. And yet these structures and systems of perception were denied. Hopefully this work will contribute to rendering visible what racism seeks to make invisible and it will help efface the lines that divide social, economic, and cultural differences into "races."

We gratefully acknowledge the permission to republish parts or all of the following:

Robert Bernasconi, "Sartre und Levinas: Philosopher gegen Rassismus und Antisemitismus" in *Verfehlte Begegnung. Levinas und Sartre als philosophischen Zeitgenossen*, ed. Thomas Bedorf und Andreas Cremonini (Munich: Wilhelm Fink, 2005): 205–22

Judith Butler, "Violence, Nonviolence: Sartre on Fanon," *Graduate Faculty Philosophy Journal* 27.1 (2006): 3–24 © Judith Butler.

George Ciccariello-Maher, "The Internal Limits of the European Gaze: Intellectuals and the Colonial Difference," *Radical Philosophy Review* 9.2 (2006): 139–65.

Lewis R. Gordon, "Sartre et l'existentialisme Noir," *Cités: Philosophie, Politique, Histoire* (2005): 85–97.

Introduction
Jonathan Judaken

To claim that Jean-Paul Sartre was a major contributor to antiracist politics, critical race studies,[1] Africana existentialism, and postcolonialism[2] may surprise some readers. Unlike the now canonic works of some of his interlocutors—Léopold Senghor and Aimé Césaire; Albert Memmi and Frantz Fanon; and Richard Wright and James Baldwin—Sartre contributed no major theoretical treatise on these topics. He offered no systematic and coherent account of racism and ventured no programmatic approach to undoing its manifold operations. And yet, as the chapters in this volume show, there are few figures who have had a greater influence on the critical theories applied to "race"[3] and whose own praxis served so consistently to destabilize racial and colonial oppression.

So why have Sartre's writings on "race" and racism not been given the salience they deserve? First, new directions in race theory opened up in the 1980s,[4] a period in which Sartre's work was doubly eclipsed: by approaches influenced by structuralism and poststructuralism,[5] and by Sartre's long commitment to a radical Marxist politics that seemed to be crashing like the Berlin Wall.[6] Second, beyond *Réflexions sur la question juive* (*Antisemite and Jew*), Sartre wrote no major tome on the topic of racism per se. Many of his key insights were interspersed in prefaces to the works of others and in his anticolonial interventions. While the most important of these were collected in *Situations V* (*Colonialism and Neocolonialism*), this text was only relatively recently translated into English.[7] Third, Sartre was a "dead white male." He had no lived experience of the racial gaze or institutionalized discrimination, and it has been primarily those victimized by racism who have emerged as its most eloquent critics and most listened to voices, for they know of what they speak.

This volume provides a corrective to this lacuna. It not only offers an overview of Sartre's approach to racism but also considers the trajectories of his influence on other theorists, and suggests the fecundity of his antiracist strategies for combating racism today. As such, *Race after Sartre* will certainly be of interest to Sartre scholars, since the effort to elucidate rigorously his approach to "race" has only recently been taken up.[8] In several chapters, Sartre is situated historically, and the impact of his involvements opposing antisemitism, colonialism, and racism, and his struggles alongside immigrants and minorities on the evolution of his oeuvre is explored. All of the chapters treat Sartre sympathetically, even as they broach the criticisms that have been raised concerning his thought.

The book demonstrates once again Sartre's ability to write powerfully and compellingly against oppression. His strident interventions remain a model of Leftist politics in a globalized age when "racialized social systems"[9] continue to operate at the micro and macro levels. Moreover, Sartre's novel and perceptive theories about the psychology of prejudice, the configurations of racial formations, and the mechanisms by which racism is rearticulated in a de jure postsegregationist, postcolonial, racially heterogeneous world are enumerated.[10] Because of this, *Race after Sartre* will also appeal to scholars concerned with the philosophy of "race," critical race theories, postcolonial theory, intellectual history, and French and Francophone literature.

The Stages on Sartre's Way

As these chapters attest, Sartre's phenomenology of the racial oppressor and his revolutionary solutions to alienation, marginalization, and systemic exploitation changed over time. "In 1944 he thought that any situation could be transcended by a subjective movement," notes Simone de Beauvoir, but by "1951, he knew that circumstances sometimes rob us of our transcendence; against them, no individual salvation is possible, only a collective struggle."[11] Three key vectors affected this shift in how Sartre viewed racism and antisemitism: the changing contexts he lived through, the political struggles he was immersed in, and the transformations in his intellectual itinerary from existentialism to existential Marxism.

The historical situations in which he wrote about antisemitism and racism underwent powerful transformations from the 1930s to the 1970s. Born on June 21, 1905, he was baptized Jean-Paul-Charles-Aymard Sartre. After his father died in 1906, he was raised by his doting mother and his Protestant grandfather, Charles Schweitzer, to become a greater intellectual figure than Albert Schweitzer, his Nobel Prize–winning cousin. A Dreyfusard, but still fond of Jewish jokes,[12] his grandfather home-schooled the young Sartre in the classics until he entered the training grounds for France's intellectual elite in Paris—Lycée Henri-IV and Louis-le-Grand—where

Sartre began to publish his earliest works even before entering the École Normale Supérieure (ENS) in 1924. Sartre's entourage included the brilliant Beauvoir, Paul Nizan, and Raymond Aron. This cadre sought to transcend the neo-Kantianism of Léon Brunschvicg that then reigned supreme at the ENS and within academic philosophy in France without recourse to the subjectivism of Henri Bergson. Sartre, in particular, wanted to overcome the false dichotomy between subject and object.

Providing the methodological route was the introduction into France of Husserlian and Heideggerian phenomenology.[13] The classic, albeit somewhat mythical story[14] of Sartre's own introduction to phenomenology was recounted by Beauvoir in *La force de l'âge* (*Prime of Life*):

> Sartre was greatly attracted by what he had heard of German phenomenology. Raymond Aron, preparing a thesis on history, was studying Husserl. When he came to Paris (1932), we spent an evening together at the Bec de Gaz, rue Montparnasse; we ordered the specialty of the house: apricot cocktails. Aron pointed to his glass: "You see, my friend, if you are a phenomenologist, you can talk about this cocktail, and that is philosophy." Sartre grew pale with excitement, or nearly so. This was precisely what he had wished for years: to talk of things as he touched them and that this was philosophy. Aron convinced him that this was exactly what fitted his preoccupations: to transcend the opposition of idealism and realism, to affirm at the same time the sovereignty of consciousness and the presence of the world as given to us. On the boulevard Saint Michel he [Sartre] bought the book on Husserl by Levinas, and he was in such a hurry to inform himself that, while walking, he leafed through the book, whose pages he had not even cut.... Sartre decided to study it seriously, and at Aron's instigation, he took the necessary steps for succeeding his "friend" at the Institute Français de Berlin the following year.[15]

He would spend 1933 and 1934 in Berlin as the Nazis consolidated power, immersing himself in Husserl's *Ideas*. He also attended a few of Heidegger's lectures the year he served as the Nazi-appointed rector of the University of Freiburg. The product of this labor was a radicalization and critique of Husserl's transcendental ego, *La Transcendance de l'ego* (*The Transcendence of the Ego*, 1937). "Consciousness is purely and simply consciousness of being conscious of that object," Sartre maintained.[16] Consciousness thus has no interiority; for Sartre *it is nothing* other than its intentional activity. The existential implications of this insight were worked out in Sartre's modernist masterpiece, the philosophical novel *La nauseé* (*Nausea*, 1938),[17] which gave him his first dose of literary renown, even as France was itself becoming polarized by the threat of fascism rising. It would be followed shortly by *Le Mur* (*The Wall*, 1939), which included a novella, *L'enfance d'un chef*

("Childhood of a Leader"), that was a biting critique of the extreme Right, as well as the antisemitism that circulated widely across the political spectrum in the 1930s. This text was Sartre's most overt political engagement of the interwar years, and it established the contours of his existential critique of antisemitism.[18]

Sartre would become an intellectual star in 1943,[19] the year he published his magnum opus *L'être et le néant* (*Being and Nothingness*). The same year the first of his plays, *Les mouches* (*The Flies*), was staged in the heart of Nazi-occupied Paris. His sustained elaboration of freedom as what constituted the human condition flew in the face of both Nazi and Vichy ideology, with indigenous French "state antisemitism" becoming a pillar of the new regime.[20] Sartre spent the war years, in his words, as a "writer who resisted, not a resistor who wrote."[21] His prolific output under the jackboot of the Nazis—two novels, two plays, five screenplays, eleven literary-critical articles—made him an international celebrity following World War II.[22]

As the iron curtain of the Cold War descended, Sartre became a vociferous critic of colonialism. He was also an early and forceful patron of the negritude intellectuals. He served on the editorial board of *Présence Africaine*, the major journal and later publishing house of black francophone writers and artists founded by Alioune Diop. Elevating its visibility in the French intellectual field, he contributed the preface "Présence noire" ("Black Presence") to the first issue of the review in 1947.[23] "Orphée noir" ("Black Orpheus"), Sartre's preface to Léopold Senghor's 1948 *Anthologie de la nouvelle poésie nègre et malgache de langue française* (Anthology of African and West Indian Poets Writing in French) was largely responsible for introducing the negritude movement to the world. Césaire, who is credited with coining the term, later explained its origins:

> It must not be forgotten that the word "negritude" was, at first, a riposte. The word "*nègre*" had been thrown at us as an insult, and we picked it up and turned it into a positive concept.... We thought that it was an injustice to say that Africa had done nothing, that Africa did not count in the evolution of the world, that Africa had not invented anything of value. It was also an immense injustice, and an enormous error, to think that nothing of value could ever come out of Africa.[24]

Negritude was a movement of black solidarity and a search for an authentic black self that began with the negation of racism. Negritude writers revolted against the European colonial order and the hierarchy of values it imposed on its African subjects, ultimately seeking a transvaluation of all values that would lead to an essential humanity beyond racialism.[25]

Sartre also directly intervened in the anticolonial struggle. His first close work with the Parti Communiste Français came in 1951 when he joined the campaign to free Henri Martin, a Communist sailor who was imprisoned for disbursing leaflets denouncing French involvement in Indochina. He was one of the earliest critics of the Franco-Algerian war (1954–1962), advocating on behalf of his younger colleague Francis Jeanson's strident condemnation of French colonial policy in *L'Algérie hors la loi* (Outlaw Algeria, 1955).[26] In 1955, Sartre joined the Comité d'action contre la poursuite de la guerre en Afrique du Nord (Action Committee against the War in North Africa). On January 27, 1956, he made his first major public critique at a rally "for peace in Algeria," later published in *Les Temps modernes* as "Colonialism is a System."[27] Articulating here what he would reiterate in his preface to Albert Memmi's classic book *Portrait du colonisé précédé de portrait du colonisateur (The Colonizer and Colonized)*, he argued that since both racism and exploitation were intrinsic to the colonial system, it could not be reformed but needed to be smashed.

When General Jacques Massu was given full police power to destroy the terrorist networks in Algeria in 1957, thus beginning the Battle of Algiers, repeated scandals concerning the use of terror and torture in the Franco-Algerian war resulted in a shift in the tide of opposition to continuing the conflict. This was unmistakable when Raymond Aron, who in 1956 signed a manifesto in support of *Algérie française*, published *La Tragédie algérienne* (The Algerian Tragedy) advocating Algerian independence.[28] By 1958, the war in Algeria had destabilized the Third Republic. But Sartre was deeply disillusioned by the Left's continuing failure to unequivocally support the national liberation struggle. His dismay peeked with the popularity of General de Gaulle's assumption of office in June with unlimited powers for six months and a mandate to revise the constitution.

By 1959, Sartre advocated unbridled support of the Front de Liberation Nationale (FLN). He was one of the first signatories of the manifesto of 121 intellectuals who supported the "Declaration of the Right of Insubordination in the Algerian War" in 1960. The failure of the French to embrace the aims of the FLN led to the radicalization of his position apparent in his preface to Frantz Fanon's *Les damnées de la terre* (*The Wretched of the Earth*, 1961). His intransigence led to him being targeted by the *Organisation Armée Secrète* (OAS), a group of military officers and *pied noir* (Algerian settler) extremists, formed in 1961 to use terror tactics to bring down the regime that was ending French Algeria. They bombed the offices of *Les Temps modernes* on May 13, 1961 and Sartre's apartment on rue Bonaparte in St. Germain-des-Prés on two occasions: July 19, 1961 and January 7, 1962.

By the late 1960s Sartre had begun to consider how neocolonialist structures enabled European domination and control to continue even after imperial rule had officially ended. In his last activist years in the early 1970s, before the onset of his blindness and his death in 1980, one of his most sustained political campaigns focused on the struggles of immigrants returning to the postcolonial metropole. He was beginning to discern the importance of migrant labor and to sketch the contours of the "new racism"[29] that characterizes the age of globalization.

From Existential Phenomenology to Existential Marxism

Sartre's evolving views on antisemitism and racism developed over these years in relation to his changing comrades in struggle as well. Differing contexts led him to elective affinities with a wide diversity of groups who faced varied kinds of oppression and often dissimilar situations and whose fight for freedom was animated by ideologies and ends that were sometimes crosscutting. In the late 1930s and through World War II, Sartre was part of the nonaligned constellation of antifascists. In the Cold War, he battled alongside the workers of the world and national liberation fighters struggling for independence from France from Indochina to Algeria. By the early 1960s, Sartre was the global ambassador for "Third World" insurgents from Cuba to the Congo. By the late sixties, he embraced *gauchist* (New Leftist) student revolutionaries from Berkeley to Berlin to the barricades of Paris. And by the early 1970s, Sartre had come to see how globalization created "interior colonies" in the metropolitan centers of the industrialized and postindustrial North.

Adjusting his philosophical framework in relationship to these shifting situations and struggles, Sartre's theoretical perspective changed from an emphasis on existential phenomenology to existential Marxism. What remained constant was an effort to grasp what was at the heart of his existentialism: the possibility of human freedom in the face of lived constraints. Sartre distilled the axioms of his existentialism in his famous lecture *L'existentialisme est un humanisme* (*Existentialism is a Humanism*), delivered on October 29, 1945, at the *Club Maintenant* and remembered afterward as the cultural event of the year. In a series of pithy formulations, Sartre announced the key themes of existentialism: "existence precedes essence," "man is nothing else than the ensemble of his acts," humanity is "condemned to be free," but as such we are all responsible for the choices we make of ourselves, often not in situations of our own choosing.

Full apprehension of this entails anxiety, so most flee our accountability. We numb ourselves through work, or anesthetize ourselves through the media or conspicuous consumption, or repress our responsibility for the downtrodden, or deny our complicity for the horrors committed in our name by our governments. In short, we live in "bad faith" pursuing whatever will fill the void at the heart of the human condition. Or we adopt the viewpoint of racists who blame their condition on Others who are deemed culpable for the social and psychological ills that plague society. But as Sartre so elegantly crystallized it, "if existence really does precede essence, man is responsible for what he is ... and when we say that a man is responsible for himself, we do not only mean that he is responsible for his own individuality, but that he is responsible for all men."[30] Racism made plain, however, that all people were not free, and the lived constraints on some people's freedom were obviously significantly more pronounced than on others'.

Therefore, in the course of the prefaces he wrote for Senghor, Memmi, and Fanon, as well as in the wake of his political interventions in the key struggles of the Cold War and decolonization, Sartre began to reexamine the theoretical foundations of his thought, specifically the relations between the individual, society, and history. What did not change were his existential commitments to freedom as constitutive of the human condition, his phenomenological conception of consciousness, his critique of determinism—whether by natural, social, or supernatural laws—and his emphasis on creating the self through an interiorization and subjectivation of the external conditions that shape humans. But how Sartre came to understand the factors that condition this process were deepened. Asked to write an article on "The Situation of Existentialism in 1957" for a Polish review, he contributed an essay that he would eventually elaborate as *Questions de Méthode* (*Search for a Method*), his epistemological preamble to his *Critique de la raison dialectique* (*Critique of Dialectical Reason*, 1960). His prologue repeatedly reiterated, "Marxism is ... the philosophy of our time."

Marxism offered the best method for comprehending the present, Sartre averred, but it needed to be resuscitated from the stultifying dogmatism of Stalinism or any reductive or mechanical laws of history. He wanted to show simultaneously how the world makes humans and how humans make their world. This would be accomplished by reintroducing the individual within the dialectic in order to understand how history was made by individuals who were also products of the history that individuals had made. Existentialism thus had to be rethought within the frame of Marxism, since the "'analysis' of a situation," he argued "is not enough and that it is but the first moment in an effort at synthetic reconstruction."[31] What was required was a more sophisticated understanding of the mediations between economic determinations and concrete action, with the family serving the mediating role, and where social context and class position are constitutive factors of individual development (30–31).[32] Akin to Wilhelm Dilthey, who sought to formulate a "critique of historical reason" in order to understand "objective mind,"[33] Sartre wanted a theory that would account for the relative autonomy of institutions, customs, the state, the law, ideology, religion, language, art, and philosophy. He sought to show how these in turn were mediated to the individual through the family.

Consequently, Sartre's political interventions and specifically his opposition to colonialism and neocolonialism, as well as his philosophical engagement with a series of interlocutors on the political question of liberation, the ontological question of agency, the ethical question of responsibility, and the epistemological question of history altered how he framed the dialectical relationship between individual and society, consciousness and history, and ethics and politics. As *Race after Sartre* elaborates, attention to racism and its discontents therefore illuminates the Sartrean oeuvre while Sartre's critical acumen discloses anew the workings of racist exploitation. And it does so in ways that offer powerful insights into Sartre's work as an informing horizon for critical approaches to racism and for rethinking race in a postcolonial age.

Sartre in His Time and in Ours

In this volume Sartre is scrutinized as our contemporary. His philosophical reflections are not examined as the antiquated repository of a great mind no longer relevant. All of the chapters examine Sartre's work as a vital resource for the most pressing political questions today, where race and racism continue to shape the social configuration: from the riots in France in November 2005 to the response to Hurricane Katrina to today's "global apartheid"; from the wider issues of immigration and racism in the age of globalization to the outsourcing of torture in liberal societies; from the stolen elections by Bush in Florida in 2000 to the racial inequities in incarceration; from the policies of affirmative action to the possibility of a "colorblind" society; from reparations for slavery and apartheid to the Truth and Reconciliation Commission in South Africa; and from the role of intellectuals in speaking for or with the oppressed to enabling the subaltern to speak in their own critical idioms.

The title of the collection connotes at least three axes of interrogation. First, the category of *"race"* will be examined through Sartre's work because in a series of seminal texts (*Being and Nothingness, Antisemite and Jew*, his preface to Senghor's anthology of negritude poetry, his prefaces to the works of Memmi, Fanon, and Lumumba, *Critique of Dialectical Reason*, among others) he anticipated and made possible much of the crucial work that is being undertaken in "race" critical theories and postcolonialism: (1) he was among the first to argue that "race" is a social construct; (2) he insisted that "race" is formed by social struggles and informs processes of inclusion and exclusion, racial subjectification and subjection; (3) he developed the dialectic of the gaze as intrinsic to defining the individual and collective Self and Other; (4) he was an early critic of the shortcomings of the liberal, humanist, Enlightenment tradition for combating racism; (5) he examined how racism was shaped in discourse—considering the semiology of the racialized other and the necessity to deconstruct these stereotypes; (6) he also maintained that discrimination was institutionalized in the structures and rituals of everyday life; (7) he saw how the system of rules and norms establishing hierarchy and subjugation within the social order could be revealed from the perspective of the racially oppressed; and (8) his vision broadened over time to an appreciation of how race and racism function within the neocolonial global order.

Consequently, a number of the contributors consider race *after* Sartre because his work provides a machinery of concepts and a set of axioms that need to be developed in thinking about racialization and the politics of antiracism today: from his existential approach to freedom, responsibility, bad faith, the situation, and the dialectic of human recognition engendered by the gaze to his later Marxist emphasis on dialectical history, praxis, need, the practico-inert, idea hexis, groups-in-fusion, and seriality. Moreover, Sartre's antifoundationalist critique of essentialism was a crucial step toward the decentering of subjectivity so pivotal to poststructuralism and, in turn, postcolonialism. These theories have led to reconsiderations of the interplay between cultural identities and social structures. Sartre was the most visible intellectual in the world reflecting on the transformation of these structures after Auschwitz and during decolonization, and his insights shaped how these issues have come to be considered in his wake, even when this influence remains unacknowledged.

But finally, *Sartre* himself also constitutes a privileged site for thinking about the dead ends of certain roads to freedom from the racialized social order. His work evinces the slipperiness and links of stereotyping because while he was a sophisticated critic of antisemitism and racism, he occasionally repeated certain antisemitic and racist motifs. His radical activism also poses the question of the limits of violence and the shortcuts of terrorism since Sartre advocated revolutionary violence as a means to overcome the systematic dehumanization and exploitation of the oppressed that in his later work he saw as the kernel of racism, which in Algeria and the Congo, to name only two prominent examples where he supported such measures, had horrific consequences.

Sartre's Questions and Ours

There are diverse approaches taken here by a motley collection of contributors: philosophers, intellectual historians, literary scholars, cultural critics; men and women; Europeans, Americans, Africans, African Americans, Afro-Asians, Afro-Irish-Amero-Indians; Jews, non-Jews, and nonbelievers; young and more established academics. Their differing methodological and epistemological interests consequently intersect with the issues raised by race after Sartre from a variety of perspectives and toward different ends. While this leads to some contrasting viewpoints about the same texts or contexts, for the most part it results in a prismatic approach where the many hues of Sartre's work and impact are delineated. Ultimately, what most unites the pieces are the ways that Sartre's considerations of racism and colonialism involve one in a tangle of ethical and political problems. This problem-oriented slant gives the volume its vitality and animates the links between the parts and pieces.

To what extent are racism and antisemitism congruent forms of stigmatizing the Other and to what extent do their histories diverge? Richard King's *Race, Culture and the Intellectuals*, which provides an overview of theories of racism and antisemitism from Auschwitz through the Civil Rights Movement, maintains that "the epistemological, psychological, historical, and ideological roots of racism, antisemitism and Eurocentrism proved to be quite disparate."[34] But most of the writers he considers focused on *either* antisemitism or racism. One of Sartre's virtues, however, was to have considered both, drawing upon the concepts and guidelines of his interventions into antisemitism in his later antiracist, anticolonial, and postcolonial works. Several of the chapters (Jonathan Judaken, Steve Martinot, Christian Delacampagne, Robert Bernasconi) develop the cross-filiations between these differing forms of ostracism, even as they are aware of the differences between these modalities of racialization.

What responsibility do the citizens or descendants of racist states have to those victimized in the name of racial ideology? Sartre's writings in the immediate aftermath of the Holocaust and Hiroshima broached the problem Karl Jaspers had addressed in *Die Schuldfrage (The Question of German Guilt*, 1946) about what he called "metaphysical guilt" or what Bernasconi names "hyperbolic responsibility." We are collectively responsible for the oppression that is committed in our name, Sartre reminded us time and again. In the case of Jim Crow America, Nazi Germany, *Algérie française*, or South Africa, which Mabogo P. More explores at length here, what are the avenues to truth and reconciliation and what limits does the racial order impose upon achieving them?

What are the links between the use of torture and the racial order that imposes its rule through these brutal measures? In the aftermath of Abu Ghraib and the program of "extraordinary rendition" sanctioned by the highest rungs of the American political and military establishment, Sartre's writings on the topic once more sting with a new urgency as both Judith Butler and Judaken explore. How are we to reconcile modern liberal democracy and the righteous sanctification of medieval methods for the extraction of "information"? Sartre taught that torture is about dehumanization, not gathering facts. The torturer is merely the most visibly violent face of the imposition of power whose end is systemic dispossession and expropriation that ultimately can only legitimate itself by racism.

What do the occlusions within Sartre's own "antiracist racism" indicate about the ways in which racism as a parasitic ideology is able to perpetuate itself? At times, his own work reiterates stereotypes of "the Jew" or "the African" as a characterological type. He sometimes valorized as necessary the prejudices that the oppressed merely inverse and return in their image of the oppressor. But he also suggested that what W. E. B. Du Bois called the "conservation of the races" was necessary in the form of embracing in pride the status of the subordinate class or group, at least until racialism was overcome. He thus squarely apprehended the antinomies that linger in the contemporary politics of affirmative action or in calls for a "colorblind" society. And what of the legitimacy of the counterviolence of the oppressed in reclaiming their humanity after a subhuman existence? In addressing these dilemmas to Sartre's oeuvre, a number of the contributors (Bernasconi, Butler, Delacampagne, Richard Watts) examine not only how they demarcate closures in Sartre's thinking, but openings to unexamined assumptions within Western civilization about racialized Others.

And what defines "the West," Europe, France, or America, and what place does race and racism have in these political spaces? Indeed, all of the overdetermined questions of identity revolve around this vexed query. Here, Sartre's antiracist and anticolonialist writings and interventions fold onto the new terrain of not only postcolonial theory, but also postcontinental philosophy. For via Sartre's canonical location within the Western philosophical and cultural tradition, all of his companions and interlocutors are admitted into that sacred realm. But via their interventions that inspired his own, Sartre also opens those traditions to what has been excluded, repressed, marginalized, or oppressed. Simultaneously a new Africana and postcontinental tradition is demarcated, as Lewis Gordon, George Ciccariello-Maher, and More sketch. Gordon's genealogy of Sartre's impact on black existential thought, the theorization of race, and the development of antiracist theory, explored also by Delacampagne and Bernasconi, indicates the effects that Sartre's input had on reforging the boundaries of philosophy and intellectual history.

What then is Sartre's place within the map of postcolonial thought? Both Watts and Butler survey key interventions that have defined the Francophone postcolonial field, discerning how Sartre inhabits its margins but nonetheless casts a shadow across the postcolonial topography. In examining the borders of violence/nonviolence, difference/indifference, insider/outsider, and center/periphery, they each consider what his prefaces or "paratexts"[35] imply for a host of complicated issues: Does Sartre in his mode of address reiterate the very gesture of dehumanization at the core of racism? Does he interpolate a frenzied fraternal order, a masculinist mob, who are the audience who must hear his appeal to listen to the words Fanon offers in *The Wretched of the Earth* or that the negritude poets sound? Has Sartre squelched the freedom of the colonized in an overly reductive view of the processes of history? Does his valorization of violence as the deterministic blowback of colonial exploitation paradoxically deny agency to colonial insurgents?

How also did the impact of Sartre's own self-reflexive examination of these questions impact the development of his philosophical and political agenda? While several chapters explicitly trace the stages on Sartre's way, many of the contributors offer their own version of the changes within Sartre's oeuvre. His work clearly shifted from an emphasis on the existential phenomenology of racial oppression defined by the structure of the gaze toward racism as the "idea hexis" of economic exploitation (i.e., the stereotypes, images, myths, and sound bites that help legitimate the institutionalization of white superiority). In the course of these cleavages, Sartre created a tool box of concepts, theorems, and strategies for understanding the operations of race and racism that are not only helpful in understanding his opus but in engaging with the ongoing racialized structures of domination that we face in the world today.

The Pieces of the Puzzle

The structure of the book is straightforward: It is divided into four parts with the first chapter in each offering a general overview, some aspects of which are then explored in greater detail in what follows. The first section, "Sartre on Race and Racism," provides a survey of Sartre's positions as they unfolded over his lifetime. Judaken's first chapter argues that there were four overlapping phases that are nonetheless heuristically useful to separate in order to define the major texts, concepts, and precepts that Sartre worked through in his antiracist writings: (1) anti-antisemitism, (2) anticolonialist existential humanism, (3) Third World radicalism, (4) antiracist alter-globalization. The chapter offers an intellectual history of "Sartre on Racism" that explicates the key notions and theorems of Sartre's understanding of race as they evolved in his major works on the topic over time and provides a systematic overview of Sartre's approach to racism that sets the stage for all the other contributions.

Having surveyed the oeuvre as a whole, the chapters that follow magnify particularly neglected aspects of Sartre's work. In "Skin for Sale," Martinot examines closely his much-neglected dramatic work *The Respectful Prostitute* (1946), exploring how Sartre may well have been accused of anti-

Americanism when the play was produced precisely because, properly understood, it lays bare the mechanisms of white supremacy in American society. Racism, Martinot argues, is a complex set of processes of internal white bonding and *The Respectful Prostitute* brilliantly and incisively dramatizes these. He not only uses the theatrical piece as a point of entry into Sartre's understanding of racism, but also outlines how the social structures of ethical inversion, criminalization of the victim, derogation, and "consensus, myth and membership in the white socius constitute the framework in which a person understands himself or recognizes himself as 'white.'" He thereby helps us to understand the social production of whiteness as the basis of white supremacy and white supremacy as the basis of racism.

Paige Arthur in "The Persistence of Colonialism" focuses on Sartre's last years of militant activism in the early 1970s when his political interventions addressed the policies and treatment of non-European immigrant laborers in France and also engaged the question of autonomist regional movements within Europe. She examines how his last works knitted together issues of racism and regionalism within the analytical framework of "interior colonialism." By the mid-1970s, however, Sartre's failing health dovetailed with the general collapse of the revolutionary Left. The Parti Socialiste came to co-opt struggles for immigrant rights and regional autonomy. But in doing so, they rejected the culturally particularist arguments of Sartre and the *gauchistes* in favor of universalist claims of national identity purportedly open to all, conjoining socialism to values of liberalism, often articulated around the theme of human rights, with culturalist arguments consigned to the shadows. This nexus would predominate for the next intellectual generation. Contextualizing Sartre's efforts in the early 1970s, Arthur shows how these circumstantial pieces nonetheless "marked in a rather prescient way many of the issues that would dominate political discussion concerning relations with non-Western countries and peoples for the coming decade and beyond: the social, economic, and cultural problems of immigration; the contemporary conjuncture of racism with economic and demographic pressures pushing and pulling people across borders; the persistence of colonialism, whether on the level of economics (neocolonialism) or the level of ideas (as a model for social oppression and exclusion); and, finally, the possibility of freedom for the least favored of the world, beaten down in this case by poverty and exploitation, but in other cases, by repressive governments in their home countries."

The essays in Part II elaborate upon some of the resources within Sartre's body of work for antiracist theory. Delacampagne in his "Race: From Philosophy to History" offers a genealogy, focusing primarily on the history of antisemitism but insisting on its essential overlaps with racism. He examines how it was originally "philosophers with a historical turn of mind, whose theoretical insights were later empirically grounded by the efforts of historians" that elucidated how "race" functions as an historical construct and thus how Sartre was intrinsic in establishing some of the foundational axioms for combating racism. Robert Bernasconi, in contrast, bemoans the fact that philosophers have contributed at least as much to the history of racism as to antiracism. His chapter on "Sartre and Levinas" focuses on how both these thinkers can be mobilized to destabilize, disrupt, and disarm racism. He maintains against other commentators, notably Alain Finkielkraut, that Sartre and Levinas are not as radically opposed to each other as is usually claimed. Bernasconi is attentive to their different philosophical agendas, specifically on the issue of racism: Levinas emphasizes that racism is a denial of ethical responsibility before the Other, a rebuff of alterity and one's concomitant ethical moral obligations; whereas for Sartre the germ of racism is the denial of the freedom of the Other. In short, they divide over whether politics or ethics comes first. But Bernasconi insists that their differences should not foreclose what they shared in the fight against racism, since "both Sartre and Levinas offer an alternative to the so-called Enlightenment universalist approach by emphasizing the positive role played by the bodily within a synthetic or holistic account of identity to which one is nevertheless not reduced."

Ciccariello-Maher's "European Intellectuals and Colonial Difference" explores the internal antinomies of European conceptions of humanism and antihumanism. Focusing first on the debate between Sartre and Foucault on the universal versus the specific intellectual, Ciccariello-Maher maintains that Sartre's understanding of "the situation" bolsters his position against some of the charges laid by Foucault. He then compares Sartre's and Foucault's conceptions of the gaze. He argues that Foucault's notion of the power relations of the gaze worked out from *The Birth of the Clinic* through *Discipline and Punish* and Sartre's later existential Marxist understanding were crucially anticipated by Fanon. Fanon is then leveraged to insist that both Foucault and "Sartre's totalization remain bound to Eurocentrism" because they had not fully digested the implication of their own situation as European intellectuals. Fanon, on the other hand, emphasized "the concreteness and historical ladenness of the gaze, which is asymmetrical in terms of power, but which invokes not only a history of classification, but that of a colonial classification based on phenotype." In the final turn of the chapter, Césaire is marshaled alongside Fanon, to construe an alter-humanism that no longer reinscribes "philosophical agency within its traditional European *locus*."

Part III, "Sartre and Africana Existentialism," follows the trajectory opened by Ciccariello-Maher's chapter in considering the impact of Sartre on the black existentialist tradition. Gordon's "Sartre and Black Existentialism" is an encomium to Sartre the Africana existentialist, since Gordon argues that black existentialism is not only existentialism produced by blacks. Sartre was a black existentialist for many reasons: (1) because he was a committed antiracist from his early works on antisemitism to his interventions against the discrimination of immigrant Africans in France; (2) he engaged with black cultural forms, specifically poetry, literature, philosophy, and jazz; (3) he had a profound impact on non-European intellectuals from America, the Caribbean, Latin America, and Africa; (4) he was an important influence on liberation theorists, including black liberationists like Fanon and Angela Davis; and (5) in and out of the academy, the whole black existentialist tradition that Gordon sketches was engaged with Sartre's writing, as he was engaged with black existentialism, providing a cross-fertilization that offers some of the richest resources for thinking about race and racism.

This fertile ground is then delved into in More's "Sartre and South African Apartheid," which considers how Sartre's philosophical vocabulary and analyses of oppression influenced the Black Consciousness Movement, particularly Steve Biko. Biko, like Sartre, sought to register the systemic nature of apartheid and how its webs of privilege and subordination implicated everyone at every level. Both also emphasized an expansive conception of human agency and its correlate "collective responsibility." More applies these considerations as a critical corrective to the Truth and Reconciliation Commission, arguing that in the end it served as a mechanism to achieve national reconciliation by compromising the truth and reinforcing the alienation of blacks from economic and social justice, which remains an ongoing struggle in South Africa.

From postcolonial South Africa to two central moments of the postcolonial Francophone canon, in Part IV, "Sartre and the Postcolonial Turn," Watts and Butler in turn investigate "Black Orpheus," his famous preface on behalf of negritude poetry and his preface to Fanon's *The Wretched of the Earth*. By contextualizing "Black Orpheus" within the history of prefaces by European patrons of colonial literature, Watts's "Difference/Indifference" problematizes the now facile dismissal of Sartre's text as a "poisoned gift." While sensitive to the ways that Sartre's tack was panoptic and sometimes cast into shadow the writers he sought to bring into the light of critical discourse, Watts offers an alternative way of reading Sartre's dialectic, following Denis Hollier, that sees it not as insisting on the dissipation of difference but, rather, as appreciating how differences are conditioned within the dialectics of history. He compares Sartre's "allographic paratexts" with those of Edouard Glissant, who reacting against the Sartrean tradition often sought to remain in the shadows in his paratexts, privileging a rhetoric that inscribed horizontality rather than hierarchy, but whose relational conception of differences paradoxically smothers the possibility of a critical engagement with "race" more emphatically than does Sartre.

Judith Butler's "Violence, Nonviolence" thinks alongside Sartre and Fanon (and Homi Bhabha) about a range of issues broached in their texts: their mode of address, their understanding of dehumanization and subjectivization, the shortcomings of both liberal humanism and violent insurgency, and the tensions within revolutionary violence as a response to systemic violence. While attuned to their differences, she is critical of both Sartre's and Fanon's masculinism and salvationist visions of violence, but nevertheless finds the resources for her critique within their own texts. For Sartre it was his futural vision of a community defined as an "infinite unity of mutual needs," while she heeds Fanon's call for an epistemic and political openness that is at once bodily and conscious. She affirms in both Sartre and Fanon the acknowledgment of our embodiment that presages the undoing of the binaries between colonizer/colonized and masculine/feminine, and the movement toward what Butler calls "a recorporalization of humanism." Her redemptive reading gestures toward a world in which mutual needs may be recognized, and the address to others as "you" may take the place of the abstract humanist talk about "man."

But this outline of the structure and contents of the book cannot do justice to the acumen that Sartre and his commentators evince as interpreters of the injustices of racism. The reader of the volume is therefore offered an entrée into Sartre's thought, the tools of his conceptual armory, a deeper appreciation of his place within race critical theories and postcolonialism, and the example of his engagements in the ongoing struggle to fight racism.

Ergo tolle lege!

Notes

1. By "critical race studies," I mean the vast body of scholarship on the historical evolution and contemporary expression of race as a social category for discriminating, organizing, regulating, and maintaining social differences. By revealing that racial categories emerge in specific contexts that are connected to power, politics, economics, and culture, these scholars have destabilized those categories as natural or transhistorical. The point is to disclose how race operates in differing situations and texts, in order to undermine the force of racism. For a useful overview on this scholarship, see David Theo Goldberg and John Solomos, eds., *A Companion to Race and Ethnic Studies* (Malden, Mass.: Blackwell, 2002).
2. For a good sense of this canon and how Sartre remains largely absent from it, see the most widely used anthology in the field by Bill Aschcroft, Gareth Griffiths, and Helen Tiffin, eds, *The Postcolonial Studies Reader* (London and New York: Routledge, 1995); see also, Leela Gandhi, *Postcolonial Theory: A Critical Introduction* (New York: Columbia University Press, 1998); Bart MooreGilbert, *Postcolonial Theory: Contexts, Practices, Politics* (London: Verso, 1998); Ania Loomba, *Colonialism/Postcolonialism* (London: Routledge, 1998); Henry Schwarz and Sangeeta Ray, *A Companion to Postcolonial Studies* (Oxford: Blackwell, 2000); Gaurav Desai and Supriya Nair, eds., *Post-*

colonialisms: An Anthology of Cultural Theory and Criticism (New Brunswick: Rutgers University Press, 2005). For the importance of Sartre's contributions to postcolonialism, see Robert J. C. Young, *White Mythologies: Writing History and the West* (London and New York: Routledge, 2004), 61–82, and Simon Gikandi, "Poststructuralism and Postcolonial Discourse," *The Cambridge Companion to Postcolonial Literary Studies*, ed. Neil Lazarus (Cambridge: Cambridge University Press, 2004), 100–10.

3. Following Henry Louis Gates Jr., I write "race" and "the Jew" in quotes to indicate that these are constructed categories and that to *describe* "the Jew" or "the black" or "the white" also *inscribes* the category as a marker of difference whether based on language, belief system, artistic tradition, or gene pool. See Henry Louis Gates Jr., "Introduction: Writing 'Race' and the Difference It Makes" in *"Race," Writing and Difference*, ed. Henry Louis Gates Jr. (Chicago: University of Chicago Press, 1986), 5. See also Berel Lang, "From Grammar to Antisemitism: On the 'the' in 'the Jews.' " Originally published in *Midstream* v. 49.4 (May–June 2003). Available at: http://www.wzo.org.il/en/resources/view.asp?id=1489. Accessed July 4, 2006.

Following a now common practice among scholars, I do not hyphenate antisemitism throughout this volume because, as Shmuel Almog, put it, "If you use the hyphenated form you consider the words 'Semitism', 'Semite', 'Semitic' as meaningful. They supposedly convey an image of a real substance, of a real group of people, 'Semites', who are said to be a race. This is a misnomer: firstly, because 'semitic' or 'aryan' were originally *language groups*, not *people*; but mainly because in antisemitic parlance, 'Semites' really stands for Jews, simply that.... So the hyphen, or rather its omission, conveys a message: if you hyphenate your 'anti-Semitism' you attach some credence to the very foundation on which the whole thing rests. Strike out the hyphen and you will treat antisemitism for what it really is—a generic name for modern Jew-hatred." See Shmuel Almog, "What's in a Hyphen," in *Sicsa Report: The Newsletter of the Vidal Sassoon International Study of Antisemitism* (Summer 1989), n.2: 1–2. To attain uniformity, I have altered the spelling of titles of works to accommodate this spelling as well.

4. Two useful anthologies that bring this literature together are David Theo Goldberg, ed., *Anatomy of Racism* (Minneapolis and London: University of Minnesota Press, 1990), and Philomena Essed and David Theo Goldberg, *Race Critical Theories: Text and Context* (Oxford: Blackwell, 2002).

5. For the ways that structuralism and poststructuralism defined themselves in opposition to Sartre there is an ample literature. For one excellent treatment, see François Dosse, *History of Structuralism*, vol. 1: *The Rising Sign*, trans. Deborah Glassman (Minneapolis: University of Minnesota Press, 1997). For one among many examples of the ways that postcolonialism, alongside poststructuralism and deconstruction, has defined itself in opposition to Sartre, see Gayatri Chakravorty Spivak, *A Critique of Postcolonial Reason: Toward a History of the Vanishing Present* (Cambridge, Mass.: Harvard University Press, 1999), 171, 173.

6. On Sartre's commitment to Marxism, see Mark Poster, *Existential Marxism in Postwar France* (Princeon: Princeton University Press, 1975), and Mark Poster, *Sartre's Marxism* (Cambridge: Cambridge University Press, 1982); Ronald Aronson, *Philosophy in the World* (London: New Left, 1980); and Ian Birshall, *Sartre against Stalinism* (New York and Oxford: Berghahn, 2004).

7. *Situations V: Colonialisme et néo-colonialisme* (Paris: Galimard, 1964), trans. Azzedine Haddour, Steve Brewer and Terry McWilliams (London and New York: Routledge, 2000).

8. The major exceptions to this in English are most importantly the works of Lewis Gordon, including *Bad Faith and Antiblack Racism* (New Jersey: Humanities, 1995); *Fanon and the Crisis of European Man: An Essay on Philosophy and the Human Sciences* (New York and London: Routledge, 1995), especially chapter 2; and Lewis Gordon, *Existentia Africana: Understanding Africana Existential Thought* (New York and London: Routledge, 2000), 9, 73–79, 109–13, 119–34, and passim. See also Robert Bernasconi's excellent article "Sartre's Gaze Returned: The Transformation of the Phenomenology of Racism," *Graduate Faculty Philosophy Journal* 10.2 (1995), reprinted in William McBride, ed., *Existentialist Ethics* (New York: Garland, 1997), 359–79; And finally, Jonathan Judaken, *Jean-Paul Sartre and the Jewish Question: Anti-antisemitism and the Politics of the French Intellectual* (Lincoln and London: University of Nebraska Press, 2006). Some other recent works in English are cited in chapter 1. In French, see the important book by Nouredine Lemouchi, *Jean-Paul Sartre et le tiers monde: rhétorique d'un discours anticolonialiste* (Paris: L'Harmattan, 1996).
9. Eduardo Bonilla-Silva, "Rethinking Racism: Towards a Structural Interpretation," *American Sociological Review* 62.3 (June 1997): 465–80.
10. On the latter point, see Howard Winant, "Race and Race Theory," *Annual Review of Sociology* 26 (2000): 169–85, 171. See also Michael Omi and Howard Winant, *Racial Formation in the United States: From the 1960s to the 1990s* (New York: Routledge, 1994).
11. Simone de Beauvoir, *La force de choses*, 1 (Paris: Gallimard, 1963), 333.
12. Sartre discussed this in a posthumously published interview with Arlette Elkaïm-Sartre, Benny Lévy, and Ely Ben-Gal, published in the annex of Eli Ben-Gal, *Mardi Chez Sartre: Un Hébreu à Paris, 1967–1980* (Paris: Flammarion, 1992).
13. See Eugene H. Frickey, "The Origins of Phenomenology in France, 1920–1940," PhD diss, Indiana University, 1979. On Sartre's place within the phenomenological movement, see Herbert Spiegelberg's *The Phenomenological Movement* (The Hague: Nijhoss, 1982), 445–515. See also, Martin Jay, *Marxism and Totality: The Adventures of a Concept from Lukács to Habermas* (Berkeley and Los Angeles: University of California Press, 1984), 334–36.
14. Ethan Kleinberg, *Generation Existential: Heidegger's Philosophy in France, 1927–1961* (Ithaca: Cornell University Press, 2005), 116–19, makes clear that Sartre had already encountered the work of both Husserl and Heidegger earlier.
15. Simone de Beauvoir, *La force de l'âge* (Paris: Gallimard, 1960), 141–42, trans. Peter Green, *The Prime of Life* (Cleveland: World, 1962), 112.
16. Jean-Paul Sartre, *The Transcendence of the Ego* (New York: Octagon, 1972), 40.
17. Jean-Paul Sartre, *The Philosophy of Jean-Paul Sartre*, ed. and intro. Robert Denoon Cumming (New York: Random House, 1965), 15: "The structure of the story *Nausea* reproduces the reflexive aspiration of consciousness in Sartre's philosophy: *Nausea* is a novel (at the higher reflexive level) about the prereflective experiences that led up to the writing of the novel. Proust's novel has a comparable structure. But in Proust (as in Husserl) experience is recaptured in its necessary structure by the reflective movement which transcends experience. Thus Proust's *recherche* is successfully completed in his terminal volume, *Le Temps retrouvé*. But Sartre has his ostensible protagonist in *Nausea*, Roquentin, tell the story to show that one cannot in fact 'catch time by the tail'. Further-

more, the true protagonist, nausea itself, is (one of its manifestations) the reflexive experience of the discrepancy between the necessary structure of the story as told (as a work of art) and the sense of contingency—of the indeterminacy of the future—which is the experience of the sloppiness of living one's life that one seeks to alleviate by telling the story about it. This discrepancy, which self-consciousness (as well as Proust and the literary tradition) obscures by its loquacity, is preserved in *Nausea*. The novel is not completed with the novel, which ends with Roquentin's aspiration to regain his past experience by writing the novel, but his actual future left dangling."

18. Philip Thody, *Sartre: A Biographical Introduction* (New York: Scribner's, 1971), 55, contends that "*L'Enfance d'un Chef* (sic) is, in this respect, the most openly political of all Sartre's prewar writings." Jean-François Sirinelli argues that Sartre became concerned with historical events and politics in the course of writing *Le Mur* and dates his turn to 1937. See Jean-François Sirinelli, *Deux intellectuals dans le siècle: Sartre et Aron* (Paris: Fayard, 1995), 146–47.
19. On this point, see Ingrid Galster, ed., *La naissance du "phénomène Sartre": Raison d'un succèc, 1939–1945* (Paris: Éditions du Seuil, 2001).
20. On the cultural politics of the Vichy period and how French intellectuals responded to it, see Jonathan Judaken, "Intellectuals, Culture and the Vichy Years: Reappraisals and New Perspectives," *Contemporary French Civilization*, ed. Denis Provencher and Andrew Sabonet, special issue *France, 1940–1944: The Ambiguous Legacy* 31.2 (Fall 2007): 83–115.
21. The oft-cited phrase is from the interviews with John Gerassi. See the citations in Gerassi, *Jean-Paul Sartre: Hated Conscience of His Century, volume 1: Protestant or Protestor?* (Chicago and London: University of Chicago Press, 1989), 179, 187. See also Jean-Paul Sartre, *Oeuvres romanesques* (Paris: Gallimard, 1981), lviii. Thanks to Dennis Gilbert and William McBride for the references when I needed them.
22. Andrew Leak, *Jean-Paul Sartre* (London: Reaktion, 2006), 63–65.
23. On *Présence Africaine*, see V. Y. Mudimbe's *The Surreptitious Speech: Présence Africaine and the Politics of Otherness, 1947–1987* (Chicago: University of Chicago Press, 1992).
24. Aimé Césaire, "Entretien et débat," at the Maison Helvétique in 1967. Cited in Bennetta Jules-Rosette, "Jean-Paul Sartre and the Philosophy of Négritude: Race, Self, and Society," *Theory and Society* 36.3 (June 2007).
25. See Abiola Irele, "A Defence of Negritude," *Transition* no. 13 (March–April 1964): 9–11. On the distinction between "racialism" and different modes of racism, see Kwame Anthony Appiah, "Racisms" in David Theo Goldberg, ed., *Anatomy of Racism* (Minneapolis: University of Minnesota Press, 1990). See also the way that Tzvetan Todorov delineates the distinction between "racialism" and "racism," in *On Human Diversity: Nationalism, Racism and Exoticism in French Thought* (Cambridge, Mass.: Harvard University Press, 1993), 90–95.
26. Collette and Francis Jeanson, *L'Algérie hors la loi* (Paris: Éditions du Seuil, 1955).
27. Jean-Paul Sartre, "Le Colonialisme est un système," *Les Temps modernes* (March-April 1956): 1371–86. Reproduced in Sartre, *Situations V* (Paris: Gallimard, 1964), 25–48. Translated as *Colonialism and Neocolonialism* (London and New York: Routledge, 2001). On the Comité d'action, see James Le Sueur, *Uncivil War: Intellectuals and Identity Politics during the Decolonization of Algeria* (Philadelphia: University of Pennsylvania Press, 2001), 31–54.
28. Raymond Aron, *La Tragédie algérienne* (Paris: Plon, 1957).

29. Martin Baker, *The New Racism: Conservatism and the Ideology of the Tribes* (London: Junction, 1981); Amy E. Ansell, *New Right, New Racism: Race and Reaction in the United States and Britain* (New York: New York University Press, 1997); Eduardo Bonilla-Silva, *Racism without Racists: Color-Blind Racism and the Persistence of Racial Inequality in the United States* (New York: Rowman and Littlefield, 2003); Patricia Hill Collins, *Black Sexual Politics: African Americans, Gender, and the New Racism* (New York: Routledge, 2005).
30. Jean-Paul Sartre, *L'existentialisme est un humanisme* (Paris: Nagel, 1946), 24, trans. Bernard Frechtman, "Existentialism" in *Existentialism and Human Emotions* (New York: Philosophical Library), 9–51, 16.
31. Jean-Paul Sartre, *Search for a Method*, trans. Hazel Barnes (New York: Vintage, 1963), 27. Cited parenthetically hereafter.
32. On this point and the basic premises of the *Méthode*, see Mark Poster, *Existential Marxism in Postwar France*, 272 and 264–74.
33. Rhiannon Goldthorpe makes this point in "Understanding the Committed Writer" in Christina Howells, ed., *The Cambridge Companion to Sartre* (Cambridge, England: Cambridge University Press, 1992), 151.
34. Richard H. King, *Race, Culture and the Intellectuals, 1940–1970* (Baltimore and London: Johns Hopkins University Press, 2004), 306 and passim.
35. Richard Watt's develops Gérard Genette's term in *Packaging Post/Coloniality: The Manufacture of Literary Identity in the Francophone World* (Lanham: Lexington, 2005). By the "paratext" Watt's means the various mechanisms for the packaging of books, including "titles, covers, illustrations, promotional summaries, epigraphs, dedications, and, most significantly, prefaces that make the unadorned text a book" (2), since these paratexts announce the work, situate it, and impose or at least suggest an interpretative frame.

Part I

Sartre on Race and Racism

Chapter 1

Sartre on Racism
From Existential Phenomenology to Globalization and "the New Racism"

Jonathan Judaken

In early November 2005, our television screens were suddenly ablaze with cars on fire and the burning rage of the ghettoized *banlieues* that surround the urban centers of France. On October 27, 2005, the deaths of Zyed Benna, 17, and Bouna Traoré, 15, electrocuted fleeing the *flics* (cops) in Clichy-sous-Bois,[1] sparked the pent-up wrath of the mostly Maghrebin and West African immigrant youth that erupted nightly over the next month: The damage included over 8,400 torched vehicles and 2,600 arrests in nearly 100 towns across France.[2] In contrast to the neoconservative commentary on the riots,[3] "the rage expressed by young men from the *cités* does not spring from antiimperialist Arab nationalism or some sort of anti-Western jihadism," Paul Silverstein and Chantal Tetreault maintain, "but rather from lifetimes of rampant unemployment, school failure, police harassment and everyday discrimination that tends to treat the youths as the *racaille* [scum]" that then Interior Minister Nicolas Sarkozy labeled them.[4] To end the violence, Prime Minister Dominique de Villepin announced a state of emergency on November 7. In doing so, he invoked an April 1955 law created in order to eliminate support for the budding Algerian war of independence, a provision that was extended for an additional three months on November 15 by the National Assembly.

Did we witness the reprise of colonial legislation in the postcolonial metropole because colonialism has been deterritorialized in the age of globalization? Jean-Paul Sartre, in an article written in 1973 called "Le Nouveau Racisme" (translated as "France and a Matter of Racism"), an intervention in response to the killing of Mohamad Diab by a French police sergeant, suggested more than thirty years ago that there was a nexus between the postcolonial situation and racism. Racism legitimated the exploitation that underpinned colonialism, he declared. Decolonization should have taught Europeans that "the impoverished and weaponless colonials ... are no more subhuman than we." Instead, Sartre declared, another colonialism has been established on our own soil. We bring in workers from poor European countries such as Spain and Portugal, or from our old colonies to do the unpleasant work the French workers no longer want to do. Underpaid, threatened with expulsion if they protest, and crowded into filthy lodgings, it has been necessary to justify their overexploitation which is now an important cog in the machine of French capitalism. Thus a new racism has been born which would like the immigrants to live in terror, and to rob them of the desire to protest against the living conditions that have been forced upon them.

Reading Sartre's analysis after the November riots is haunting. "This outburst is the inevitable result of the racism that has re-emerged during the last ten years in the administration and the police and which originates in the economy," he fumed. He called upon the French to rise up against this neoracism, to protest its institutionalization "by the power structure," to show that "a point of no return has been reached, that racism must be crushed." To fail to do so, he insisted, meant that we "deserve the government of fear that the bourgeoisie gave us."[5]

As we see, Sartre was intransigent in his impassioned remonstrations against racism until his last days. But the theoretical underpinning of his stances evolved over the course of his commitments. This chapter traces that evolution, suggesting four *overlapping* phases to Sartre's antiracist interventions.[6] In so doing, I insist that both his blindnesses and insights have much to teach us when it is still the case that, as one young Moroccan put it in a discussion on French television about the fate of African immigrants in France, "our color is our pain."[7] The color line at the dawn of the twenty-first century is evidently still one of the great problems that define our age of globalization. And there is still much to learn from Sartre about the differing concepts he mobilized in order to name racism's distinct modalities, about how to assess racism, about where to target our critiques, and about how to combat it.

Sartre's Anti-antisemitism

Phase 1, Sartre's anti-antisemitism, stemmed from his existential phenomenology, which he developed over the course of the 1930s. He was a lycée teacher publishing philosophical treatises on the role of the imagination and perception in consciousness when in 1933–34 he spent the academic year in Germany just as Hitler rose to power. He returned to a France increasingly polarized over fascism and antisemitism. Only the signposts of the era can be mentioned here: the Stavinsky affair; the riots of February 6, 1934; the accession to power of the Popular Front (1936–1938), headed by the first socialist and Jewish premier, Léon Blum. Blum embodied the associative logic of stereotyping that enabled the opponents of the Popular Front to tar the French Republic with a series of interchangeable epithets, exemplified by fascist Jacques Doriot's condemning what he called the "pluto-Judeo-Bolshevik coalition" that he claimed ruled France.[8]

Sartre's response to this widespread antisemitic discourse was his first overtly politicized work, the novella *L'Enfance d'un chef* ("The Childhood of a Leader," 1939).[9] The story is an ironic *Bildungsroman* deeply critical of the Action Française's shock troops, the Camelots du roi,[10] and the politics of the extreme Right more generally who defined their Frenchness against the abject image of "the Jew."[11]

The literary portrait of Lucien Fleurier, the would-be *chef* of the story and the archetype of the *salaud* (bastard)—whom Sartre never tired of decrying—would reach fruition in his famous theoretical treatise on antisemitism, *Réflexions sur la question juive* (*Antisemite and Jew*, 1946). His "Portrait de l'antisémite," Sartre's phenomenological description of the racial oppressor, was the first concrete application of the key existential axioms regarding the relation of Self and Other articulated in *L'Être et le Néant* (*Being and Nothingness*, 1943) and the crystallization of Sartre's anti-antisemitism.[12] "The most striking feature of Sartre's fight resides less in his victory than in the new weapons he deploys," Emmanuel Levinas proclaimed in applauding Sartre's essay, since "antisemitism is attacked with existentialist arguments."[13]

Sartre developed these existentialist arguments in his philosophical magnum opus *Being and Nothingness*, which was, as the subtitle proclaims, a "phenomenological essay on ontology."[14] Here he articulated the philosophical underpinnings at work in his existential-phenomenological critique of antisemitism and racism: his ontological description of human freedom, his existential analysis of responsibility, and his concepts of "bad faith," "the situation," and the dialectic of human recognition between Self and Other engendered by "the look." The first half of *Being and Nothingness* is concerned with defining the central categories of Sartre's ontology through an elaboration of the distinction between the object world, which Sartre calls the in-itself (*être-en-soi*) and the perceiving subject, which he names the for-itself (*être-pour-soi*). There is also a third kind of being that Sartre discusses, which occupies the second half of *Being and Nothingness*, being-for-others (*être-pour-autrui*).

The gaze determines the basic structure of being-for-others. I see others and see them seeing me and know that they judge my choices. The Other's gaze turns me into an object in his/her world, a character in his/her life drama, and thereby takes away my freedom to freely determine my own essence. When I am looked at (*être regardé*), I become objectified and my subjectivity is fixed by my being-for-others; this can be avoided by returning the gaze and objectifying the Other. On the basis of this structure, Sartre describes all concrete relations with others as forms of struggle. Indifference is impossible: it is a mode of self-deception that refuses to see that others gaze at me, a refusal to accept that I am alienated from my own objectivity. My desire for this objectivity—my desire to be the foundation of my own existence, to constitute my-self as an essence, to be an *en-soi-pour-soi*, is the quintessence of self-deception or what Sartre calls *mauvaise foi* (bad faith)—and it is animated by the human desire to be God. This desire creates the inherent conflict in my concrete relations with others. There are fundamentally only two kinds of response to the gaze of Others: to make oneself the kind of object that you would like to be perceived as (which in its severe form Sartre names "masochism") or to desire the pure instrumental appropriation of the Other (which in its ultimate manifestation is named "sadism"). Masochism is the desire to be the object of the gaze of the other, while sadism is the desire to objectify the other, achieved at its extreme through violence.

In the final part of *Being and Nothingness*, Sartre concretizes this discussion more explicitly around the relation between the antisemitic gaze and the Jewish Other. It takes place in the context of a larger discussion about "freedom and facticity: the situation." In this section, he makes clear that the conception of freedom that he is developing is not an abstract freedom divorced from the strictures upon individual choices. Freedom is always situated and conditioned by the individual's perceived "situation." There are specific factors that Sartre outlines that determine one's situation: a persons *place* in the world, their *past*, the *environment*, and all *others* that shape their context.

In the subsection on "my fellowman" Sartre explicitly uses the example of the relation between the antisemite and "the Jew" to explicate the struggle for recognition and the objective limits of freedom in a situation:

> It is only by my recognizing the *freedom* of antisemites (whatever use they may make of it) and by my assuming this *being-a-Jew* that I am a Jew for them; it is only thus that being-a-Jew will appear as the external objective limit of the situation. If, on the contrary, it pleases me to consider the antisemites as pure *objects*, then my being-a-Jew disappears immediately to give place to the simple consciousness (of) being a free, unqualifiable transcendence. To recognize others and, if I am a Jew, to assume my being-a-Jew are one and the same. (675)

Sartre thus explains that a limit of the Jewish situation is the gaze of the antisemitic Other, who defines "the Jew" in accord with an essence of being-a-Jew. "The Jew," can refuse this designation. However, "the Jew" cannot deny that the antisemite perceives him as a Jew. The question for "the Jew" becomes how s/he responds to this limit factor in his/her situation.

Sartre goes on to tackle this question: "How then shall I experience the objective limits of my being: Jew, Aryan, ugly, handsome, kind, a civil servant, untouchable, etc.?" The objectification of your being, the designation of your essence by an Other, does not define who you are for-yourself. These labels conferred upon us by Others require "an interiorization and a subjectivizing" (675). Every essence ascribed to us by others, Sartre categorically insists, must be conferred with a meaning for us. In short, "a Jew is not a Jew *first* in order to be *subsequently* ashamed or proud; it is his pride of being a Jew, his shame, or his indifference which will reveal to him his being-a-Jew; and this being-a-Jew is nothing outside the free manner of adopting it" (677). In other words, the Jewish situation is like the condition of all humans for whom there are objective conditions which structure our choices—class, race, place, the body, and the gaze of the Other. But ultimately these only have the meaning that an individual confers upon them. The difference for "the Jew" is that this meaning is always doubled: it is a question not only of the meaning of human existence, but what it means to be-a-Jew, and how this shapes one's humanity.

While Sartre's mention of Jews and Judaism are relatively scant in the body of his enormous ontological description of the human condition, he is explicit about its implications for the antisemite and draws some provisional conclusions for Jews. The antisemite's bad faith is that he wants to be God: to have an absolute foundation for the meaning of his existence. As such, he embodies the quintessence of bad faith by seeking to found his essence in his sadistic appropriation of "the Jew," which at its extreme leads to a violent hatred for "the Jew," that at bottom is a hatred of all alterity. "The Jew" must respond to his situation by defining the meaning of his Jewishness and his humanity—always a double responsibility—knowing that Others will define his choices in part by how they perceive "the Jew," thus conferring upon Jews the facticity of their being-a-Jew.

Antisemite and Jew would elaborate upon what Sartre had sketched as examples in his ontological description, applying systematically for the first time the categories of *Being and Nothingness* to a concrete situation. Sartre argued that antisemitism does not rest solely upon economic, historical, religious, or political foundations, but rather demands an existential analysis of the antisemite and "the Jew." In undertaking this examination, he argued that the fundamental cause of antisemitism is the *mauvaise foi* (bad faith) of the antisemite: his fear and flight from the human condition.[15] Rather than face his own finitude and freedom, the antisemite, like Lucien in "The Childhood of a Leader," adopts in advance a "certain idea of the Jew, of his nature and of his role in society" (14/13) and through a process of projection and transference chooses himself through this image. In accord with a Manichean logic, he defines himself through abjection, opposing his identity to the impurity, depravity, corruption, pollution, impiety, ugliness, untruth, racial deviance, urbanity, or foreignness of "the Jew," whom he deems threatens essential Frenchness.[16] Through this negative image, the antisemite explains his experience of the world. With this model of the degraded and perverse Other, he "is under no necessity to look for his personality within himself. He has chosen ... to be nothing save the fear he inspires in others" (24/21). Antisemitism consequently boils down to a "basic fear of oneself and of truth" (21/19), a fear of all humans' fundamental ontological freedom. Antisemitism is therefore the paradigmatic form of bad faith in the face of the human condition.

On the basis of these axioms, the *Réflexions* instantiated several key theorems of Sartre's antiracism: first, that there is no biological, cultural, or metaphysical reality to "race"; it is a social construct.[17] Second, Sartre was nonetheless aware that "race" for the racist is constitutive of reality. As such, he called racism a "passion" whose bad faith is akin to religious faith and therefore not amenable to any rational evidence that opposes the racist's Manichean and conspiratorial logic.[18] Third, Sartre's *Réflexions* also castigated what he labeled the "politics of assimilation"[19]—the Enlightenment and liberal tradition that defined Franco-Judaism and Jewish emancipation—contending that it ultimately eliminated Jewishness through its universal and abstract principles that did not recognize Jewish difference. He thus decried any polity based upon homogeneity, normalization, or what goes by the name today in France of *intégration*. Fourth, conjoined to this proposition, Sartre also announced that the fight against racism must be waged in the name of liberty, not based on the abstract axioms of liberalism (i.e., human rights, constitutionalism, equality of opportunity, equality before the law, etc.), but rather on the existential conception of freedom at the root of human existence. And finally, he maintained that the primary responsibility to combat antisemitism lay with the dominant culture whose own freedom was contingent upon the freedom of all in their midst. "The fate of the Jews is *his* fate. Not one Frenchman will be free," he thundered at the conclusion of his *Réflexions*, "so long as the Jews do not enjoy the fullness of their rights" (185/153).[20]

Anticolonialist Existential Humanism

Beyond the occasional allusion to his *Réflexions*, and his involvement in the Arab-Israeli conflict, Sartre would write little about the Jewish Question in the period from 1945 to 1960.[21] This second phase of his antiracism was nonetheless significantly indebted to his critique of antisemitism. "Replace the Jew with the Black, the antisemite with the supporter of slavery," he claimed, "and there would be nothing essential to be cut from my book [on the Jewish Question]."[22] The phase of anticolonialist existential humanism was based primarily on developing a key axiom in *L'existentialisme est un humanisme* (*Existentialism is a Humanism*, 1946) where Sartre maintained, "if existence really does precede essence, man is responsible for what he is ... and when we say that a man is responsible for himself, we do not only mean that he is responsible for his own individuality, but that he is responsible for all men."[23] This claim—that each individual's freedom is dependent upon the freedom of all—made clear the meaning of the concluding lines of the *Réflexions*.

This imperative underlay his antiracist anticolonialism, which figured racial oppression as a central lever in (colonial) domination in his occasional writings on racism in America (1945), in *La Putain respectueuse* (*The Respectful Prostitute*, 1946), in his excursus on "The Oppression of Blacks in the United States," in *Cahiers pour une morale* (*Notebooks for an Ethics*, 1947–1948), in "Présence noire" ("Black Presence," 1947), "Orphée noir" ("Black Orpheus," 1948), and in most of his other early writings on colonialism and decolonization gathered in *Situations V* (*Colonialism and Neo-Colonialism*, 1964). We will consider only a few examples from this period to establish further key theorems of Sartre's antiracism.

In the immediate postwar period, Sartre's existential phenomenological analysis of antisemitism would be applied to the racial oppression of blacks in many of the same terms that structured his scrutiny of antisemitism. His key concepts remained freedom, responsibility, bad faith, the situation, and the dialectic of human recognition engendered by the gaze. In "Retour des États Unis: Ce qui j'ai appris du problème noir" ("Return from the United States," 1945), the structure of the look still defined his philosophical assessment of the situation of black Americans. Sartre described how under Jim Crow blacks were treated as "untouchables" who when you "cross them in the streets ... you do not return their stares. Or if by chance their eyes meet yours, it seems to you that they do not see you and it is better for them and you that you pretend not to have noticed them."[24] Blacks function like "machines": they serve whites; they shine their shoes and operate their elevators. To Sartre, this was the ultimate example of the sadistic reification of the Other and its attendant bad faith and alienation that he had assessed in *Being in Nothingness* and had applied to the situation of Jews.[25]

But a new element began to emerge in Sartre's discussions of racism in the United States. He started to address the *institutionalized oppression* of blacks: their differential treatment as citizens with no rights, who live in a state of "semislavery" (87) in the South, with only slightly better conditions in the segregated North. Segregation provided the legal framework for the separation of populations and for blacks' unequal access to education, services, goods, housing, healthcare, theaters, restaurants, cinemas, and libraries with the effect that "the majority of them live in horrible misery" (84). Sartre described the material conditions of subordination and disenfranchisement resulting from "the economic structure of the country," insisting that "it is that which one must examine first" (87). Thus, while he had discussed economic factors in his assessment of antisemitism in his *Réflexions*, it was in his writings on the conditions of African-Americans in the United States that he first went into some detail about where and how racialized subjects live, which he maintained conditioned the racial state.[26]

Sartre would elaborate upon the institutionalized oppression of blacks in the United States in an excursus included in his *Notebooks for an Ethics*.[27] Addressing the domination of blacks under slavery, he sought to explain how through legal prescriptions covering matrimony, civic and military duties, and through the governing norms of social interaction, the legalization of oppression makes it seem legitimate. Making racial oppression lawful puts it in a realm beyond discussion, making it sacred, and therefore part of the natural order of things. In articulating this argument, Sartre distinguishes violence, which "cannot be defined apart from some relation to the laws that it violates (human or natural laws)" from oppression. Oppression is institutional: "It suffices that the oppressing class legitimate its oppression by law and that the oppressed class, out of weakness, complicity, ignorance, or any other reason, obeys these laws and implicitly or explicitly recognizes them through its behavior" (579/561).

Sartre was stumbling toward seeing race not as an idea, but as an ideology, not only as a phenomenon of consciousness, but as a product of behaviors, practices, rituals, folkways, and symbols institutionalized daily. In this he anticipated the argument of Barbara Fields, among others, that slavery created racism (and not the other way around), since people are more readily perceived as inferior by nature when they are already seen as oppressed.[28] In short, for Sartre, "the abject institution of slavery, lived through, reworked, and rearranged," transformed "itself into a concrete relation, a type of existence, a social architecture" (583/564–65) that structured social relationships and thereby provided the oppressor with a good conscience.

But the analysis of the institutional character of slavery did not supplant the dialectic of the gaze that underpinned the existential phenomenology of racism. With a copy of Gunnar Myrdal's *An American Dilemma* at hand as the springboard upon which many of his reflections are constructed,[29] Sartre still focused on the different modalities of the bad faith of slavery. Slave masters justified the institution by claiming that it was blacks who sold other blacks into slavery; they deployed the Hamitic myth; they suggested that Africans were not Christians and therefore not privy to the same ethical norms; in short, they contended that blacks were "submen" (580/562–63). The concepts of *Being and Nothingness* are still apparent, as Sartre examined how under slavery and segregation the for-itself "freezes the other into an object" (581/563). He also described the "limited transcendence" of both master and slave.

Nevertheless he clearly sought to go beyond the limits of the Hegelian dialectic as well.[30] "In reality, Hegel saw just one side of the slave: his labor," Sartre claimed. As a result, "his whole theory is wrong, or rather it applies to the proletarian, not to the slave" (586/566). Sartre, like Marx, therefore flipped Hegel on his head when he asserted that "oppression is *institutional*" because it functions through a set of norms and rules that make possible "a certain way of living out a relation with the other" (589/570). Antiracism thus depended upon transforming the structures of oppression, which themselves conditioned the structures of perception. "To see clearly in an unjustifiable situation," Sartre averred in an arresting formulation, "it is not sufficient that the oppressor look at it openly and honestly, he must also change the structure of his eyes" (590–91/571).

But Sartre's antiracism would continue to focus primarily on dismantling racist structures of perception in this period, as is apparent in "Black Orpheus," his famous celebration of negritude poetry written as a preface to Léopold Sédar Senghor's *Anthologie de la nouvelle poésie nègre et malgache de langue française* (Anthology of African and West Indian Poets Writing in French).[31] As "Black Orpheus" makes plain, much of his early writing on colonialism would continue to revolve around the same conflict that he characterized for Jews: the struggle with how the dominant culture imposes itself, how this is internalized, and how colonial subjects can liberate themselves. In "Black Orpheus," however, he did take a more definitive step in the direction of the argument that defined his politics in the postwar period: the demand that the writer reveal the world from the perspective of the oppressed.[32] The standpoint of "the Jew," "the African," the colonized, and the worker offer a critical lens through which to view the system of oppression.

Similar to his *Réflexions*, "Black Orpheus" positioned the intellectual as a critic of established values and norms, which exclude and repress through the pathologization and exploitation of the subaltern. There are homologies in his analysis of blackness and Jewishness. Both are defined by what they oppose: racial oppression and antisemitism. Negritude is a critique of the cultural discourses and institutional practices and policies that repress the African in the European world. Since race is intrinsic to their oppression, Sartre is emphatic that blacks must first be made conscious of their race and therefore, "anti-racist racism is the only road that will lead to the abolition of racial differences" (xiv/18). In a counterpart to his discussion of authentic Jewishness, since the oppression of blacks has depended upon the vilification of blackness, there must first be a moment of pride in being black. As Abiola Irele incisively put it, "Sartre's term ["antiracist racism"] therefore meant a negro racial pride designed to destroy racialism itself."[33]

Sartre does, however, emphasize a difference of degree between the alienation of Jews and blacks, for "a Jew—a white man among white men—can deny that he is a Jew, can declare himself a man among men. The Negro cannot deny that he is a Negro, nor can he claim that he is part of some abstract colorless humanity: he is black" (xiv/18). But while the possibility of assimilation is thus greater for Jews, as he maintained in his *Réflexions*, it is ultimately destined to fail. In a fashion not dissimilar to what Sartre described for Jews, repressed by European culture, blacks develop what W.E.B. Du Bois called "double-consciousness"[34] and what Sartre describes as the split consciousness of their "double exile" (xvi/20). Exiles from Africa, they are exiled within Europe. Sartre calls negritude "Orphic because the negro's tireless descent into himself makes me think of Orpheus going to claim Eurydice from Pluto" (xvii/22). This Orphic journey into the self is undertaken "to ruin systematically the European knowledge he has acquired, and this spiritual destruction symbolizes the great future taking-up of arms by which black men will destroy their chains" (xviii/22).

One of the radically new claims of "Black Orpheus" is that if blacks have nothing to lose but their chains, this will depend upon negritude writers deconstructing how blackness is figured within the semiotic system of the West. Sartre's semiology of the racialized Other as a sign within the system of colonial oppression thereby anticipated certain deconstructive and postcolonial analyses. Since he is writing about black Francophone poets, he argues that these diasporic critics must use the oppressor's language for their resistance, utilizing the master's tools to dismantle his house.[35] Negritude poets exploit the failures of European culture to name black experience and this misunderstanding, Sartre claims, facilitates our ability to see the whole civilization and its discontents.

Negritude poetry pushes the French poetic tradition from Mallamé's symbolism to surrealism that is about the "autodestruction of language" (xx/25) in new directions. Negritude writers traverse the "short-circuits of language" (xx/26) because within the semantic field that defines the key terms of colonial and racial discourse—exile/home, black/white, and native/colonist—there are already prescribed positions of hierarchy and subordination. Negritude negates the semiotics of whiteness, which is identified with humanity, light, truth, virtue, essence, and spirit, as opposed to the carnal flesh, inessential, deviant, dark bestiality of blackness. Negritude poetry upsets this hierarchy by valorizing the secondary and inferior terms. There is thus a self-destruction of the semiotic system in negritude, analogous to Duchamp's art and surrealism. Negritude is thus a poetry of negativity: a refusal and destabilization of colonial and racist signification, upsetting and reorienting our concepts of blackness.

Sartre argues, however, that because their critique happens in language, negritude poets are destined to reestablish "the hierarchy they have just upset" (xxii/27). But just as was the case with his writing on Jewishness, where he recycles certain antisemitic motifs,[36] Sartre contributes to this restabilization by unproblematically accepting stereotypical conceptions of blackness and Africa. As Stuart Zane Charmé acutely puts it:

> Repeating the same strategy that had produced *Antisemite and Jew*, Sartre remained on the level of myth or symbol rather than history. Like the Jew, the black's primary mythic function was to embody simultaneously the victimization by, and the negation of, white European culture and the colonialism it supported.[37]

Sartre's depiction of blackness as the negation of white supremacy serves to destabilize white, European, bourgeois hegemony. In the process, however, he reinscribes typological constructions of blackness that figure for him the negativity of European values.[38] He thus identifies "the black" with primitivism and he resorts to images of blacks as natural man and unchaste woman whose identification with nature and *Eros* have an emancipatory function not only for blacks, but also for repressed Europeans. Sartre says, for example, that the blacks "wild and free looks that judge our world" (x/14) do so by plunging "man back into the seething breast of Nature" (xxv/31). Blacks have "timeless instincts, a simple manifestation of universal and eternal fecundity" (xxxviii/46). His identification of blacks with nature, sexuality, a phallic order, instinct, creation, and rhythm are justified by him as a necessary stage within what he calls "Universal History."

But this ultimately mired Sartre's patronage of negritude in the quagmires that result from his strategic essentialism—his "antiracist racism"—that he advanced as a means to undo racialism. In *Peau noire, masques blancs* (*Black Skin, White Masks*, 1952), Frantz Fanon sharply criticized Sartre for failing to condemn some of his hackneyed images of blackness. Fanon blamed the effacing of what he called "the lived experience of blackness" on Sartre's dialectic with its totalizing and universalizing logic that he construed as the foundational problem in Sartre's writing on behalf of the black Other.[39] The historical specificity of the Other, "the lived experience of blackness," is sacrificed to a mythological and ahistorical depiction within the logic of Sartre's dialectic. Fanon's rejoinder served as a warning that when Sartre abandoned his existentialist premises, even doing so for strategic political ends elucidated by his dialectic of history, he risked falling into the trap of racist discourse.

Sartre's other early anticolonial writings would elaborate on the need for avoiding these traps through the demystification of stereotyping that he referred to as "the picturesque" in his preface to Henri Cartier-Bresson's *D'une Chine à l'autre* ("From One China to Another," 1954).[40] Stereotyping "scorned collectively" (7/17). Cartier-Bresson's virtue was to provide snapshots of a society in transition that exploded the exoticism and "convenient label[s]" (9/18) of typologies. Assedine Haddour thus rightly praises Sartre for prefiguring "the arguments of Roland Barthes in 'Myth Today' and Edward Said in *Orientalism*, i.e. [criticizing] the fabricated quality of the mythic idea and its orientalizing intent."[41] This is crucial, for as Sartre maintained, "What separates has to be learned; what unites can be seen in an instant" (12/20). He concluded the piece by rejoicing in the Chinese revolution that Cartier-Bresson's album documented as it moved from the countryside into the municipal capitals of China, since it offered hope for overcoming the archipelago of "capitals of poverty" that defined the Third World.

Sartre's antiracist anticolonialism thus elaborated upon some of the perceptive pronouncements of his anti-antisemitism at the same time that he expanded his conception of racism. The keystone of this phase was his leap from his earlier emphasis on individual existential freedom toward his existential humanism, insisting that the freedom of the individual is dependent upon the freedom of all. Second, while he continued to hold that the kernel of racism is the sadistic reification of the other in an effort to deny their freedom, he also clarified that seeing things from the perspective of the marginalized and oppressed helps to divulge the structures of oppression in a society. Third, he asserted that a first step to overcoming racism by racialized groups is to embrace their collective identity as part of the struggle against racism; an "antiracist racism" was thus necessary to destroy racialism. But antiracism on the basis of a strategic essentialism also risked reduplicating racism, unless it was marshaled as part of a committed effort to explode the racial order as a whole. Fourth, as such Sartre venerated the novel efforts of poets and writers to deconstruct the semiotics of race in order to detonate the stereotypes that underpin racism. But it was in his immediate postwar writings on racism in the United States that Sartre first broached axioms that would shape the next phase of his reflections on racism. Here, he schematically explored how oppression was institutionalized and as such how racism was part of the social architecture. He contended that racism was not only conditional upon the stereotypes or roles that are assigned to oppressed groups, but is woven into the fabric of practices, rituals, symbols, and institutions that structure social systems. Antiracism thus depends upon transforming the structures of oppression, which themselves condition structures of perception.

Third World Radicalism

By the late 1950s, as Sartre's defense of the Algerian revolution became more unbridled and as the conflict became more violent on both sides, the terms of his understanding of racism changed more clearly in the direction of an emphasis on racialized social structures. A transitional text was his preface to Albert Memmi's classic analysis *Portrait du colonisé précédé du colonisateur* (*The Colonizer and the Colonized*, 1957).[42] Sartre commended Memmi's inquiry, which is clearly modeled on Sartre's intersubjective dialectic of the gaze. Memmi's existential premises concerning freedom and authenticity in a specific situation are also derived from Sartrean precepts. The *Réflexions* also remained foundational for the two portraits Memmi draws: the colonizer is not unlike the portrait of the antisemite and the situation of the colonized overlaps with Sartre's portrait of "the Jew." But Sartre is nevertheless critical of Memmi's subtle psychological depiction of the dynamic relationship within colonization and how this results in the interiorization of colonial hegemony. "The whole difference between us arises," Sartre asserts in a critical footnote, "because he sees a situation where I see a system" (27/xxv).

Sartre had made this shift in his thinking by the time of his speech "Colonialisme est une système" ("Colonialism is a System," 1956), which reflected the subsuming of his existential-phenomenological analysis within his developing existential Marxist framework. In his remarks made at a protest rally held at the Salle Wagram against continuing the war in Algeria he stressed, "Colonization is neither a series of chance occurrences nor the statistical result of thousands of individual undertakings," or choices in isolated situations. "It is a system," he continued, "which was put in place around the middle of the nineteenth century, began to bear fruit in about 1880, [and] started to decline after the First World War."[43]

In the third phase of his antiracist works, Sartre described the mechanisms and material effects of colonial exploitation in far more detail than his earlier writing on institutionalized racism in the United States. He labored to show that each of the signs of the European civilizing mission—the roads, French schools, and public heath and hygiene—were, in fact, means for colonial domination.[44] But nothing was more central to the colonial system than the systematic dispossession of Arab land and the concomitant mechanization of colonial agriculture. Colonial exploitation was thus experienced as "methodical and rigorous: expelled from their lands, restricted to unproductive soil, obliged to work for derisory wages, the fear of unemployment discourages ... [colonial] revolts" (37/39). Consequently, for many Algerians, their only alternative was to emigrate to France where they worked to send back money to support their families in Algeria. Sartre thus explained, as Tony Smith sums it up, "the congruence between economic spoliation, cultural imperialism, and political domination of the native Muslims by the French invaders and colonizers ... where cultural antagonism compounded class struggle with aspects of race warfare."[45]

Sartre's shift from the analysis of the colonial "situation" to a "system" carried over into his understanding of racism. If capitalism had to become colonialist to expand its markets and the sources of its raw materials, its ideological justification was liberalism, which purported to uphold universal human rights that could only logically be denied Algerians in light of a racist rationale.[46] "One of the functions of racism," Sartre therefore claimed "is to compensate the latent universalism of bourgeois liberalism." Hence "since all human beings have the same rights, the Algerian will be made subhuman" (CS, 44/45).

But in his preface to Memmi, he made clear that the racist rationale is itself a function of the system of exploitation: "Colonialism denies human rights to human beings whom it has subdued by violence, and keeps them by force in a state of misery and ignorance that Marx would rightly call a subhuman condition. Racism is ingrained in action, institutions, and in the nature of the colonialist methods of production and exchange" (26/xxiv). While racism operates psychically, conditioning how we perceive and receive the Other, serving to dehumanize colonial and racialized subjects so that human rights and equality need not be extended to them, Sartre's point now is unequivocally that racism is enmeshed in the power structure and material system of oppression itself. Discrimination functions not only cognitively and intersubjectively, but within institutions and everyday practices and policies. The racist colonial system "is embodied in a million colonists, children and grandchildren of colonists, who have been shaped by colonialism and who think, speak and act according to the very principles of the colonial system" (CS, 43/44). The racist system therefore shaped both the colonized and the colonizer, infecting all "with its racism" (CS, 47/47). This was nowhere more apparent than in the methods that were used by the French to pacify resistance to colonialization.

Sartre responded to the reciprocal reign of terror that began to characterize the French-Algerian conflict by the time of the Battle of Algiers (1957) by insisting that torture was a product of systemic violence and dehumanization that in turn produced inhuman acts. This could only be overcome through a revolution against the system of exploitation that might restore our humanity. In "Vous êtes formidables" ("You are Wonderful"), he insisted that all who failed to denounce "the cynical and systematic use of absolute violence," which included "pillaging, rape, reprisals against the civilian population, summary executions, [and the] use of torture to extract confessions or information" were complicitous with the system because none could deny ignorance.[47]

He goes on to analyze the different modalities of elision, evasion, and denial about torture in liberal societies that nonetheless produced a "troubled conscience" that ultimately cannot repress "the game of hide and seek that we play, the lamps that we dim, this painful bad faith" (65/60). All who fail to rail against torture are blameworthy of what Jaspers in *The Question of German Guilt* called the "metaphysical guilt" of those who acquiesce when categorical injustice is committed in their name: "False naiveté, flight, bad faith, solitude, silence, a complicity at once rejected and accepted, that is what we called, in 1945, collective responsibility" (66/60), he reminded his readers.

In his introduction to Henri Alleg's *La Question* (*The Question*, 1958), he would elaborate on how torture was the ossification of a system of exploitation whose connective tissue was racism.[48] "In this way," Sartre expounded about torture, "exploitation puts the exploiter at the mercy of his victim, and the dependence itself begets racialism" (120/32). He explained that torture is not really about producing information, but instead is about destroying human dignity (118/30), which ultimately is the only thing that can legitimate the system of exploitation. The purpose of torture is not to make a person talk, but "rather to humiliate them, to crush their pride and drag them down to animal level. The body may live, but the spirit must be killed. To train, discipline and chastise; these are the words which obsess" the torturers Sartre insists (121/33).

Torture is merely the most brutal and crude mechanism in the system of domination. In this sense, "Torture was simply the expression of racial hatred" (121/33), just as racial hatred was the means to justify treating some people as animals or cogs in a machine. As such, torture ultimately ends up destroying the human being who hates, just as exploitation cannot but result in enmeshing the exploiter, for "hate is a magnetic field: it has ... corroded them and enslaved them [both]" (122/34). In the end then, torture reveals the limits and the ends of systemic exploitation and how racism was imbricated within it: "Torture was imposed here by circumstances and demanded by racial hatred. In some ways it is the essence of the conflict and expresses its deepest truth" (124–25/36).

In short, by the late 1950s, Sartre conceived of racism not as a mythical blinder that legitimates oppression; he argued that it is a central pillar in the structure of exploitation itself. The conception of the institutionalization of racism and its enmeshment in the system of production and exchange goes beyond the terms of his earlier reflections on antisemitism and his support of the negritude negation of colonialism, elaborating on what he first explored in his writing on racism in the United States, reaching full fruition in his existential Marxist writings.

The theoretical elaboration of his existentialist Marxist position was most developed in *Critique de la raison dialectique* (*Critique of Dialectical Reason*, 1960), where a new series of concepts governed Sartre's analysis: dialectical history, praxis, the practico-inert, totalization, and seriality.[49] The *Critique* sought to explain how humans make history and in turn are made by that history. Or as Sartre put it, he wanted to explain the "permanent and dialectical unity of freedom and necessity." Developing what he called after Henri Lefebvre the progressive-regressive method, dialectical history moved back and forth between the social totality and the individual in search of the mediations that could account for historical configurations. Humans are always set in specific situations, which they interpret and act upon. This "subjective process of self-definition through action in the world" defines praxis, which as Martin Jay explains, translates Sartre's notion of the for-itself in *Being and Nothingness* into the terms of the *Critique*. The accumulated result of human action is the practico-inert. "Like Marx's concept of capital as dead labor or Sartre's own earlier notion of the in-itself," Jay elaborates, "the practico-inert confronts man as an irreducible other, despite his role in its creation."[50] Most people thus lead atomized, alienated lives, an existence that Herbert Marcuse called the life of "one-dimensional man," where they do little more than internalize the dead existence of the practico-inert, satisfied with themselves as the reified incarnation of prescribed social functions. Collective existence is thus dominated by what Sartre called seriality. "'Serial' collectives are agglomerations of human beings," William McBride explains, "engaged in some enterprise to which a common name can be given but which far from unifying them, reinforces their isolation."[51] Racism, Sartre maintains, is a part of "a *praxis* illuminated by a 'theory' ('biological,' 'social,' or empirical racism, it does not matter which) aiming to keep the masses in a state of molecular aggregation" (721).

Abstracting from his specific interventions into the Algerian conflict, but also reflecting on Nazi and Stalinist antisemitism, Sartre tried to elucidate what he now called "the seriality of racism" (652). Internal to the supraexploitation of colonialism was violence and appropriation that was justified through the self-reinforcing logic of racism. In the terms of the *Critique*, Sartre enumerated its unfolding: it begins as a

> structure of alienation in the *practico-inert*, it is actualized as *praxis* in colonization; and its (temporary) victory presents itself as the objectification of the practical ensemble (army, capitalists, commodity merchants, colonialists) in a

practico-inert system where it represents the fundamental structure of reciprocity between the colonialists and the colonized. (720)

This "serial exis" is engraved in the practices and institutions of the lived world, where the colonialist or antisemite "lives on an 'Island of Doctor Moreau,' surrounded by terrifying beasts created in the image of man, but botched" (720). Since the racial oppressor lives constantly with a paranoid vision that those subhumans—demonized, bestialized, and racialized to justify colonial oppression or antisemitism—are dangerous and violent, he presents the everyday violence of the racial system as well as any extreme measures that might become necessary as a legitimate self-defense to the threat of the racial other.

This criminalization of the victim engenders in turn a new mechanism of common praxis that takes the form of "agitation, publicity, the diffusion of information ... campaigns, slogans, the muted orchestration of terror as an accompaniment to orders, 'stuffing people's heads' with propaganda, etc." (642). The machinery of racial indoctrination disseminated through the mass media, inculcated in educational apparatuses, and incorporated into ordinary habits turns racism into an invisible practice of everyday norms. So "the hatred which these dummies excited in everyone belonged to the Other; but totalizing propaganda constituted this hatred into other-direction as an exigency of a totalizing ceremony" (653). Everyone within the system comes to internalize the crimes that belong to no one in particular, so collective responsibility is avoided as "serial responsibility" (654). When the material conditions of life become such that life itself becomes impossible for those whose domination is justified by racism, the only solution is revolt: "The only possible way out was to confront total negation with total negation, violence with equal violence; to negate dispersal and atomization by an initially negative unity whose content would be defined in struggle" (733).

The crystallization of Sartre's third world radicalism saw revolutionary violence as the solution to institutionalized exploitation undergirded by racism. This point of departure was apparent not only in his campaign against the French-Algerian war, but in his opposition to the Vietnam war, his support of revolutionary movements in Latin America, especially the Cuban revolution, and most emphatic in his "Préface aux *Damnés de la terre*" (preface to *The Wretched of the Earth*, 1961) and his "Lumumba et le néo-colonialisme" ("The Political Thought of Patrice Lumumba," 1963).

The clearest exemplar of this new phase in Sartre's antiracism is his introduction to Fanon's *The Wretched of the Earth*, which echoed Fanon's call for a revolutionary uprising of the Third World against Western culture in order to discover its authentic subjectivity through revolutionary violence. The camps of the opposing forces in the apocalyptic scene that Sartre draws this time are not determined by the dialectics of the gaze, but by the struggle for power itself, defined by control over limited resources.[52]

Sartre heralded a new generation of anticolonialist writers who expressed the contradictions of colonialism by showing that European moral principles and codes of conduct and the material lives of colonized peoples "did not hang together, and that [the colonized] could neither reject them completely nor yet assimilate them" (10/8). Sartre insisted that while Fanon spoke exclusively to the wretched of the earth Europeans should read the book because it explained how we are "estranged from ourselves," since in defining the non-European, Europeans do not only alienate and subjugate others. "It is enough that they show us what we have made of them for us to realize what we have made of ourselves," Sartre exclaims. The dehumanization and ostracism of racialized others, what Sartre describes as "their scars and ... their chains," (14/13) are therefore part and parcel of the creation of European identity and hegemony.

Fanon's *The Wretched of the Earth* consequently reveals how the West has shaped the rest of the modern world. His advocacy of violence is justified as the return of the repressed violence of colonialism deflected back upon the West, playing out in geo-political terms Sartre's earlier description of the inherent violence of intersubjectivity. Sartre reaffirms, "we only become what we are by the radical and deep-seated refusal of that which others have made us" (16/17). This is the key premise that animates the Sartrean dialectic of authenticity first applied in the *Réflexions*. But it also discloses what Sartre's existentialism shares with Marxism encapsulated in Marx's comment in *The Eighteenth Brumaire* that "men make their own history, but they do not make it just as they please; they do not make it under circumstances chosen by themselves, but under circumstances directly encountered, given and transmitted from the past."[53] Sartre's *Critique* was the extended elaboration of how this functions. His preface to Fanon urged that Europeans support the revolutionary blowback from the colonial encounter, for "we in Europe too are being decolonized: that is to say that the settler which is in every one of us is being savagely rooted out" (22/24). The "boomerang" (19/20) of colonial revolt was the restorative violence of "man recreating himself," (19/21) and in the face of it, Sartre recommended that Europeans "stand in judgment" (26/31) of themselves and side with the revolution that will bring about the final liberation of all humanity, not only from racism but from all structures of oppression.

Sartre's "Lumumba et le néo-colonialisme" ("The Political Thought of Patrice Mumumba," 1963) more cogently, but just as emphatically, wove together an account of systemic economic structures and racial oppression. It also celebrated revolutionary violence as necessary to forge a solution. Thus, Lumumba and Fanon are hailed together as the "two great dead men

[who] represent Africa. Not only their nations: all of their continent."⁵⁴ The preface to Lumumba's political speeches was an effort to analyze his rise and fall and to offer an account of why, ultimately, he was murdered.

Lumumba, for Sartre, was a "black Robespierre," (219/175) caught in the contradictions of his own Jacobin desire to centralize and unify the Congo, while only dimly aware of the structural forces of neocolonialism that ended up destroying him. He embodied the inconsistencies of colonialism and the paradoxes of the anticolonial struggle, but he had the potential to "stir up the people against neocapitalist mystification," which was why he had to die (247/196). Educated first by Catholic and then Protestant missionaries, incorporated into the colonial civil service, he realized at the age of twenty that he had already reached his zenith: "Above all the blacks, he would always remain beneath the whites" (202/162). Lumumba lived the contradictions of his elite status as black in a segregated and racist society:

> The registered black had no more right than the unregistered to enter European towns, unless he was working there; like them, he could not evade the curfew; when he went shopping, he met them again at the special counter reserved for blacks; like them he was a victim of segregationist practices on every occasion and in every place. (203/163)

Sartre was clear that he now thought economic exploitation was the cause of this racist segregation. He was categorical that the suffering from the daily toil for their master's benefit was worse than the pain of racist discrimination, since prejudice and inequity was a consequence of the extraction of surplus labor.

In his singular emphasis on a political solution to national independence however, Lumumba, failed to see the forest for the trees, which would have necessitated fusing his political struggle to a social revolution like that waged in Vietnam, Cuba, Angola, and Algeria. It was only a movement created through a revolutionary uprising, where "the oppressors violence begets counter-violence which at the same time turns against the enemy and against the divisions that play the enemy's game" that the cleavages of the Congo and in turn of Africa could be overcome (228/181). Sartre did not mince words. One could only eliminate the vestiges of the old order "through persuasion, political education, and if necessary, through terror" (228/182). Terror was thus legitimated as the weapon of the weak.

Lumumba's failure ultimately meant that what happened in the Congo would be repeated in Africa as a whole, which was already an iteration of the neocolonialism that stymied Latin America and the Caribbean. A new indigenous elite, who conspired in Lumumba's downfall, would replace the old government but remain completely dependent upon the Europeans and the Americans. Africa would be racked by weak central governments, controlled by the bourgeoisie and large landowners aligned with the military, who would do the bidding of multinational corporations.

This neocolonial order marked the decisive reinforcement of white hegemony because separate from an appreciation of the structural forces that underpin it, the white, Western, new world order appeared to have clean hands in the murder of Lumumba. So, concluded Sartre,

> The dead Lumumba ceased to be a person and became Africa in its entirety, with its unitary will, the multiplicity of its social and political systems, its divisions, its disagreements, its power and its impotence: he was not, nor could he be, the hero of pan-Africanism: he was its martyr. His story has highlighted for everyone the profound link between independence, unity and the struggle against the multinational corporations. His death—I remember that Fanon in Rome was devastated by it—was a cry of alarm; in him, the whole continent died and was resurrected. (252/200)

The hope of salvation, for Sartre, rested upon the realization of the infrastructure of neocolonialism and its resistance in a series of interconnected armed uprisings.

So by the period of Sartre's commitment to third world radicalism he had come to think of racism not as a situation, a dyad between individuals, or a product of beliefs and ideas, but the substratum of a system of exploitation. Torture, he argued, is merely the most vicious product of racial systems, brutally enacting the cruel logic of racism, which begins with demeaning human dignity, but whose violence also reveals the contradictions of a racial system. Overcoming this violent system of oppression, Sartre preached, is only possible through a violent revolution whose redemptive bloodshed salves the wounds of the oppressed and whose future wholeness is fashioned by their commitment to overcome exploitation in the name of human freedom. When those like Lumumba, keenly sensitive to the racism of the colonial system, nonetheless only conceive their struggle in the narrow terms of national liberation struggles rather than as tactical points within a neocolonial global order, they are destined to fail. For Sartre's vision had now broadened to see that power rests with the owners of the means of production, the military, and the lapdogs in the government who do their bidding, all of whom are readily used and abused by multinational corporations.

Antiracist Alter-Globalization

By the middle of the 1960s, Sartre's writing began to emphasize a new modality of racism, connected to shifts in the global conditions of labor. The contours of this fourth phase can be gleaned from his opposition to apartheid in South Africa. On November 9, 1966, he participated with Emmanuel d'Astier de la Vigerie and Jean-Jacques Félice in a press conference that was followed by a public gathering organized by the Comité de liaison contre l'aparheid. Sartre's intervention fulminated against what he said, "is today a cancer that risks becoming in a short period of time a generalized cancer: it is apartheid practiced systematically by South Africa." Apartheid was, therefore, a specific social arrangement of ideas, practices, and institutions that could spread globally.

Sartre obviously identified the essential element of apartheid as "integral racism and the absolute superiority of whites." But, he persisted, "This doctrine is born of the facts themselves: the necessity to procure cheap labor." Apartheid was, consequently, an ideology that was "nothing more than the very product of the economy and of [a system of racist] practice[s]. But it rebounds on itself, since it makes the white man treat himself like a subhuman being, by ... developing his racism on all fronts": against Jews, against the English, against communists, and so on. He decried a white, racist minority exercising its slavish oppression over the majority of blacks. He also denounced the hypocrisy of the French government, who under the pretense of supporting national sovereignty would do nothing about the situation in South Africa, but who continued to supply arms to the South African government in contravention of the resolutions of the United Nations. In concluding, he called for solidarity with the heroes fighting against apartheid: "It is necessary that these men, whose heroism is to fight in solitude, know that they are not alone, that not only the UN condemns apartheid, but that private organizations in all corners of the world, trade unions, Church organizations, and people in general, without distinction of who they are [condemn it]."[55]

Sartre would later follow up his intervention against the apartheid system with his support for the black power movement at a rally held at Mutualité on Monday, April 30, 1968, organized by the French committee in support of the Student Nonviolent Coordinating Committee (SNCC) in the United States. To the two thousand who gathered to show their solidarity, Sartre averred, "It is the same aggressor that oppresses thirty million Vietnamese and twenty million blacks." The oppression of blacks, he went on, is a metonym of "the third world that the Americans have introduced in their own home."[56]

Subsequent interventions in this last phase of his antiracism would clarify the parallels Sartre found between the racism akin to that in South Africa and what he began to label the "interior colonies" of capitalist countries. For example, on the occasion of the appearance in 1970 of *Livre des travailleurs africains en France*, prefaced by Albert Memmi, a debate was organized under the title, "Le Tiers-Monde commence en banlieue" ("The Third World Begins in the Suburbs"). Sartre's intercession, originally titled, "Les Pays capitalistes et leurs colonies intérieures," ("The Capitalist Countries and their Interior Colonies"), made evident the connection between postcolonial immigration—legal and illegal—and colonialism. Immigration is a necessary consequence of colonization, he contended, since the impoverishment of the colonies required that the dispossessed pursue economic opportunities. Indeed, he insisted that the shadow workforce of illegal aliens was a function of a systematic "politics of immigration." Often no matter how skilled, immigrants were confined to jobs that French workers were loath to take. As such, rather than being integrated as a class, they were rejected as a group. "This is how," Sartre explained, "one developed a racism that is very useful to capital" (305).

While many in France derided the racism in the United States, claiming that Americans had de facto colonies in their country, France, he cautioned, was "in the midst of trying to reconstitute within her borders the colonies she had lost."[57] He explicitly compared blacks in the United States and immigrants in France as members of the lumpenproletariat who suffered from the iniquities of deplorable housing conditions, low salaries, and racist discrimination, segregated in ghettos defined by systemic unemployment, criminalized solutions to poverty, and educational failure. Sartre's key point was clear, then, that the case of African immigrant workers as well as other immigrants who suffered from discrimination was "not only due to racism" but was "a necessity of French economic capitalism" (302). Sartre's focus on the "interior colonies" that characterize the metropolitan centers of late capitalism thus highlighted the generalizable structures of apartheid.

According to Michel Contat and Michel Rybalka, between January 1970 and July 1971 alone, Sartre participated in fifteen meetings, press conferences, demonstrations, or as a part of diverse delegations, signing twelve petitions, messages, or telegrams of solidarity, testifying at four trials of immigrant militants, and writing short circumstantial articles, communiqués, or public declarations about immigrant workers in France.[58] This was clearly one of his last significant political initiatives while he was physically able. While these interventions by Sartre were episodic and never resulted in a significant article on how racism continued to function in an era of mobile labor and production, his conception of interior colonization sketched the contours of racial formations in the global economy. As the recent insurgency in France as well as Hurricane Katrina have made clear, these conditions are very much still with us. Slavoj Žižek acutely distilled them in his response to Hurricane Katrina:

> The segregation of the people is the reality of economic globalization. This new racism of the developed world is in a way much more brutal than the previous one: Its implicit legitimatization is neither naturalist (the "natural" superiority of the developed West) nor culturalist (we in the West also want to preserve our cultural identity). Rather, it's an unabashed economic egotism—the fundamental divide is the one between those included into the sphere of (relative) economic prosperity and those excluded from it.[59]

In addition to the specific cultural, legal, political, and institutional factors inside France or inside the United States or elsewhere, Sartre's final clarion calls against racism thirty years ago remind us to think about these problems as a product of global capitalism. South African President Thabo Mkebi suggested the same thing. In opening the World Summit for Sustainable Development in Johannesburg on August 26, 2002, Mbeki issued a call to end what he called the "global apartheid" between rich and poor created by the primitive neoliberal rule of survival of the fittest. "A global human society based on poverty for many and prosperity for a few, characterized by islands of wealth, surrounded by a sea of poverty, is unsustainable," he remonstrated. Mbeki was lending his voice to a prophetic tradition of which Sartre was always an audacious contributor.

What I want to suggest in concluding is that in the age of globalization, we ought to read Sartre's remonstrations against racism backward. We must begin with the extraordinary divide between the so-called Third World and the First World that Mbeki called "global apartheid" and the institutionalized injustices that undergird globalized capitalism. Reading Sartre helps to remind us of the sometimes subtle and often ferocious ways in which racism is a crucial ratchet in the mechanics of the system of oppression in our global age. But his earlier work serves as a lever against his advocacy of the shortcuts of terroristic violence that he came to believe were part of restorative justice in such an age. The postcolonial situation has made evident that revolutionary violence, especially the violence of terrorism, is most often *not* therapeutic in healing the scarred body politic of colonial subjects (witness, for example, Algeria or the Congo today), even in response to state-sponsored terrorism.

Moreover, racism continues to insinuate itself not only into the material structures of exploitation, but into the psychic and cultural structures of how we perceive the individual and collective Self and Other, and not only in the West, as the export of the so-called new antisemitism into the Arab world makes plain, as does what some are calling the "class apartheid" that has insinuated itself into the new South Africa.[60] Sartre reminds us that solutions to these problems cannot come in the form of a retrenchment into the politics of assimilation, but will depend upon a deconstructive transvaluation of the signs and strictures of race wherever they rear their ugly face. Only this persistent work of undermining the "passion" of racism, by revealing at once the groundlessness of this social construct and how it is nonetheless socially mobilized, will enable us to someday gingerly walk the roads to freedom that Sartre so valiantly helped to pave.

Notes

1. The impoverished and segregated northeastern suburb of Paris, Clichy-sous-Bois has a population where 50 percent "are under the age of twenty, unemployment is above 40 percent and identity checks and police harassment are a daily experience." See Naima Bouteldja, "Explosion in the suburbs: The Riots in France are the Result of Years of Racism, Poverty and Police Brutality," *Guardian Weekly* (November 11–17, 2005), 6.
2. Paul Silverstein and Chantal Tetreault, "Urban Violence in France," *Middle East Report Online*, November 2005.
3. See Daniel Pipes, "Reflections on the Revolution in France," *New York Sun*, November 8, 2005; Frank Gaffney and Alex Alexiev, "Farewell to Europe?" *Washington Times*, November 10, 2005; Charles Krauthammer, "What the Uprising Wants," *Time*, November 13, 2005; Fouad Ajami, "The Boys of Nowhere," *US News and World Report*, November 21, 2005.
4. Silverstein and Tetreault, "Urban Violence in France."
5. Jean-Paul Sartre, "France and a Matter of Racism," *New York Times*, March 11, 1973.
6. It is important to stress that these phases were not discrete and they did not develop in a neat chronological order. The key theorems that undergird each are distillations of my own analysis. Breaking up Sartre's developing conception of racism into these four phases is a heuristic devise in order to demarcate the evolution in his thinking on the subject, but also to extract his major insights for political ends.
7. See Marie-Béatrice Baudet, "Jobs at Heart of French Crisis," *Guardian Weekly* (November 25–December 1, 2005): 29. Baudet draws upon the work of French sociologists like Dominique Meurs, Ariane Pailhé, Patrick Simon, and Eric Maurin who have shown the lack of intergenerational mobility and the persistence of inequality for African and Turkish immigrants in France. The article explains that non-European laborers run the risk of falling into a "spiral of precariousness" since North African immigrants were 79 percent more likely to find themselves unemployed than the indigenous French.

    Since the *modèle républicain d'intégration* is the sacred creed of France's strict Republicanism, the official collection of data based upon religious or ethnic origin is prohibited. It is nonetheless clear from the statistics that have been amassed that African immigrants have overwhelmingly fallen into labor-intensive jobs and unskilled labor positions in the service sector, including telemarketing, catering, and retailing. Ethnic minorities are significantly under-represented in the five million jobs in the public sector (government officials, military and police, teachers, forestry) because these positions are limited to French nationals and 26 percent of public servants follow their parents into those same public sector positions, the figure being even higher (32.5 percent) for management positions.

Even the neoconservative alarmist work of Gabriel Schoenfeld concedes the statistics on institutionalized inequality in France. With Muslims now close to 10 percent of the population, "half of [all] unemployed workers are Muslim, a rate more than double the national average. Those who do succeed in gaining employment are mostly concentrated in low-paying, low-prestige, unskilled jobs." In addition, "housing for Muslims is universally bleak and overcrowded. A large fraction of France's Muslims live in urban *foyers*, dismal housing projects for unaccompanied foreign workers that are seedbeds of violence and criminality." The result is that "over half of prison inmates and 43 percent of the residents of juvenile justice facilities are 'foreign-born,' a euphemism for Muslims." The source for Schoenfeld's statistics is Christopher Caldwell, "Allah Mode," *Weekly Standard*, July 15, 2002. See Gabriel Schoenfeld, *The Return of Antisemitism* (San Francisco: Encounter, 2004), 60–61. Schoenfeld is unquestionably right about the return of antisemitism, but his analysis of it is distorted and misguided. For my analysis, see "So What's New?: Rethinking the 'New Antisemitism' in a Global Age" in Jonathan Judaken, ed., *Naming Race, Naming Racisms* (New York and London: Routledge, 2008).

For an excellent comprehensive analysis of Muslims in France today, see Jonathan Laurence and Justin Vaisse, *Integrating Islam: Political and Religious Challenges in Contemporary France* (Washington, D.C.: Brookings Institution Press, 2006).

8. Robert Soucy, "Functional Hating: French Fascist Demonology between the Wars," *Contemporary French Civilization* 23.2 (Summer/Fall, 1999): 158–176, 158.

9. Jean-Paul Sartre, *L'enfance d'un chef* in *Le Mur* (Paris: Gallimard, 1939), trans. Lloyd Alexander, *The Wall* (New York: New Directions, 1948). See Jonathan Judaken, *Jean-Paul Sartre and the Jewish Question: Anti-antisemitism and the Politics of the French Intellectual* (Lincoln: University of Nebraska Press, 2006), chapter 1, where I argue that contrary to the canonical interpretation of Sartre's work, he was politicized during the 1930s. The claim that he was not can only be sustained if you separate Sartre's literature and consequently the realm of culture from politics, which is dubious, especially in a cultural context like France where the two are so intertwined.

It should be added here that Sartre's *L'Enfance d'un chef* and its influence in particular on his *Réflexions sur la question juive* makes evident that it was not Sartre's first visit to the United States in 1945 and his engagement with the racism against African-Africans that engendered his political activism in general nor his antiracism in particular. Annie Cohen-Solal makes this argument in *Sartre 1905–1980* (Paris: Gallimard, 1985), 318–19, trans. A. Cancogni *Sartre: A Life* (London: Heinemann, 1987), 241: "It is far from home, far from his daily reality and his socio-historical connivances, that his first endorsement of a purely social cause takes place." Robert Bernasconi's outstanding article also echoes this point. See "Sartre's Gaze Returned: The Transformation of the Phenomenology of Racism," *Graduate Faculty Philosophy Journal* 10.2 (1995), reprinted in William McBride, ed., *Existentialist Ethics* (New York: Garland, 1997), 359–79, 359.

10. The Action Française was the most important organization of the extreme Right in France in the first quarter of the twentieth century. See Eugen Weber, *The Action Française: Royalism and Reaction in Twentieth-Century France* (Stanford: Stanford University Press, 1962); Paul Mazgaj, *The Action Française and Revolutionary Syndicalism* (Chapel Hill: University of North Carolina Press, 1979); and Michel Winock, "*L'Action française*" in *Histoire de l'ex-*

trême droite en France, Michel Winock, ed. (Paris: Éditions du Seuil, 1991), 125–56.

11. I write "the Jew" in quotes to indicate that it is a constructed category and that to *describe* "the Jew" also *inscribes* the category as a marker of difference whether based on language, belief system, artistic tradition, or gene pool. On this point in relation to 'race,' see Henry Louis Gates Jr., "Introduction: Writing 'Race' and the Difference It Makes," in *"Race," Writing and Difference*, ed. Henry Louis Gates Jr. (Chicago: University of Chicago Press, 1986), 5. See also Berel Lang, "From Grammar to Antisemitism: On the 'the' in 'the Jews.'" Originally published in *Midstream* 49.4 (May–June 2003). Available at: http://www.wzo.org.il/en/resources/view.asp?id=1489. Accessed July 4, 2006.

12. Jean-Paul Sartre, "Portrait de l'antisémite" was first published in *Les Temps modernes* 3 (December 1945): 442–70. Jean-Paul Sartre, *Réflexions sur la question juive* (Paris: Gallimard Folio/Essais, 1954), trans. George Becker, *Antisemite and Jew* (New York: Schocken, 1948). Cited parenthetically hereafter. In the case of all of Sartre's texts, I have cited the French text first and then the English, altering the translations where necessary.

13. Levinas's response was recently translated by Denis Hollier and Rosalind Krauss as "Existentialism and Antisemitism" in *October 87* (Winter 1999): 27–31, 28. It was collected in Emmanuel Levinas, *Les Imprévus de l'histoire* (Paris: Fata Morgana, 1994): 103–106.

14. Jean-Paul Sartre, *L'être et le néant: Essai d'ontologie phénoménologique* (Paris: Gallimard, 1943), trans. Hazel Barnes, *Being and Nothingness* (New York: Washington Square Books, 1956). The citations to the English translation are parenthetical hereafter.

15. Lewis R. Gordon teases out the different modalities of bad faith at work in racism in his "Sartrean Bad Faith and Antiblack Racism," in S. Galt Crowell, ed., *The Prism of the Self* (Amsterdam: Kluwer Academic Publishers), 107–29. Reprinted in McBride, *Existentialist Ethics*, 336–38. I would abstract and itemize the forms of bad faith he discusses as follows: (1) the effort to flee the freedom and responsibility constitutive of the human condition by reifying Others (which Sartre calls "sadism") or accepting how you are objectified by Others (which Sartre names "masochism"); (2) the evasion of the gaze of the Other, which in racialized contexts can take the form of "exotizing and romanticizing of the Other in a way that denies his freedom to judge"; (3) the denial of the social world in the form of solipsism or pure alienated individuality; (4) "emphasizing abstract humanity over concrete human beings or of focusing upon the corporeality and facticity of human beings as though they were devoid of other possibilities.... Thus, a person in bad faith could love humanity in the abstract while torturing human beings in the flesh"; (5) the epistemological claim that underpins much of racist discourse, which claims to speak from the perspective of objective truth and thus fudges the question of evidence, which from an existentialist perspective is always situated and perspectival.

16. Sander Gilman has done the best work on the associative logic of stereotyping and why certain characteristics are stressed in typologies of the Other. Among his many works, see in particular "What Are Stereotypes and Why Use Texts to Study Them" in *Difference and Pathology: Stereotypes of Sexuality, Race and Madness* (Ithaca and London: Cornell University Press, 1985).

17. On the evolution in Sartre's understanding of the social construction of race, see Donna-Dale Marcano, "Sartre and the Social Construction of Race" in Robert Bernasconi with Sybol Cook, eds., *Race and Racism in Continental*

Philosophy (Bloomington and Indianapolis: Indiana University Press, 2003), 214–26. Her essay explores "two models of group constitution employed by Sartre, the first from *Antisemite and Jew*, which bases group constitution and identity on the gaze of the dominant Others, and the second from his later work *Critique of Dialectical Reason*, volume 1, which places the group as a prominent facilitator of history that *produces* itself in the domain of the Other. For the later Sartre, the genesis of groups is found in the events, the materiality, and the group members' work and antagonisms, set against a background of need and an effort at concerted praxis" (214).

18. See Sartre, *Réflexions/Antisemite and Jew*, 22/19. Bernard-Henri Lévy emphasizes this point in *Le Siècle de Sartre* (Paris: Bernard Grasset, 2000), 403, trans. Andrew Brown, *Sartre: The Philosopher of the Twentieth Century* (London: Polity, 2003), 304.
19. This is translated in the English as "policy of assimilation," (57), but in the French is "politique d'assimilation" (67).
20. There are numerous shortcomings in Sartre's *Réflexions*, which are detailed in chapter 4 of my *Jean-Paul Sartre and the Jewish Question*. In recent discussions, these have sometimes foreclosed the important insights of Sartre's text, which I attempt to highlight as well. For an assessment of the critical literature and responses to the *Réflexions* in French as a means to trace the Jewish Question in postwar France, see chapter 8 of *Jean-Paul Sartre and the Jewish Question*. There is also an important critical literature of the work in English, including Harold Rosenberg, "Does the Jew Exist? Sartre's Morality Play about Antisemitism," *Commentary* 7.1 (January 1949): 8–18; Joseph Sungolowsky, "Criticism of *Antisemite and Jew*," *Yale French Studies* 30 (Fall–Winter 1962–63): 68–72; Elaine Marks, "The Limits of Ideology and Sensibility: J. P. Sartre's *Réflexions sur la Question Juive* and E. M. Cioran's *Un peuple de Solitaires*," *French Review* 45.4 (1972): 779–88; Stuart Zane Charmé, *Vulgarity and Authenticity: Dimensions of Otherness in the World of Jean-Paul Sartre* (Amherst: University of Massachusetts Press, 1991), 105–44; Susan Rubin Suleiman, "The Jew in Jean-Paul Sartre's *Réflexions sur la question juive*: An Exercise in Historical Reading" in *The Jew in the Text: Modernity and the Construction of Identity*, ed. and intro. Linda Nochlin and Tamar Garb (London: Thames and Hudson, 1995), 208–15; there are also several important contributions in the special issue of *October* commemorating the fiftieth anniversary of *Antisemite and Jew*: *October* 87 (Winter 1999).
21. On this period, see chapter 5 of my *Jean-Paul Sartre and the Jewish Question* and chapter 6 for Sartre's interventions into the Arab-Israeli conflict. Works in which Sartre does address antisemitism in this period are primarily works of fiction. See *Le Scénario Freud*, ed. J.-B. Pontalis (Paris: Gallimard, 1984), trans. Quintin Hoare, *The Freud Scenario* (Chicago: University of Chicago Press, 1985), and *Les Séquestrés d'Altona* (Paris; Gallimard, 1960), trans. Sylvia and George Leeson, *The Condemned of Altona* (New York: Knopf, 1961). I cite his discussion in the *Critique of Dialectical Reason* below.
22. Cited in M. Watteau, "Situation raciales et condition de l'homme dans l'oeuvre de Jean-Paul Sartre," *Présence africaine* 2 (January 1948): 228.
23. Jean-Paul Sartre, *L'existentialisme est un humanisme* (Paris: Nagel, 1946), 24, trans. Bernard Frechtman, "Existentialism" in *Existentialism and Human Emotions* (New York: Philosophical Library), 9–51, 16.
24. Jean-Paul Sartre, "Retour des Etats Unis: Ce qui j'ai appris du problème noir," *Le Figaro* (June 16, 1945), 2, trans. T. Denean Sharpley-Whiting in *Existence in Black : An Anthology of Black Existential Philosophy*, ed. Lewis Gordon

(New York: Routledge, 1997): 83–87. The page numbers to the English translation are cited parenthetically hereafter.
25. See Sartre, *L'être et le néant*, 85–111, 431–503, and *Being and Nothingness*, 86–116, 471–556.
26. On the central role that the state plays in racism, see David Theo Goldberg, *The Racial State* (Oxford: Blackwell, 2002). On the term "racialization," see 12, n.1: "it might characterize in some contexts simply the attribution of racial meanings or values to social conditions or arrangements, or the distinction between social groups in racial terms. In other contexts it is used to impute exclusionary or derogatory implications to social conditions thus characterized."
27. Jean-Paul Sartre, "La violence revolutionnaire," in *Cahiers pour une morale* (Paris: Gallimard, 1983), 579–94, trans. David Pellauer, "Revolutionary Violence" in *Notebooks for an Ethics* (Chicago: University of Chicago Press, 1992), 561–74. Cited parenthetically hereafter. These *Notebooks* were written in 1947 and 1948 and were Sartre's initial efforts to formulate an ethics on the basis of the ontology developed in *Being and Nothingness*. The difficulty was to explore what imperatives might derive from Sartre's ontological indicatives. The only pages of the *Notebooks* published in Sartre's lifetime were taken from this excursus. See Jean-Paul Sartre, "Le Noir et Le Blanc aux États-Unis," *Combat*, June 16, 1949. Charmé, *Vulgarity and Authenticity*, 197, n. 5, suggests that this excursus on the oppression of blacks in the United States may have been part of an article, "Concerning Slavery," which was announced by *Présence africaine* in 1949, but which never appeared.
28. Barbara Jeanne Fields, "Slavery, Race and Ideology in the United States of America," *New Left Review* 181 (May/June 1990): 95–118, 106. Fields explains that ideology is not the same as doctrine or dogma, but the "vocabulary of day-to-day action and experience.... Doctrine or dogma may be imposed ... ideology is a distillate of experience" (111–12). Thus racial ideology was the distillation of the experience of the oppression of slavery. As such, "racial ideology supplied the means of explaining slavery to people whose terrain was a republic founded on radical doctrines of liberty and natural rights" (114), since "when self-evident laws of nature guarantee freedom, only equally self-evident laws of equally self-evident nature can account for its denial" (107).
29. Gunnar Myrdal, *An American Dilemma: The Negro Problem and Modern Democracy* (New York: Harper and Row, 1944). Myrdal's central thesis was that America was committed to what he called the "American Creed," which he summed up as a "belief in equality and in the rights to liberty" (vol. 1, 8), and the "American dilemma" arose from the contradictions of this creed with America's de facto racist caste system, along with other local and community interests and prejudices that overrode the belief in the creed. On Myrdal and the debate his work occasioned, see Richard H. King, *Race, Culture and the Intellectuals, 1940–1970* (Baltimore and Washington D.C.: Woodrow Wilson Center Press and Johns Hopkins University Press, 2004), 21–48.
30. For an excellent discussion of Fanon's critique of the Hegelian dialectic in *Black Skin, White Masks*, see Kelly Oliver, "Alienation and Its Double; or The Secretion of Race" in Robert Bernasconi with Sybol Cook, eds., *Race and Racism in Continental Philosophy*, 176–95, 177–78.
31. Jean-Paul Sartre, "Orphée noir," preface to Léopold Sédar Senghor, *Anthologie de la nouvelle poésie nègre et malgache de langue française* (Paris: Presses Universitaires de France, 1977), trans. John MacCombie, "Black Orpheus,"

The Massachusetts Review 6 (Autumn 1964–65), 13–52. Cited parenthetically hereafter.
32. This is a step beyond Sartre's position in *What is Literature?* where he holds that the task of the writer is to bear witness to the limits and possibilities of freedom in his/her age.
33. Abiola Irele, "A Defence of Negritude: A Propos of *Black Orpheus* by Jean-Paul Sartre," *Transition* 13 (March–April, 1964): 9–11, 9. On the distinction between "racialism" and different modes of racism, see Kwame Anthony Appiah, "Racisms" in David Theo Goldberg, ed., *Anatomy of Racism* (Minneapolis: University of Minnesota Press, 1990). See also the way that Tzvetan Todorov delineates the distinction between "racialism" and "racism," in *On Human Diversity: Nationalism, Racism and Exoticism in French Thought* (Cambridge, Mass.: Harvard University Press, 1993), 90–95.
34. W. E. B. Du Bois in *The Souls of Black Folks* (New York: Bedford/St. Martin's, 1997) argues that African-Americans were "born with a veil, and gifted with a second-sight in this American World." Second sight, however, "yields him [the African-American] no true self-consciousness, but only lets him see himself through the revelation of the other world. It is a peculiar sensation, this double consciousness." Du Bois continues, "this sense of always looking at one's self through the eyes of others, of measuring one's soul by the tape of a world that looks on in amused contempt and pity. One ever feels his two-ness—an American, a Negro; two souls, two thoughts, two unreconciled strivings; two warring ideals in one dark body, whose dogged strength alone keeps it from being torn asunder" (38).
35. Audre Lorde famously denied this in her article "The Master's Tools Will Never Dismantle the Master's House," in *This Bridge Called My Back: Writings By Radical Women of Color*, ed. Cherrie Moraga and Gloria Anzaldúa (New York: Kitchen Table, 1983), 98–101.
36. For a taxonomy of these motifs, see chapter 4 of my *Jean-Paul Sartre and the Jewish Question*.
37. Stuart Zane Charmé, *Vulgarity and Authenticity: Dimensions of Otherness in the World of Jean-Paul Sartre* (Amherst: University of Massachusetts Press, 1991), 202.
38. Several recent critics have accused Sartre of reiterating a notion of an essential black character. See for example, Francis A Joppa, "Sartre et les milieux intellectuels de l'Afrique noire," *Présence francophone* 25 (1989): 7–28, 21, and Christopher L. Miller, "Theories of Africans: The Question of Literary Anthropology," in Henry Louis Gates Jr., ed., *"Race," Writing and Difference* (Chicago: University of Chicago Press, 1986). Henry Louis Gates Jr. thus stipulates in "Talkin' That Talk," *Critical Inquiry* 13.1 (Autumn 1986): 203–10, 207, "Sartre's fantasies of 'the being' of 'the' African in *Black Orpheus* are racialist, as is his consideration of Richard Wright's 'split' audience in *What Is Literature?*"
39. Frantz Fanon, *Peau noire, masques blancs* (Paris: Éditions du Seuil, 1952), 110, trans. *Black Skin, White Masks*, trans. Charles Man Markmann (New York: Grove, 1967), 135.
40. Jean-Paul Sartre, "Préface" in *D'une Chine à l'autre* by Henri Cartier-Bresson (Paris: Robert Delpire, 1954), reprinted as "D'une Chine à l'autre" in *Situations V: Colonialisme et néo-colonialisme* (Paris: Galimard, 1964), trans. Azzedine Haddour, Steve Brewer, and Terry McWilliams (London and New York: Routledge 2001). Cited parenthetically hereafter.
41. Azzedine Haddour, "Introduction: Remembering Sartre," in Jean-Paul Sartre, *Colonialism and Neocolonialism*, 1.

42. Jean-Paul Sartre, "Préface," in Albert Memmi, *Portrait du colonisé précédé de portrait du colonisateur* (Paris: Payot, 1973), trans. Howard Greenfeld, "Introduction," in *The Colonizer and the Colonized* (Boston: Beacon, 1991 [1965]). Cited parenthetically hereafter.
43. Jean-Paul Sartre, "Le colonialisme est un système," *Les Temps modernes* 123 (March–April 1956), reprinted as "Le colonialisme est un système," in *Situations V*, 25–48, 26, trans. "Colonialism Is a System" in *Colonialism and Neo-colonialism*, 31. Cited parenthetically hereafter as CS.
44. For a fully developed version of this argument, see Michael Adas, *Machines As the Measure of Men* (Ithaca: Cornell University Press, 1989).
45. Tony Smith, "Idealism and People's War: Sartre on Algeria," *Political Theory* 1.4 (November 1973): 426–49, 428–29.
46. For the notion that universalism and equality contains the potential of an exclusionary logic, see George M. Fredrickson, *Racism: A Short History* (Princeton: Princeton University Press, 2002): "If equality is the norm in the spiritual or temporal realms (or in both at the same time), and there are groups of people within the society who are so despised or disparaged that the upholders of the norms feel compelled to make them exceptions to the promise or realization of equality, they can be denied the prospect of equal status only if they allegedly possess some extraordinary deficiency that makes them less than fully human. It is uniquely in the West that we find the dialectical interaction between a premise of equality and an intense prejudice toward certain groups that would seem to be a precondition for the full flowering of racism as an ideology or worldview" (12).
47. Sartre originally wrote this piece at the request of *Le Monde* to comment on a collection of statements and documents on the methods of pacification used by reservists called *Des Rappelés témoignent* (*Mobilized Reservists Bear Witness*). When *Le Monde* rejected the article as an incitement to violence, Sartre published it in *Les Temps modernes* 135 (May 1957), and reprinted it in *Situations V* as "Vous êtes formidables," 57–67, 57, trans. in *Colonialism and Neocolonialism* as "You Are Wonderful," 54–61, 54. Cited parenthetically hereafter.
48. Jean-Paul Sartre, "Une victoire," in Henri Alleg, *La Question* (Lausanne: La cite, 1958), trans. John Calder, "A Victory," in Henri Alleg, *The Question* (New York: Brazillier, 1958). Cited parenthetically hereafter.
49. See in particular, Jean-Paul Sartre, *Critique de la raison dialectique* (Paris: Gallimard, 1960), 726–38 and 797–814, trans. Alan Sheridan-Smith, *Critique of Dialectical Reason*, vol. 1 (New York: Verso, 1976), 642–54 and 716–34. Cited parenthetically hereafter.
50. Martin Jay, "From Totality to Totalization: Sartre" in *Marxism and Totality: The Adventures of a Concept from Lukács to Habermas* (Berkeley and Los Angeles: University of California Press, 1984), 351.
51. William McBride, *Sartre's Political Theory* (Bloomington: Indiana University Press, 1991), 136.
52. Jean-Paul Sartre, "Préface" in Frantz Fanon, *Les damnés de la terre* (Paris: François Maspero, 1961), 9, trans. Constance Farrington, "Preface" in Frantz Fanon, *The Wretched of the Earth* (New York: Grove, 1963), 7. Cited parenthetically hereafter.
53. Karl Marx, *The Eighteenth Brumaire of Louis Bonaparte* (New York: International Publishers, 1987), 15.
54. Jean-Paul Sartre, "Lumumba et le néo-colonialisme," preface to *Discours de Lumumba* (Paris: Présence Africaine, 1963), reprinted as "La pensée politique de Patrice Lumumba," in *Situations V*, 194–253, 194, trans. "The Political

Thought of Patrice Lumumba" in *Colonialism and Neocolonialism*, 156. Cited parenthetically hereafter.
55. The text was published in *Christianisme social* 74.11–12 (1966): 623–30, and as "Ceux qui sont aux prises avec l'apartheid doivent savoir qu'ils ne sont pas seuls," *Droit et liberté* 257 (December 1966): 8–9. My citations are to this text. Extracts were also cited in the short article by Jean Geoffroy, "Sartre et l'apartheid," *Le Nouvel Observateur* 105, 16–22 (November 1966): 6.
    It should be remembered that Sartre considered donating the money from the Nobel Prize he was awarded (and then decided to reject) to an anti-apartheid group in London. See "L'Ecrivain doit refuser de se laisser transformer en institution" *Le Monde*, October 24, 1964.
56. "Meeting en faveur du 'Pouvoir noir,'" *Le Monde*, May 2, 1968, 3.
57. Jean-Paul Sartre, "Les Pays capitalists et leur colonies intérieures" *Tricontinental*, Paris, 1970, reprinted as "Le tiers-monde commence en banlieue" *Situations VIII* (Paris: Gallimard, 1972), 302. References are to this text and cited parenthetically hereafter.
58. Michel Contat and Michel Rybalka, Supplement to *Ecrits de Sartre, Le Magazine littéraire* 55–56 (Summer 1971). Cited in Noureddine Lamouchi, *Jean-Paul Sartre et le tiers monde: Rhétorique d'un discours anticolonialiste* (Paris: L'Harmattan, 1996), 170.
59. Slavoj Žižek, "The Subject Supposed to Loot and Rape: Reality and Fantasy in New Orleans." http://www.inthesetimes.com/site/main/article/2361.
60. On this point, see Gillian Hart, "Changing Concepts of Articulation: Political Stakes in South Africa Today," *Review of African Political Economy* 111: 85–101. I am grateful to her also for the following references: Patrick Bond, *Talk Left, Walk Right* (Scottsville, South Africa: University of Kwa-Zulu-Natal Press, 2004), and Jeremy Seekings and Nicoli Nattrass, *Class, Race and Inequality in South Africa* (New Haven: Yale University Press, 2005).

Chapter 2

Skin for Sale

Race and *The Respectful Prostitute*

Steve Martinot

In 1946, Sartre wrote a little-known play called *La Putain respecteuse* (*The Respectful Prostitute*) about racism in the United States. When it was produced in the United States, Sartre was accused of anti-Americanism. It was an accusation that suggested that he might have hit close to home with the play. Commentary on the play has been sparse, perhaps for the same reason.[1]

Racism and racialized domination were much on Sartre's mind in the wake of World War II. In 1946, he published *Réflexions sur la question juive* (*Antisemite and Jew*), in which he addresses antisemitism not in its extreme Nazi incarnation but in its quotidian appearance in France. In 1948, he wrote an introduction to a volume of African and Afro-Caribbean poetry (*Orphée noir* "Black Orpheus"), in which he attempted to show the white European mind how it was seen by those it had colonized, exploited, and silenced. And in his *Cahiers pour une morale* (*Notebooks for an Ethics*), written in 1948, he addressed the phenomenology of the mind of the racial oppressor.[2]

But "race" and "racism" were not welcome issues in the United States at that time. The United States did not desire to have its leadership in the Nuremberg trials of Nazi leaders besmirched by attention to Jim Crow and the chain gangs of its own southern states. Furthermore, though some people had realized that the modern concept of "race" was a fabrication, a way of rationalizing European colonialist seizure of other peoples' lands by inventing a biological European superiority—an idea that should have received wide acceptance in the wake of the Nazi onslaught—it would be a few decades before it would be more fully intelligible in the United States. Though articulated by thinkers such as W. E. B. Du Bois or David Walker, the idea that "race" was not "natural," but rather a political process of inferiorization and degradation of people of color by whites for the purpose of white superiority, would have to wait until mass (civil rights) movements had ended Jim Crow to become acceptable.[3]

55

Part of what Sartre saw, and presented in his play, was the operation of whiteness as a social structure. Even when the barbarity with which white supremacy would institutionally defend itself against civil rights movements had been clearly revealed to the world, the idea that "race" and whiteness were social structures would still be resisted by most white people.[4] It is perhaps appropriate that someone from outside the United States would see what those within it could not. For them, whiteness as a social structure would be hard to see to the extent to which it was itself the lens through which they looked, the filter through which they saw the world.

In offering a critical analysis of *The Respectful Prostitute*, I will try to do three things: (1) analyze the components of Sartre's insight into the structure of whiteness and white supremacy; (2) relate the elements of that structure to their present form in contemporary events; and (3) link his insights to other of his philosophical writings, in order to more fully explicate them, as well as to fill out the space of the play's understanding of white racialized identity.

The Structure of Whiteness

The play takes place in a southern town, in the apartment of a prostitute named Lizzie, who has recently arrived by train from the north. The drama unfolds at three discursive levels: that of an unnamed black man's insights into the sociology of the town, that of the structural cohesion of the town's white people, and finally, that of the internal mythology and content of that white cohesion. The black man's insights bracket the action of the play as preface and epilogue.

As the curtain rises, the black man appears at Lizzie's door and simply asks her to tell the truth: that he hadn't done anything. He explains that the streets are full of white people, that strangers are talking to each other as old friends, and that when that happens, a black man is going to die. Thus, Sartre contextualizes his play by invoking the calm white sociability that portends racial violence.[5] When the black man reappears at the end of the play, he is indeed seeking refuge from a lynch mob that has germinated with an inexorability that transcends any and all real issues.

The rest of the first scene takes place between Lizzie and the town's white elite. Her first client, who had been hiding when the black man knocked, is a white man named Fred who had picked her up in a dancehall the night before. He is the rich son of the local senator. He distrusts women, evinces shame at his night with Lizzie, suggests he does not enjoy sex, and appears to be expecting the police to show up. He keeps the blinds drawn against the light of day, and plays mind games about erasing all memory of the night before. Lizzie, on the other hand, is an honest sex worker. She does not want to defraud a customer, nor lie about people. She is, however, very impressed by wealth (as opposed to mere money). When her client, Fred, offers her only ten dollars for the night, she becomes enraged at his underestimation of her talents; but her mood shifts quickly when he tells her he is a senator's son (RP, 258). Wealth obsessively regulates her emotions.

Fred's ulterior motive for picking her up at the dance hall is to have her affirm his second-hand account of what happened on the train she arrived on. In his story, two black men had assaulted Lizzie. Some white men had come to her rescue, and when one of the black men pulled a knife, one of the white men shot him to death. The other then escaped. Lizzie's first-hand account differs considerably. According to her, four white men had gotten on the train and started to molest her. When they noticed that two black men were in the car watching them, they abandoned Lizzie and started a fight with the black men. Because the black men seemed to be defending themselves successfully, one of the white men pulled a gun and shot one of the black men, killing him. The other black man then jumped off the train as it approached the town.

Fred wants Lizzie to affirm his version, which will clear the shooter of wrongdoing. Otherwise, Fred says, he goes to prison, and the black man goes free. Lizzie demands that her account be respected as the truth. Fred argues that "there is no truth; there's only whites and blacks" (RP, 262). When Lizzie refuses to "rat" on anyone, Fred responds that she will have to give one of them away in any case, in choosing which story to affirm. She responds by affirming that the black man had done nothing. And Fred rejoins that a black person has always "done something" (RP, 263).

Fred explains that in the south, whites have to stand together. And his first injunction to Lizzie is that "you can't punish a fellow of your own race" (RP, 262). For Fred, to kill a black person is not to commit murder, while to fail to exonerate the shooter would be to "protect" the black man. When she scoffs that she's not going to take the side of some guy who put his hands all over her, Fred responds: "You do things like that without thinking; they don't count. Thomas [the shooter] is a leading citizen; that's what counts" (RP, 262). Thomas is in fact Fred's cousin, and Fred offers Lizzie five hundred dollars to exonerate him. At that moment, Lizzie realizes what is going on, and why he had picked her up the night before. But she is caught in a double bind: with either choice, she betrays someone, and thus betrays her principles.

As a spokesman for the sanctity of whiteness, Fred's bad faith is clear. Regardless of truth, morality, law, or experience, yet in the name of all that, white solidarity takes precedence. White solidarity and the social order become one, a domain of consensus. It is the bad faith of that consensus that puts Lizzie in a double bind. The demand that she stand on the side of the white man is more than white solidarity; it is a demand for the preservation of the social order. She is caught between her sense of ethics and a social structure that discounts any such ethics in the name of its own integrity.

As she realizes the trap she is in, the police arrive with a written statement for Lizzie to sign. She is told that if she doesn't sign the statement, Thomas will be charged with murder. Since the statement is carried by the police, and has a judge's official sanction, it is clear that Thomas's exoneration has already been arranged by the political elite of the town (i.e., Fred's family, the police, and the judge), working in concert. In other words, the story exonerating Thomas is more than merely an alibi. It is white society's allegiance to itself. Thomas's actions of molesting women and killing black men are ignorable because he is white. The ideological requirements of race trump experiential truth or justice.

Herein lies a part of the town's racialized structure. White social cohesion and its exoneration from criminality are two sides of the same coin. Fred's claim that a black person has always "done something" is seamlessly linked to the counterassumption that whatever a white person does to a black person (even killing him) is to have done nothing. There is an inversion of criminality. A black man is (has already been) criminalized in order to decriminalize a white man's murder of another black man. Or, to state it as a general maxim: *Racial domination decriminalizes itself by criminalizing its victims.*[6]

One can see this same ethos today expressed in many ways. Take, for instance, the contemporary ideology of judicial and political "colorblindness." The "colorblindness" idea proclaims that race has been transcended through civil rights legislation. It does not matter that social vestiges or structures of segregation remain in effect. When black or brown people raise the issue of racism or racial discrimination because they find themselves still subjected to it, they are countermanding the white proclamation and are thus at fault. Indeed, they themselves are now labeled "racist" for having brought it up. Thus the white proclamation of colorblindness exonerates itself by condemning any black person who questions it. If the one color "colorblindness" can still "see" is white, its edict of equality (as white) implies that only whiteness counts. In other words, the corruption of racial domination gets purified through just such an ethical inversion as Sartre had presented.

It is a corruption that the play even extends to Lizzie's profession. When Lizzie reviles Fred for his bribe, it is because she realizes he took her to bed for even more nefarious purposes than his prurience. The corruption required to keep the white social order intact extends even to a betrayal of prostitution.

As Sartre explains in the *Notebooks for an Ethics*, in order for those who dominate to have a good conscience, they have to be able to make those they dominate wrong, a priori. All virtue has to be drained from the oppressed, so that their deficiency becomes sufficient reason to dominate them (Ethics, 562). Enslavement, torture, segregation, and criminalization are the means whereby the dominated are shown to be devoid of virtue or humanity. White supremacy imposes a "bestial" existence on others in order to render itself "civilized" (Ethics, 569). But in so constructing itself, white racialized identity shows its truly parasitic nature. Though it seeks to reduce black people to a form of social nonexistence, black people remain indispensable for the maintenance of white racialized identity as a social structure. Their victimization is the instrumentality by which white social sanctity, the very identity of its social order, is constructed.

Thus, the white characters in the play continually disdain black people to each other, deploying derogatory expressions as if paying dues to white membership. This habitual attitude of disparagement is not simply to reflect a white sense of power. It provides for the suspension of bad conscience.

And underneath it, a structure of impunity looms into view. The ability to dispense with ethics, the ability to be a law unto oneself, goes beyond the structuring of social cohesion around required consensus. And this provides a more disturbing link to the present. *In the confluence of these structures of ethical inversion, derogation, and impunity, the play appears deplorably familiar.* Indeed, nothing about it seems foreign, or unfamiliar, or farfetched. Its structural familiarity links firmly to the present.

For instance, we have the case of Mumia Abu-Jamal. Abu-Jamal was a black journalist convicted in a tainted trial of killing a police officer in Philadelphia, in an incident in which Mumia himself was shot, and his own gun remained unfired; he sits on death row despite recanted testimony, evidence of judicial malfeasance, tampering with evidence, and the fact that a white man has come forward admitting to the deed. Mumia's journalistic focus had been on police brutality against the black community in Philadelphia. To silence his testimony of police criminality, he himself was criminalized as a "cop killer." The entire judicial establishment of Pennsylvania, from police departments to the state Supreme Court, has cohered in refusing to allow a retrial, to preserve its original conviction intact. The state and national police departments continually express outrage that a "cop killer" should be granted any rights at all, while no expression of outrage at patent injustice has emerged from within any state institution.[7] In other words, beyond simply reflecting institutional racism, this case *represents a structure of social consensus on institutional impunity with respect to both police brutality and the suppression of its critics.* "Racism" becomes too impoverished a term for what that "impunity" represents.

As an element of social structure, the ethical inversion Sartre has dramatized echoes repeatedly in the play, as it does in our world.[8] For instance, it recurs in the criminalization of Lizzie; she becomes the victimizer of Thomas when she refuses to exonerate him. To persuade her, the men show her pictures of Thomas, refer to phrenology, and attempt to impress her with the ontological superiority of the man she will be sending to prison. She who had been the victim of Thomas's molestations, and seen him murder someone, is to be given the onus for his imprisonment. And if he is to be her "victim," then the law will impugn her through prosecution.

In a similar fashion, many whites have claimed to be the victims of affirmative action legislation, feeling that it discriminates against them. Thus, they choose to see affirmative action's attempt to undo past discriminations and exclusions as a quota system, while refusing to see the system it sought to replace and compensate for (Jim Crow segregation) as itself a 100 percent quota system for the benefit of whites. At this abstract level, the ethical inversions of the white social machinery manage to transform bad faith into citizenship and honor; they mark the structural core of how white society has been ordered.

When Lizzie persists in refusing to sign (though facing jail on prostitution charges), the men start to rough her up.

The Ontology of Whiteness

While the play's agon occurs between white people (in conflict over white consensus), the black man remains the mediating entity in its unfolding struggle. Black people in general are the indispensable other at the core of white sociality, as the existential target of white self-decriminalization. But the black man from the train is not charged with raping Lizzie simply because he was there ("rape" being the catch-all charge against black men under Jim Crow).[9] He was attacked for other reasons. Something else happened on that train, which for Sartre is central to the phenomenology of domination. The black men on the train "saw" the white men. At the moment of molesting Lizzie, the white men were subjected to the look of the black other. It is that which domination finds unacceptable.

For Sartre, it is in the "look" of the other that one apprehends another as a subject.[10] Sartre's account of the "look" resolves a previously intractable philosophical problem: how to account for another subject without falling prey to the solipsism of attributing one's own subjectivity to the other. Finding oneself in the look of another, one apprehends the other as a subject by recognizing oneself as an object for that subject (BN, 262). It is not that one "encounters" the other's subjectivity; one apprehends the other as subject through the other's effect on oneself through the look.

Between individuals of equal social standing, the look can be returned, reestablishing one's own subjectivity by seeing the other as an object—in potentially endless exchange. It can also be returned to grant the other the subjectivity apprehended in the other's look, in a returned look that accepts one's own objectivization by the other as a dimension of one's retrieved subjectivity, a granting of subjectivity that the other's re-returned look can also reciprocate, as a form of dialogic conjunction (BN, 283ff). Sartre recognized that an essential aspect of domination or oppression of another consists in reducing him/her to subhuman status through a denial of subjectivity itself. This means prohibiting both the other's look and the very possibility of dialogic interaction. The subordinate is denied the possibility of making the dominant an object for him/herself. No recognition for being a subjectivity in one's own right, able to see the dominant as an object, is admitted (Ethics, 567). The limited subjectivity the other is permitted will only extend to the performance of tasks assigned, as well as expressions of gratitude and respect for the oppressor, so that the latter need not confront his refusal of humanity to the oppressed. The corollary is that no respect or kindness can be shown toward the oppressed because it would signify that the oppressed had been fully human all along (Ethics, 572).

White supremacy relies upon the denial of subjectivity to black people. Sartre reiterates this point in "Black Orpheus." He notes that white privilege consists in "seeing [the other] without being seen."[11] That is, those white supremacy racializes for its own identity and stability must be denied recognition as subjects. To look at white people is to violate that prohibition. The Other of racism is obsessively looked at (even in absence), and appropriated as a pure object, while being refused the recognition of being able to look back. In the play, when Fred claims that a black person has always "done something," the violation of the prohibition against the look forms an important part of the substance to his blanket indictment. To have looked constitutes a violation of the rule of whiteness. Each transgression of this law becomes an act of insurrection against white supremacy. On the train, the two black men were assumed to have presented themselves as subjects, for which they were to be punished by the white men. As Sartre puts it in the *Critique of Dialectical Reason,* colonialism is a sentence passed on the colonized apriori.[12]

The inversions of ethical values that introduce fraudulence at the heart of white consensus and social cohesion emerge naturally from this refusal of reciprocity. White supremacy has insisted on segregation and disenfranchisement (which has also included barring black people from testifying against white people in court) as its logical extension. And conversely, the general white blindness to the oppressions of white supremacy is licensed by that same refusal of reciprocity.

This is quite different from the Hegelian master-slave dialectic. Hegel's dialectic depends upon a mutual recognition between the dominant and the subordinate, though the terms of that recognition may be disparate or even incommensurable. Each achieves a sense of social being through the other.

But racialization—what whites as a group do to those they designate as nonwhite in order to constitute themselves as white (see note 3)—becomes a subject-object relation in which recognition is unidirectional. For Sartre, the "master/slave" relation applies primarily to workers within a capitalist framework, who stand in reciprocal relation to capitalists across the objects of capital (the means of production) (Ethics, 566).

To understand "race" as a social structure means to understand it as a social relation between the collective or consensual white socius and the objectified other as racialized (Ethics, 570). It cannot be a relation between subjectivities or modes of consciousness since its subject-object character prohibits reciprocity or mutual recognition. It is to this structure that DuBois alluded when he spoke of double consciousness. For DuBois, to be black in the United States is always to see oneself through the eyes of another. While one remains a subjectivity for oneself among black people, one apprehends oneself as an object for whites.[13]

In this structure of racialization, with its inversion of ethics and curtailment of subjectivity, there is inherent violence. It is a gratuitous violence, however. For those targeted by it, it seems to come out of nowhere, with no overt source or motivation. (In that sense, the black man's initial plea, at the beginning of the play, that he "hadn't done anything," symbolizes the condition of all racialized and colonized people.) For the white perpetrators, on the other hand, who choose to see a black person's assumption of subjectivity as an act of insurgency, their violence appears as "counterviolence" or self-defense. In the play, Thomas's invention of a knife in the black man's hand was an automatic justification for the shooting, masking Thomas's retaliation for having been seen molesting Lizzie. In effect, to be white means to constitute one's racialized identity (that is, one's white subjectivity in the Sartrean sense of the "fundamental project" (BN, 463)) through the construction of a threat one locates in black people and in any black autonomy that can be suppressed.

But the structure goes beyond threat. As Sartre shows in the *Ethics*, one becomes conscious of society, and of one's socialization, through the look of others (Ethics, 111). For whites, since black people are to be prohibited the look, they can only become conscious of their social framework through other whites. All social dynamics occur only through interaction with other whites. In the *Critique*, Sartre argues that because each member of the colonized (black) group is seen as a threat to all colonizers (whites) (CDR, 302), whites are faced with the continual necessity not only of enforcing their domination on those who would throw it off if they could, but of demonstrating to each other that it is still enforceable. The apprehension of a threat (of black subjectivity) generates an ever-renewed demand for white solidarity and consensus. *White society must constantly imbue itself with a sense of threat in order to reproduce the mutual recognition and allegiance essential to white identity as such.*

This is the role of racism. "Racism is the colonial interest lived as a link of all the colonists" (CDR, 300). That is, "racism" is a social technology designed not only to maintain the system of social categorizations called "race," but to be the means whereby white racialized identity is continually reconstituted through its construction of a threat. The existence of the racialized other as a threat, through denial of the other's subjectivity, provides the fundamental condition for the survival of white social cohesion. In other words, "racialization" is the white deployment of others (designated nonwhite) who, in being appropriated as objects, pose the possibility of a threat through which whites can constitute themselves as white. Though racism may be called "prejudice" toward others, its hostility and contempt really express a narcissistic, blind, and gratuitous social reaffirmation of white identity and membership—as a relation between whites. Furthermore, Sartre argues, each refusal to recognize the (nonwhite, or colonized) other as a subjectivity marks an "impotence" because it testifies to a subjectivity devoid of the ability to constitute itself as a subjectivity without that other as its object (CDR, 302).

For a white person to truly grasp how this happens in his/her own mind, and to stop it, would mean to cease being white, because it would mean granting the subjectivity and humanity to others that whiteness withholds. All bad faith would have to be brought to an end. One would have to stop racializing black people, while guaranteeing their autonomy to define themselves however they see fit, whether that was to continue their former racialization as black (or Native American, or Latino, etc.) or not, insofar as their own racial consciousness has been the major way they have honorably and courageously survived white supremacy.

What Sartre sought to do, in both *Antisemite and Jew*, and "Black Orpheus," was to take steps toward the restoration of the subjectivity of the colonized, by placing European colonialism in its look. His purpose was to make the structure of white (colonialist) self-racialization clear to the Eurocentric mind. However, there is a problem with this. In the anthology that "Black Orpheus" introduces, the look is oblique, since the contributors are speaking to each other about "what concerns them," which does not include Europe. Indeed, it expresses a disregard for European pretensions to being the center of the world by turning away from Europe and concerning itself with its own thinking and experience.

Sartre in effect renarrativizes these writers by turning them back on Europe so that Europe can see itself as seen; that is, see itself as an object for those it had for centuries objectified. Sartre himself then becomes the look of the decolonized eyes rendering Europe an object for itself. He appropriates the look of these black poets, replacing their oblique look with his own. Thus, he imposes his own Eurocentric gaze on their decolonizing act of "turning away" from Eurocentrism. Against the strength of the black refusal of European hegemony that he celebrates in the volume, he reintegrates a Eurocentric historicity. In *Peau Noire, Masques Blancs* (*Black Skin, White Masks*), Frantz Fanon would later censure Sartre for seeing a people's struggle for its own being as merely a stage in an historical dialectic,[14] which ignored the alternate ontologies that grounded opposition to Eurocentric thought, and which emerged in various ways from African anticolonialist struggles.

In pointing this out, Fanon sought to extricate Sartre from a more general entrapment in a Eurocentric dialectic. In *Antisemite and Jew*, for instance, though Sartre recognizes the relationality of antisemitism, he can only propose a programmatic response that remains wholly inadequate to the structure of that relationality. He sees no further than the Marxian dialectic, and blandly proclaims that antisemitism will only be eliminated with the elimination of class society (ASJ, 150). Sartre correctly argues that for the antisemite, the character of the other ("the Jew"), or even the nature of Judaism, is wholly contingent. But in offering his dialectical programmatic, he reveals little sense of the profound cultural transformation necessary. It is not only the denigration of an other that counts for the racist, but a larger complex of social structures by which the racist (or antisemite) constructs his/her own social identity. *The relation of social identity to a social order as a cultural order* is what Sartre addresses in *The Respectful Prostitute*.

The Mythos of U.S. Whiteness

In the play, what ultimately breaks through Lizzie's resistance is a third level of discourse nested within the racializing structure of appropriation and decriminalization of whiteness. White racialized identity lives not only in its forms of social cohesion, the allegiance and consensus it demands among whites; it provides itself with a cultural content, a system of mythologies and technologies to govern the social performance of whiteness. They appear in the words of the Senator (Fred's father), who arrives just as the police begin to assault Lizzie. He stops them, and approaches Lizzie in wholly different terms.

The Senator begins by questioning Lizzie briefly, to ascertain that she is sure of her story. He neither rejects her account nor impugns her honor. Thus, he begins by granting her autonomy, a subjectivity of her own, as the first step in integrating her into the white socius of the town. At the same time, he shifts the victim again (for the third time). Where, for Fred, Thomas is to be Lizzie's victim if she does not sign the paper, the Senator makes

Lizzie's victim a mythical woman waiting passively somewhere for Lizzie to choose. He introduces this woman as he starts to leave Lizzie's apartment by saying, offhand, "Poor Mary." And Lizzie falls for it. The Senator turns back for his command performance.

Mary is Thomas's mother, a rich but helpless woman ostensibly caught in Lizzie's clutches because Lizzie controls Thomas's fate. The Senator assures Lizzie that the imprisonment of her son will kill her. Not only will Lizzie be victimizing a "leading citizen," but motherhood itself will fall to her power. Looking Lizzie right in the eyes, he expatiates on what he envisions Lizzie herself is thinking of what Mary would be thinking of Lizzie (in gratitude) if Lizzie would save her son by signing the paper. Where the double thinking of simple inversion is sufficient for the subject-object relation between white and black, a triple thinking of the situation is necessary between whites—a fictionalization of consciousness rather than a denial of it. The Senator renarrativizes Lizzie's desire, making her be the one who desires innocence and citizenship above all else (a hegemonic state contingent on accepting the unethical and the criminal as legitimate), while couching it in her "desire" to preserve the white mother's mythic purity, whose gratitude will make Lizzie whole and honorable. Lizzie will be granted both innocence and citizenship through "Mother" Mary. The angel is invoked to offer the sinner entry into heaven. By informing Lizzie of what she is herself thinking about someone else who is allegedly thinking about her, he is placing Lizzie in the look of the mother, through which Lizzie is provided with a "white consciousness." Though the Senator first seems to respect her story and to grant her autonomy in it, he is far from doing so. By making her the focus of how other white people see her, he incorporates her into the seriality of white society and makes her white in his terms.

Citizenship in the town and allegiance to whiteness are not what Lizzie wants, which is why she is able to resist the demands of political power. But she wants to be considered good at her profession, and would like the elite, to which Mary belongs, to recognize her as a good person. That would require that she receive the gratitude of the matriarch for having paid obeisance.

In his play, *Huis clos* (*No Exit*), Sartre investigates the modes by which one arrives at a desired identity through others, rather than through one's self-enacted authentic being in the world. A desired identity is dependent upon the thoughts and opinions of others, and is thus an abandonment of one's freedom. In *No Exit*, each character seeks in bad faith to be known as someone other than who they are, needing another to grant it. In *The Respectful Prostitute*, the Senator turns this around. By looking in Lizzie's eyes, he performs the act of making her "look" the object of his own, making her subjectivity his object. He tells her what she wants, and who she wants to be, by his look, and his narrativization of Mary's look, rather than withholding it, as the characters do to each other in *No Exit*. Lizzie is to be given a new identity, one she has not desired, through a woman she does not know.

The "Mother" is a mythic figure in the play, the avatar for the white socius. Fred jealously controls how his mother is to be mentioned, and by whom. He pleads in the name of his mother to sanctify himself when he is at a disadvantage—for instance, when Lizzie holds a gun on him. He threatens Lizzie when she impugns his mother for not having taught him sufficient respect for women. Thomas's mother embodies the "good family" Thomas comes from, and which will crumble if his acts of killing are to be considered culpable murders. The mother is the avatar for inborn social virtue, ultimately embodying the biologization of whiteness.

To supplement the mother, the Senator also provides a world-historic framework. He invokes an equally mythic "Uncle Sam," whom he casts in a beatifying Socratic role (and here, the Hegelian Eurocentric dialectic finds its proper place). Through the Senator's voice, Uncle Sam asks Lizzie, since she has to choose between two men, Thomas and the black man, how she is to determine who the "better" man is. She finds herself trapped in the circle of white supremacy: Thomas is the better man because he is a leading citizen, and he is a leading citizen because he is the better man. Faced with this totalized and essentializing circle (adjoined to a decriminalizing ethical inversion and an invocation of a mythic mother), Lizzie's resolve weakens enough for the Senator to help her sign the paper. After she signs, Thomas once again becomes an honest leading citizen in the eyes of the law.

We do not have to look far for a contemporary analogue to the statement Lizzie is induced to sign (against all her principles of fairness and truth). In the 2000 election in Florida, well over one hundred thousand people of color were prevented from voting, in what amounted to massive illegal disenfranchisement.[15] The following week, the NAACP collected ten thousand sworn affidavits concerning improper obstruction from voting, far more than Bush's margin of victory. However, the Democratic Party leadership ignored this in favor of simply recounting ballots, preferring thereby to decriminalize the state's criminal disfranchisement of its own citizens, and valorize the participation of those to whom the state had limited its recognition. Thus, the Democratic Party sought to affirm its membership in whiteness. When the ballot issue was taken to the Supreme Court, the court stopped the recount procedure in violation of the Voting Rights Act of 1965, which makes it a felony to prevent all votes cast from being counted. Thus, it sustained an extant disfranchisement, exonerated an electoral ignominy, and rendered the nation complicit in an antidemocratic act. While the political entanglements of organizations (such as parties) is more complex than that of individuals in small towns, it is the relational structure inherent in these events (the play and the election) that reveals a congruence. If we spell out the allegory suggested, Thomas, Fred, and the police play the role of the Florida state government, the Senator plays the Democratic Party, Lizzie plays the role of the people manipulated by the Democratic Party to save the honor of the white state, and the paper Lizzie (the people) signs under the Democratic Party's hand and valorization plays the role of the Supreme Court decision, clearing the state of all wrongdoing. As the Senator and the others leave, Lizzie realizes that she has been had, in more ways than one.

Sartre is clear on what set Lizzie up. She has seen a man get shot to death on the train, yet this has not impressed her as much as the thought of the Senator's sister's grief at her son the killer being locked up for ten years. All her principles fall away in the face of the mythos of whiteness and the normativity of white supremacy. Against the imposition of white social identity, with all its inchoate desires and performances of belonging by which it manipulates her mind, Lizzie has no defenses. Her consciousness is already governed by her own whiteness, as racialized privilege, which the Senator plays on. Though one could see gender solidarity as well in her act, it is really gratitude that she desires from Mary, and acceptance (citizenship).

Later, when she holds a gun on Fred, intending to shoot him, he expatiates on how his family had tamed the land and the frontier, to found the white nation upon it. He tells her she can't kill the history he represents. She acquiesces, and hands him the gun. In short, she is already white in a white society, and what the Senator's recognition of her subjectivity had done is remind her of it.

The Performative Violence of Whiteness

These social structures of ethical inversion, consensus, myth, and membership in the white socius constitute the framework in which a person understands himself or recognizes himself as "white." Yet the worldly "reality" of these structures requires a social cohesion beyond the ethical inversion of impunity. What leads white people to answer the call of consensus (Lizzie's acquiescence, the townspeople collecting in the street to save Thomas; the charge of anti-Americanism levied against Sartre) is an identity involvement, for which gratuitous violence is often the adjunct. To elucidate this, let us return to the Senator's performance, which has taken Lizzie in.

When the Senator has Lizzie look him in the eyes, fictionalizing to her face what she is to be thinking at that moment, he is divesting her of subjective autonomy through what would constitute her subjectivity for him, her look; and he is inscribing his own subjectivity in her. It is a subtle form of thought control allied to the nonreciprocity of domination. He transforms her look into an instrumentality for himself. It is this instrumentality that permits her induction into the fold, through the credentials of Mother Mary's recognition and gratitude. Thus, while white racialized identity withholds recognition from those it subordinates as the condition for its own existence, it grants white identity through recognition as white. Not only is "race" something one group does to another (see note 3), but in granting whiteness to itself as membership, it recognizes whiteness as a cultural act of licensing.

In staging their performances, the "mother" is only a "prop" for both Fred and the Senator, to be used at appropriate moments (like Fred's rhetorical expressions—e.g., that a black person "has always done something"). These props (stories, expressions, and recognitions) represent what Sartre would call the "idea-hexis" of whiteness. They control the seriality of white racialized society by providing the materialities around which that seriality is constructed.

For Sartre, a serial collective requires some form of inert materiality in terms of which to form. In his prototypic example, it is the bus at whose terminal people line up, each with their own personal destinations; through the bus, they collectively attain their separate ends (CDR, 256). "Hexis" names the materiality around which each practical situation gains its social stability, the objectivity of the situation (bus routes, for instance) to which individual "praxis" addresses itself in its projects. It signifies the nature of wood that a carpenter must understand in order to be able to shape it properly, for instance, with a different understanding than s/he would have to have for cement. A basketball, soccer ball, and volleyball are all the same shape, but each acts differently; in each game, the ball has to be played differently. Each provides a different hexis around which each kind of team develops its teamwork.

"Idea-hexis" is "hexis" in the form of idea or discourse (CDR, 300). *The "idea-hexis" of whiteness is the complex of props, stories, assumptions, demands for consensus, and the language of racism to which obeisance and acceptance is required by whites.* In Sartre's account of racial domination, it is the language of racism that holds colonialist society together. The world of that language, its contempt for those it appropriates and instrumentalizes (CDR, 304), and the social values it gives itself and the other, constitute a complex history of impunity and violence by which each white person is linked to all others (CDR, 303). These links are at the same time projected as universal values.[16] And the universalized values created by white exigent consensus invoke practices of racial assault and disparagement against those excluded in advance from those universals. The idea-hexis of self-universalization (of white racialized identity) constitutes the core of white seriality, its unity in alterity (CDR, 301). It is to this "unity in alterity" that the black man refers when he describes white strangers greeting each other as friends.

They unite as strangers to reconfirm themselves as white through their serial project to kill a black man in order to exonerate a white man.

In this "unity in alterity," each grants the other credentials, as the Senator does to Lizzie. Since black (or brown) people are misrecognized or not recognized and prohibited subjectivity, and thus prohibited from granting subjectivity to whites (through reciprocity or a dialogic look), the only source left for white subjectivity is recognition of their social performance of whiteness by other whites. The Senator's performance sways Lizzie's sense of justice, accomplishing an alchemy of being where the threat of jail or physical violence had failed, because the performance offers belonging in the socius valorized by the myths of whiteness. Her incorporation in the town constitutes an act of violence insofar as it requires her to be who she is not. But in being given a white subjectivity through the Senator's mythologization of Mary, she becomes someone who can recognize herself only through the eyes of other whites. Thus, she undergoes the additional violence of being scripted by others, and judged in her performance of the script. Fred's bad faith, his racism, and his refusal of himself as a sexual being are all similar aspects of being a plaything of one's racialization, of the seriality of whiteness.

One can grasp the obsessiveness of this seriality of whiteness in the unending use of racializing derogatory terms by whites. Derogatory terms are prototypic elements of the white "idea-hexis." They are not signifiers; their purpose is only to express disdain, hate, or contempt. As Sartre explains, they cannot be translated into real thoughts, nor formulated as such (CDR, 300). Their meaning cannot be made the object of intentionalities. Without substance or meaning, their significance lies in their use. Rather than signifiers, their use constitutes acts of assault. The domain of their use is defined by the surrounding structures of white hegemony and domination, structures that give them their content as modes of assault. To speak these terms is to adopt an attitude of aggressiveness and hostility. Though they remain impoverished "verbal tools" (CDR, 304), they are the instruments by which the white social world is organized as violence (CDR, 305). Thus as idea-hexis, they provide membership in the seriality of the white socius.

Ultimately, the real referent for derogatory terms is not those assaulted by them but the socius that deploys them as hexis for itself, for the purposes of serial cohesion. Where the other (persons of color) remains essential as both a presence and the core content of white identity, the phrases, presumptions, and derogatory terms of white idea-hexis are essential to white serial sociality, to give its racialized identity form. This is what marks the structure of white racialized identity as a socius of violence. The indispensable use of derogation and hostility against the other for the purposes of white social cohesion does not only constitute the way that the white socius recognizes itself collectively but how it gives itself its meaning. Its means of hostility to the other signify that collectivity to itself; that is, its existence in seriality is maintained only through the constant invocation of (potential) violence, for which the use of derogatory terms serve as proxy.

There is a compulsiveness implicit in the performance of aggressiveness in the absence of any need, or indeed of a present target. The purpose of endlessly engaging in denigration in white speech, as a form of "noticing" black people (especially in their absence), marks an obsessiveness among whites about belonging, about confirming membership through "paying those dues." Insofar as this compulsiveness is internal to the construction of white racialized identity, it marks the insecurity of social seriality, a need for more and more props. The entire complex of comportments, of terms, myths, fictions, and fictionalizations of those one confronts, as things one does "without thinking," remain "unthought" because they are obsessive. White subjectivity finds itself doubly serialized: first, in being condemned to relate to other whites across an idea-hexis that has no meaning other than membership; and second, in relying on other whites to bestow white identity through approbation of one's performance of whiteness for them.

Herein lies the necessity of impunity, on which Thomas counted in his assault on both Lizzie and the black men on the train. In performing his whiteness (and his masculinism) as contempt and hate, he is relating to other whites (and other men) for purposes of membership, to play his role as a leading citizen. That is, his citizenship in a law-governed society (in which murder, fraudulent testimony, and tampering with evidence are all crimes) is trumped by his citizenship in the white socius. The white socius becomes fraudulent with respect to law-governed society. Thomas's (and Fred's) autonomy as persons becomes fraudulent insofar as they must mark their membership in the white socius as of a higher order than that in law-governed society. The framework of whiteness constitutes a system of norms by which one "acts" white in the eyes of other whites. It dispenses with the norms of law-governed society, which then functions merely as a "cover story" for it. It is this framework that brings the town's people into the streets searching for a victim, not only to approve Thomas, but to recognize each other. It is the doubled social framework, with its double seriality, that gives the play's action its familiarity for those in the real world, both that of 1947, and today.

To have set black people obsessively at the core of white identity (in the real world) produces the narcissistic necessity to extricate white identity from them, that is, to continually evict them from white subjectivity. But it is also to pretend to an independence in the performance of whiteness that remains dependent on other whites. This is the real content of the gratuitous violence by which whiteness maintains itself, and testifies to the depth of the alienation of white identity. *White racialized identity cannot know who or what it is, since its center lies doubly elsewhere.* This is the ground on which criminality and the inversion of criminality becomes not only possible, but indispensable.

White racialized identity condemns itself to the performance of violence for all renewal of a sense of self. Its gratuitous violence condemns it and its racism to having no real referent beyond that violence itself. Whites make reference to their history, as does Fred, but it is only a history of violence, of conquest, the seizure of land from others, the enslavement of people kidnapped from afar, and the degradation of human personhood. In the contemporary United States, the mass incarceration of black and brown people has taken the place of these other historical modes of violence, as an expression of the way white society chooses to affirm itself under the cover of being "law-governed."

The Structure of Racialized Identity

The compulsive irrationality of racialized violence, of segregation, of gratuitous hostility, of obsessive incarceration, as we have seen, reflect what Sartre calls an impotence (CDR, 302), the "violence of impotence" (CDR, 304). On top of the incapacity to simply be without the appropriation and control of the other, there is the need to feel threatened, the creation of a sense of being threatened through which to gain approbation for the violence of that appropriation. It is a double violence, conjoined in the prohibition of the other's look, the inability to withstand the potential threat attributed to that look.

The serial need for a threat, and its endless social reinvention in the subordinated other, constitutes a communal paranoia as one of the essential components of the social structure of white racialized identity. This sense of paranoia relies upon and generates (as impunity) a white solidarity against the perceived threat, which its violence concretizes, and in so doing, makes the threat seem real. All this transpires doubly in the play. The presence of the black men on the train is something that must be met with an attack, in which the four white men are immediately in concert; and when Thomas shoots one of the black men, the town closes ranks to valorize the shooting by accepting the criminalization of the black man. To have accepted the criminalization of the black man for having allegedly assaulted Lizzie is to have extended the threat to the town as a whole, where the cycle continues. Having invented this threat, the elite and the white townspeople come together, and a lynch mob forms.[17]

As represented in the play, the threat that is so essential to whiteness is always and everywhere a mythic threat, necessarily self-generated for the purposes of identification with a serial socius. When the threat becomes real, through a mass civil rights movement, for instance, the idea-hexis of white supremacy must hide because it faces a world that is no longer intelligible to it. It retreats into law-governed society, allows the state to negotiate in order to stall for time, and reorders whiteness through eventual repression. The civil rights legislations passed during the 1960s were eventually eviscerated or repealed in the 1980s, accompanied by the massive imprisonment of people of color through reinvented myths of criminalization. Today, though one-eighth of the U.S. population, black people outnumber whites in arrests, indictments, and convictions by a ratio of eight to one. As a result, the United States, with 6 percent of the world's population, holds 25 percent of the world's prisoners, 75 percent of whom are people of color.[18] The form the new impunity takes (the old form being chain gangs and Jim Crow) is a system of victimless crime laws, police profiling, and the ideology of "colorblindness." Indeed, in violating all odds and averages, the violence of the mass imprisonment of people of color signifies that white serial society has again trumped law-governed society even within the domain of law and judiciality. As long as the threat is mythic and self-generated by white society, violence in all its gratuitousness can be justified.

The final violence of the play is the appropriation of Lizzie, her dispossession as white womanhood in white society. In the last scene, Fred reappears and informs Lizzie that the mob caught a black man (a different one, but no matter) and killed him—gratuitously, for nothing more than his existence. Fred then tells Lizzie that watching the man die made him (Fred) sexually excited; so he has rushed to Lizzie's apartment to take possession of her. He expresses his intention to house her in a middle-class home to wait upon his desires, a toy to cater to his whims. Now it is in Lizzie whom Fred needs to objectify his identity, and to refuse all subjective reciprocity. Because he has little interest in sexuality, he must create an idea-hexis by which to realize himself. He reminds her that she remarked that morning that he excited her, and he makes her repeat it, to pay obeisance to it. At the very moment of seizing her, of taking control of her, he must refocus her subjectivity, as the correlate of the dependence on her that he creates for himself. The structure of that dependence, in its minuteness, is analogous to the structure of societal dependence of white racialized identity on black people.

In Fred's culminating masculinist gesture, Sartre also portrays a sense of the degenerate ecstasy (sexual or not) that drives the white mob to the violence it heaps on black people. In 1916, fifteen thousand people showed up to watch Jesse Washington be slowly tortured to death in broad daylight in front of City Hall, and then scrambled to get a piece of his charred body to take home as a souvenir.[19] Torment is at the heart of the violent construction of white identity, because death isn't sufficient to nullify the threat it has created for itself. In other words, the gratuitous violence against the mythic threat whiteness concocts for itself, which mediates its solidarist consensus, is not an aberration. It is a travesty that expresses an essential norm of the social structure of whiteness.

In its reliance on a mythic threat, white racialized identity reveals desperation, a psychological and emotional need for a tortured victim. The contemporary production of prisons, and indeed, the present modifications of the concept of prison, appear wholly natural to it in this sense. Today, imprisonment goes beyond its original juridical function as punishment for violation of the law; it has become instead the place where punishment is meted out. A convicted person is placed in prison not *as* punishment, but in order to then *be* punished beyond the fact of being imprisoned. Torture has become routine in all prisons in the United States, whether directly at the guards hands or through the instrumentality of other prisoners. And "supermax" prisons have been built whose purpose is to drive inmates' insane.[20] These practices are not a Foucauldian structure of discipline, but rather an extension of the structure of whiteness, a mode of sadism which Sartre recognized as inherent in white supremacist bad faith.

At the end of the play, a kind of existential solidarity emerges between Lizzie and the black man, both victims of a social order that lives on torment, as they listen to the mob search the town. When some of the vigilantes knock at Lizzie's door, she hides the black man and bluffs the mob. Still, she and the black man are confounded by the single-minded obsessiveness of the town in its search for this man who has done nothing. The town's hate and cohesion succeed in generating feelings of guilt in both, which almost override their determination to survive (RP, 277). When this confuses Lizzie, he assures her, "that's how it always goes with white folks" (RP, 278). It is a statement of resignation, of the inexorability of white obsessiveness, violence, and "unity in alterity." But it implicitly recognizes the fanatical superseding of the law, governed by the structure of whiteness.

Notes

1. *New York Herald Tribune*, Nov. 13, 1946. Susan Keane calls it a "difficult play for American readers" in a review in *Modern Language Journal* 66.2: 206. Even as astute a reader as Hazel Barnes gave it short shrift. In *Humanist Existentialism*, she misrepresents some important details, misconstrues the central plot motif, and expresses a strange disbelief in the gratuitousness of southern racist violence. She evidently had not yet read Ida Wells. Barnes's ultimate focus was on the extent to which Lizzie is rendered a "thing." Hazel Barnes, *Humanist Existentialism* (Lincoln: University of Nebraska Press, 1959), 73.
2. Jean-Paul Sartre, "Black Orpheus," trans. David MacCombie, *The Massachusetts Review*, 6 (Autumn 1964): 13–52; *Antisemite and Jew* (New York: Schocken, 1948), hereafter cited as ASJ; *Notebooks for an Ethics,* trans. David Pallauer (Chicago: University of Chicago Press, 1992), hereafter cited as Ethics;

"The Respectful Prostitute" in *No Exit* (New York: Vintage, 1956), hereafter cited as RP.

3. As Walter Mignolo points out in *Local Histories, Global Designs* (Princeton: Princeton University Press, 2000), the idea of "race" had originally been proposed to reduce those from whom colonialists stole land to a level at which they could no longer make a claim on that land or on their own past. See also David Walker, *Appeal to the Colored Citizens of the World* (New York: Hill and Wang, 1995); Ashley Montague, in *The Concept of Race* (New York: Collier, 1969), made an early argument that there was no biological basis for it. Recently, various critiques of whiteness as a social structure have appeared. See, for instance, David Roediger, *Wages of Whiteness* (New York: Verso, 1991); Theodore Allen, *The Invention of the White Race* (New York: Verso, 1997); and Steve Martinot, *The Rule of Racialization* (Philadelphia: Temple University Press, 2003).

It is important to understand "race" as relational. That is, it should be understood as a verb, and not a noun; the verb is "to racialize." "Race" is something one group of people does to another (necessarily with brutality, and as a justification for brutality). Insofar as race was invented in the European colonies in the Americas, it is a process whereby whites racialized themselves as white through their racialization (subordination, inferiorization, dehumanization) of others, as nonwhite. This idea of "race" as a social structure has generally remained unintelligible to most white people, which might explain the paucity of commentary on Sartre's play.

4. A contemporary form this resistance takes, at the juridical level, is the attack on affirmative action as a "quota system," and "reverse racism," conveniently refusing or ignoring the fact that the entire history of segregation amounted to a 100 percent quota system for whites. The contortions concerning the concept of "racism" that the state and various (white) citizens organizations have gone through to overturn affirmative action is astounding. For instance, the government's proclamation that the passage of civil rights legislation had produced a colorblind society was eagerly grasped by whites, who could then accuse those who still charged racial discrimination of being "racist" for having brought up the issue. Colorblindness still sees color; but the only color it can see is white. Thus, it amounts to an alternate disguised form of discrimination.

5. Those who have seen the photos of lynching mobs (and there are many) cannot avoid being struck by the festive atmosphere often surrounding the acts of torture in progress. People smile, talk among themselves, sometimes with drinks in their hands, as if content with their work, the reconstitution of their sacred social framework. *Without Sanctuary*, ed. James Allen (Santa Fe: Twin Palms, 2000); see in particular, the photo of Thomas Shipp and Abram Smith, Aug. 7, 1930, Marion, Indiana.

6. Sartre expresses another version of this in ASJ. He ventriloquizes the antisemite: "By treating the Jew as an inferior and pernicious being, I affirm at the same time that I belong to the elite.... There is nothing I have to do to merit my superiority, and neither can I lose it. It is given to me once and for all" (ASJ, 27). With respect to a black person or a Jew being rendered a priori the embodiment of evil, see ASJ, 39–40; good then consists in treating such people destructively.

7. There is an international movement attempting to get Mumia a retrial. The facts of the case, and of the movement's efforts are mostly found on webpages. Cf. www.mumia.org; www.freemumia.org; en.wikipedia.org/wikiMumia_Abu-Jamal. What is most often omitted in accounts of the case is the most glaring omission in the case itself, viz. that the police did no test for gun shot residue on Mumia's hands.

8. This structure even appears in the preparations for the invasion and occupation of Iraq. The invasion was a criminal act, an unprovoked attack on a sovereign nation; a prima facie violation of the UN Charter, and thus of the U.S. Constitution (Art. VI, sec. 2). It violated the principle of national sovereignty, whose inviolability is taught in high school civics classes throughout the United States. What made the invasion acceptable to mainstream U.S. opinion was the familiarity given it by ethical inversion. The United States decriminalized its invasion by criminalizing all Iraqis who rose in resistance against the invasion and occupation in defense of their country. Though racism or white supremacy did not play an overt role in the invasion, the structure of self-valorization axiomatic to white racialized domination as a cultural logic of the United States validated the invasion for the American mind. Cf. Steve Martinot, "The Whiteness of the Assault on Iraq," in *Socialism and Democracy* 34.2 (Summer, 2003): 165–69.
9. In 1954, for instance, a black man was charged and convicted of rape in Florida for speaking to a white woman on the telephone, and sentenced to fifteen years in prison. See *New York Times,* April 11, 1954, 8.
10. Jean-Paul Sartre, *Being and Nothingness*, trans. Hazel Barnes (New York: Philosophical Library, 1956), 262ff; hereafter cited as BN.
11. The volume is edited by Léopold Senghor, of Senegal, as an expression of black self-awareness, which Sartre labels, following Aimé Césaire, as "negritude." Negritude represents black subjectivity become aware of itself as such. Expatriot African intellectuals, encountering common elements of African thought while in Paris, and laying claim to them, transformed their identity by throwing off the inferiority complex colonialism had imposed on them, and formed what came to be known as the negritude movement. Sartre's essay played a role in establishing the meaning of the term "negritude" in Europe as such. Before that, the movement had no such logo. Sartre continued his involvement with the African expatriots, helping to found their journal, *Présence Africaine*. He is, in fact, the one who suggested that name. Sartre was not the first white European intellectual to listen to African thought. Indeed, African thought and imagery has had a profound effect on Europe, and Paris in particular, since the beginning of the century. The use of such imagery in modernist painting, cubism, and philosophy had flourished before World War II.
12. Jean-Paul Sartre, *Critique of Dialectical Reason*, trans. Alan Sheridan-Smith (London: New Left, 1976), 300; hereafter cited as CDR.
13. W. E. B. Du Bois, *The Souls of Black Folk* (New York: Fawcett, 1961), 16.
14. Frantz Fanon, *Black Skin, White Masks* (New York: Grove, 1967), 133.
15. Greg Palast, *The Best Democracy Money Can Buy* (London: Pluto, 2002).
16. The paradoxical or aporetic nature of the universal was exemplified by the debates over slavery that occurred in the United States in the early nineteenth century. Positions on slavery ranged from considering it morally evil to morally proper, from an unconscionable stain upon the United States as a democratic society to being the very essence of freedom insofar as absolute freedom means the ability to dominate absolutely. What remained unquestionable was the universal right of whites to discuss and decide the status, condition, and destiny of black people as such, without the participation of black people themselves, that is, not as universal but restricted to whites. The precedent for this "universality" emanated from the Declaration of Independence, which restricted its concept of "universal" freedom to white men by refusing to proclaim the abolition of slavery as a condition of independence. The violation of democratic principle, Fred would say, doesn't matter; all that matters is black and white.

Sartre would argue that the very existence of a debate on slavery meant that slavery was not natural and that slaves were men and not naturally slaves (Ethics, 564). For whites to debate only among themselves whether black people should be allowed the franchise, or admitted into the democratic order as participants, is already to have corrupted and destroyed that order. The law that enfranchised black people is nothing but white law; and the franchise allows black admission into what remains a white institutionality, governed by white law. As a case in point, in the wake of the civil rights movements and the Voting Rights Act, black people became a minority, along with Latinos, Native Americans, Asians, etc. (and women). But "minority" status only signifies a change in language by which the "other" is named (using the language of democratic procedure). White society defines black people as a minority a priori, prior to any vote, as a way of defining itself as the majority by exclusion (of each minority). That is, "minoritization" has the same structure as racialization. Using the rhetoric of voting strength, it constitutes the majoritarian status of an exclusionary white constituency, under the pretense of a recognized demographic. True democratic procedure would not assume a separate black voting bloc, nor categorize it as such (even if black people voted together), but recognize a majority and a "minority" only after the vote had been taken. In its present racialized sense, "majoritarian" status (self-defined by defining "minorities") simply becomes another "universal" institutionality around which exclusionary whites coalesce.

17. The profundity of the existence of this structure can be gauged by its appearance in contemporary events, and its function to make such events acceptable to the mainstream American. The invasion of Iraq was a wanton unprovoked attack on a sovereign nation, illegal under international and constitutional law. To gain acceptance for an invasion of Iraq, a paranoia was developed through invented intelligence about Iraq. An attempt at international solidarity was made, and used to develop a national consensus on the danger from that country. Then violence was promulgated in the form of a military assault, in the face of which the falseness of all initial reasons for invading dissolved. Even large elements of the antiwar movement joined the exigent solidarity that couched itself in terms of "supporting the troops"—despite the fact that every step U.S. troops took on Iraqi soil was a criminal act. The solidarity was a response to the paranoia, which then realized itself in violence that made the paranoia seem real. The violence legitimizes the paranoia, the paranoia legitimizes the racial solidarity, and the social solidarity legitimizes the violence, around and around, endlessly. Cf. Martinot, *The Rule of Racialization*, 68. Racism did not have to appear as an overt element of the invasion; it was the structure of racialization—paranoia, solidarity, and violence—that rendered the invasion acceptable because familiar, and familiar because an analogue to the structure of whiteness.
18. The most extensive and up-to-date reports on prisons in the United States are to be found at www.prisonsucks.com/factsheets.shtml. See also Angela Davis, "Masked Racism," in *Colorlines*, 1.2 (Fall 1998): 11.
19. Grace Hale, *Making Whiteness* (New York: Pantheon, 1998), 217.
20. Janis Shields, "Widespread Torture Exists in U.S. Prisons"; American Friends Service Committee Report, Nov. 11, 2005. Available at www.afsc.org; H. Bruce Franklin, "The American Prison and the Normalization of Torture" (2002), available at www.historiansagainstwar.org/resources/torture/bruce-franklin.html; and Deborah Davies, "Torture: America's Brutal Prisons" (May 23, 2005), available at http://globalresearches.ca/articles/DAV505A.html.

Chapter 3

The Persistence of Colonialism
Sartre, the Left, and Identity in Postcolonial France, 1970–1974

Paige Arthur

On November 6, 1973, Sartre lost a court battle to eight editors of the extreme right-wing weekly *Minute*. They had sued him for defamation, making death threats, and justifying the crime of destruction by explosives, and he was ordered to pay each of them a 400 franc fine.[1] The reason for the conviction was an article that had appeared in the Maoist newspaper *La Cause du peuple*. Sartre had become the director of the organ in May 1970 in an effort to keep it alive after its editors, Jean-Pierre Le Dantec and Michel Le Bris, were arrested. *Minute*, according to the article in *La Cause du peuple*, was staffed by "the poorly purged of the Liberation and those who had been in the half-pay of the OAS"—referring to the right-wing French terrorist organization that had worked to prevent Algerian independence from France in the early 1960s. The Maoists warned "all of the Kollaborators of this newspaper, director and editors alike, that ... we will not publish their addresses and leave to others the task of acting with our blessing. We will keep them, but we affirm that we will know how to use them if the need is felt."[2] The court judged that the article's threatening words had gone too far, and that Sartre as director was accountable: "While strongly pointing out the dangerous and illegal consequences risked by the consistently violent, not to mention hateful, style of the editors of *Minute* who are contesting him in this court today," the judge announced, "Sartre employed, for his part, in the article of June 21, 1972, a style and a vocabulary comparable in every way to theirs."[3]

This particular fight was merely an extension of a series of hostile exchanges between *Minute* and *La Cause du peuple*, many of which were ideological contests over the proper contents of French nationality, and thus which consistently made reference to defining and divisive historical events such as the Algerian war for independence. The political struggle over postcolonial French identity was thus already in full sway. Sartre would, in the early 1970s, operate both as an actor and as a symbol in the struggle's debates. *Minute* had been tracking the activities and pronouncements of Maoists and other *gauchistes* to whom it invariably referred under various pejorative names. But it had always had a special, enduring interest in Sartre, the "pope of the Revolution," viciously reviewing his books, acerbically commenting on his political positions, and passing along gossip on his health and personal life.[4]

Sartre was a convenient lightening rod for criticism of the radical Left, and an effective magnet for criticisms of Third Worldist sympathies. Thus, when *Minute*'s offices were bombed in May 1971, its editors blamed the "*gauchiste* dogs," but named Sartre on its front page: "Sartre, you are the criminal!" read the tabloid-style block type across an image of the building's damaged exterior. The hostilities escalated further the following month, when *Minute* made the pronouncements of *La Cause du peuple* and other *gauchiste* publications for which Sartre had also assumed responsibility for similar reasons, such as *Tout* and *J'accuse*, the centerpiece of a campaign to have Sartre jailed. "We accuse!" and "To prison, Sartre!" its June 1971 cover lines read.[5] According to the editors of *Minute*, the authorities had been indulging Sartre's incitements to "disorder, pillage, and hatred."[6] Thus, the editors surmised, it would only be by taking matters into their own hands that Sartre might be brought to "justice." As their defense attorney intimated at the trial: "I am pleased to finally see M. Sartre in front of a judge, and I regret that the prosecutor did not take the initiative in this action."[7]

The court's decision was a minor censure, taken on behalf of a group of extremist editors whose wish was to stamp out Sartre and his radical support of Third World liberation movements, immigrant workers, and cultural pluralism—as well as the democratic experimentation he and others advocated to achieve greater freedom and participation for all. As I show in this chapter, this minor censure developed over the first half of the 1970s into a broader critique of such views that spanned the Right-Left divide in France, and that strongly colored debates on the inclusiveness of French democracy.

Postcolonial Culture Wars

The battles of extreme Right and Left between *Minute* and Sartre help bring into focus some of the key political contests of the early 1970s, as well as Sartre's own function in those contests, which was both active and symbolic. One of *Minute*'s central missions was to protect and foster an integralist conception of French nationality. After all, *Minute* had been founded in April 1962 by *Algérie française* supporter Jean-François Devay, and one of its key contributors was François Brigneau, a leader of the right-wing group *Ordre Nouveau* (banned in 1973 after an anti-immigrant protest turned violent) and a founder of the *Front National* in 1972. Sartre and the *gauchistes* challenged *Minute*'s mission in two crucial ways. First, they defended the place of non-European immigrants in French society. Second, they participated in the shift of regionalism away from its traditional home on the Right, and toward a radical democratic defense of cultural pluralism. On both counts, Sartre and the *gauchistes* were interested in rethinking democratic practice in France in ways they took to be more inclusive and a direct challenge to the forces of order, and to do so they relied strongly on radical critiques of colonialism developed during the era of decolonization and adapted to new social conditions.

In keeping with these aims, *gauchiste* publications such as *La Cause du peuple* had made immigrants' working and living conditions in France a staple issue in their pages. Likewise, Sartre, continuing his decades-long concern with race and racism, took an active part in bringing attention to both the social and political stakes at work in the absorption and protection of immigrants in French society. Although Michel Wieviorka opens his book *La France raciste* with the claim that "the return of the theme of racism on the political agenda dates from the 1980s and the growth of the *Front National*,"[8] this return really should be dated a decade earlier, making the success of the *Front National* partly a consequence of that return, not its cause. The fact that the French parliament passed a law against racism in 1972 for which the *Mouvement Contre le Racisme et Pour l'Amitié Entre les Peuples* had lobbied for thirteen years suggests the political urgency of racism in the early 1970s. The law prohibited racial discrimination in employment, housing, and services, gave the government the power to disband organizations that promoted racial hatred, and extended provisions against incitement to racial violence to include racial insults.[9]

Both Sartre and his *Gauche Proletarienne* collaborators frequently invoked both the historical examples (typically, that of Algeria) and theories of colonialism in their analyses and condemnations of the mistreatment of immigrants. This importation of the radical critique of colonialism back to the Metropole was symptomatic of an important trend of the early 1970s, particularly among left-wing activists and intellectuals. Discussions of "the new racism" (the title of a 1972 essay by Sartre, published in both *La Cause du peuple* and *Le Nouvel Observateur*), for example, centered on the vexing problem of tolerance of significant non-European and non-Christian populations, making explicit reference to the residues of racism from the colonial era.[10] But the usage of the radical critique of colonialism was not confined to émigrés of the postcolonial diasporas; it was applied to national minorities within Europe as well. In the case of France, the strongest regionalist movements sprang up in Brittany and Occitanie; in these cases, separatists often used the model of "internal colonialism"—an application and modification of the core-periphery model used in dependency theory—to describe what they viewed as the historical process of both cultural and economic oppression.[11]

This chapter examines Sartre's involvement in theorizing racism and collective identity, and it explains the eclipse of his influence in intellectual discourse by the mid- to late 1970s. His interventions on behalf of immigrant workers and regionalist movements were, I show, linked both conceptually and politically for thinkers and activists involved with the radical noncommunist Left. For his part, Sartre adapted the radical critique of colonialism and racism he developed in the 1950s and early 1960s in response to the war in Algeria and Third World liberation movements to contemporary social problems in early 1970s France, as did many other *gauchistes*. Just as he had used these earlier analyses to support liberation movements abroad, Sartre sought to find ways in the postcolonial era to deepen France's democracy by highlighting and publicizing its various exclusions, thereby supporting homegrown liberation struggles. By the mid-1970s, however, a new discourse on cultural assimilation came to the fore, pushed mainly by the rising Socialist Party and its adherents: a new "universalism" that valued human rights over the protection of particular identities, and that tended to excoriate defenders of particularism on the Left as outmoded and perhaps "totalitarian" defenders of third world revolutionary practices gone awry. In the wake of this shift, Sartre's model of each human being as a "singular universal"—which he used to support cultural autonomy claims in the 1970s—was pushed aside in favor of a vision of universal tolerance fostered by supporters of the Socialist Party. I suggest that it might be worthwhile to reconsider the positions of Sartre and the *gauchistes* since, thirty years after these events, many of the same identity issues I discuss in this chapter remain contentious and unresolved.

"Reverse" Colonialism: Anti-immigrant Racism and French Identitarian Concerns

True to its ideological formation, *Minute*, whose editorial tone was often openly racist, vigorously denied the possibility of assimilating increasingly numerous non-European immigrants.[12] These immigrants, whose political visibility from the late 1960s forward was on the rise, had become important tokens in the struggle between Left and Right in the immediate postcolonial era. By the early 1970s, the stakes concerning immigrants from North Africa in particular began to be sharply contested. In January 1971, Algerian president Houari Boumedienne closed off French companies' access to Algerian oil, a step toward nationalizing the oil industry, which he ultimately took in 1973. This event led to an intensification of *Minute*'s attacks and a veritable obsession with Algerian immigrants: "Enough of Algeria!" one headline read. "They're chasing us out ... now let's chase them out!"[13] In an issue devoted to Algerians in France later that month, the contributors employed stereotypically racist arguments to define the "threat" that such immigrants posed: Algerians' "natural" way of life makes for unsanitary living conditions; refusing to live alone, whether in order to save money or because of "racial instinct," they "reconstitute their tribes"; and they are incapable of taking care of property, for example the lodgings given to them.[14]

But *Minute* was by no means alone in its concern with Algerian immigrants, nor in initiating a backlash against them driven by the Algerian government's nationalization of private enterprises. According to sociologists Alain Gillette and Abdelmalek Sayad, the French government's decision to reduce the number of entries granted to Algerian immigrants (from a net total of thirty-five thousand to twenty-five thousand) in 1971 was partly motivated by its "irritation" at such economic interference.[15] By 1973, *Minute*'s descriptions of the "problem" of Algerian immigration had become even more insistent, using terms such as "invasion" and "race war."[16] Once again, the newspaper linked its denunciation of the presence of North Africans on French soil to world events related to oil, in this case OPEC's oil shock.[17]

Certainly the rapid growth of the Algerian population to the early 1970s represented the most significant shift in the demographics of the immigrant population in France, which had traditionally been dominated by Italians, Poles, and Spaniards. Other non-European populations grew as well, including Moroccans and Tunisians, and the sub-Saharan African population went from being negligible before decolonization to sixty-five thousand by 1972. *Minute*'s and others' reactions to these changes signaled the advent of non-European immigration not just as a social but also as a political issue in France. Jean-Marie Le Pen founded the *Front National* in 1972, thereby inserting the question of the protection of an "integral" French identity directly into electoral politics, though his party did not have any significant electoral success until the 1980s—partly owing to the political schism on the extreme Right between him and *Minute*'s Brigneau beginning in 1974.

Thus, the early 1970s represented a conjuncture in which immigration, racism, xenophobia, and the politics of extremes intersected broadly. Yet it may also in some ways be a misleading conjuncture, as the historian of French immigration Gérard Noiriel points out, since it obscures the fact that France has had a long history of immigration and its concomitant problems of assimilation. Still, what seems unique about this particular period was the intense politicization of intellectuals concerning the issue of immigration, and in particular those actively doing research on it. It was in this era, Noiriel explains, that "a combination of Marxism and anticolonialism assured the fortunes of a new term, the 'immigrant worker'—little used until then. With decolonization, two previously unrelated research trends melted together: immigration studies per se and studies of the colonial world."[18]

Like *Minute*, racism was a central theme of *La Cause du peuple* in 1971, as the editors published articles calling for a "war on racism" in order to "strike back" at racists.[19] Though it is unclear what (if any) role Sartre played in the development of these articles, they nonetheless demonstrate strong affinities with his own position—taking on the issues of racism and immigration—as well as, for him, the centrality of colonialism to understanding those contemporary issues. One of Sartre's first attempts to help publicize the conditions of life and work for non-European immigrants came in 1970 when he spoke at an event celebrating the publication of the *Livre des travailleurs africains en France*.[20] The text of his speech, "The Third World Begins in the *Banlieue*," was published in *Tricontinental* later that year[21] and it marked in a rather prescient way many of the issues that would dominate political discussion concerning relations with non-Western countries and peoples for the coming decade and beyond: the social, economic, and cultural problems of immigration; the contemporary conjuncture of racism with economic and demographic pressures pushing and pulling people across borders; the persistence of colonialism, whether on the level of economics (neocolonialism) or the level of ideas (as a model for social oppression and exclusion); and, finally, the possibility of freedom for the least favored of the world, beaten down in this case by poverty and exploitation, but in other cases, by repressive governments in their home countries.

It seems likely that this text was influenced by the January 1970 deaths of five Malians living in an immigrants' foyer (or "vertical" *bidonville*, as such temporary quarters were sometimes called) in Aubervilliers. As was common practice, they had tried to use gas as a source of heat, and they died by asphyxiation. Sartre was among the intellectuals (including Michel Leiris and Jean Genet) who participated in the demonstrations organized around the immigrants' funerals on January 10, thereby drawing press attention to what was a persistent problem in France's growing *bidonvilles*.[22] In "The Third World Begins in the *Banlieue*," Sartre broadened the discussion beyond the *bidonvilles* themselves, insisting throughout on the necessity of understanding the position of African workers through the lens of colonialism. He argued that, in fact, colonial conditions had been reproduced in the metropole: the Malthusianism of the market (and lack of social protections), the insalubrious and overcrowded housing, the denial of training to improve skills, the systematic insecurity of jobs, the development of racism as a means of control—each of these conditions recreated, in Sartre's view, the colonial situation he had been describing since the mid-1950s, in particular in his classic 1956 essay "Colonialism Is a System."

As Sartre's and others' participation in demonstrations against terrible living conditions in the *bidonvilles* indicates, the "war" against racism directed at non-European immigrants, though actively promoted by *gauchiste* groups such as the *Gauche Proletarienne*, attracted support from many different quarters—even if that support did not run very deep on either the Left or the Right.[23] Sartre and other intellectuals, such as Michel Foucault, Claude Mauriac, Gilles Deleuze, Genet, and Leiris, banded together on numerous occasions in order to bring public attention to police brutality, inhuman living conditions, or racist acts. On the occasion of the shooting death of a young Arab, Mohamed Diab, by a police officer in 1972, Sartre drafted the petition/essay "The New Racism," which was signed by 137 intellectuals.

"The New Racism" incorporated many of the old themes of Sartre's polemics from the French-Algerian War, and, like "The Third World Begins in the *Banlieue*," it set contemporary racism specifically in the context of French colonialism and decolonization. According to Sartre, the "new" racism was a direct consequence of the creation of impoverished "colonies" in the metropole. In this "reverse" colonialism, it was the "colonized" French who held the power and thus set the rules for systematic exploitation and exclusion, and it was they who this time justified their power through the invention of everyday practices and terms of thinking that make the immigrant worker into a subhuman. "Thus was born a new racism," Sartre wrote, "that wanted to make the immigrants live in terror and remove their desire to protest against the conditions of life that were made for them"—echoing arguments he had employed in "Colonialism Is a System" and in more fuller form in the *Critique of Dialectical Reason*, volume 1 (1960). These somewhat sketchy ideas (in an admittedly very brief article) about reverse colonialism were not Sartre's only references in this text, however; he also made use of the memory of the French-Algerian War to argue for his point of view. "We will not accept the rebirth of this ideology of the idiotic that we knew all too well during the French-Algerian War," he wrote. And, "From 1956 to 1962, we struggled so that victory for the Algerians would be lasting. For them, first of all, but also for us: so that the shame of racism would disappear from French thinking."[24]

Sartre's take on the "new" racism fit in unlikely ways with that of his foes at *Minute*, as both of their discursive strategies relied upon understanding current social problems through the lens of colonialism. In their September 1973 nine-page portfolio on the Algerian "invasion," the writers reiterated a host of colonialist tropes to decry the intrusion of "medinas," "casbahs," and "souks" into French cities, all the while strongly denying that they were motivated by racism in any way.[25] For *Minute*, the integration of North Africans was impossible for the simple reason that "they don't want it"—they wanted, instead, to maintain their own culture, by frequenting cinemas in which "only Arabic language films are shown," for example.[26] Apparently another integral part of North African culture being imported to France were the diseases brought about by close and unhygienic living conditions, as well as an anti-Republican political life in which "the FNL [sic] is still the boss."[27]

What is important here is not the quality of the analyses offered on the issue of non-European immigration, but rather the fact that colonialism and decolonization were themselves still powerfully in play as symbolic chips in these political debates. After all, as Noiriel has taken such pains to show in *The French Melting Pot*, contests over immigrants and assimilation were nothing new; what was new in this case was that they took place in the still-vexing shadow of decolonization. Moreover, it was those very decolonized people—and not, for example, Portuguese immigrants, who by the mid-1970s were as numerous as Algerians in France[28]—who bore the brunt of the identitarian discourse taking shape in the postcolonial era. This is perhaps why racism and antiracism played a key discursive role in establishing the stakes of the debate, just as it had for anticolonialists when they were fighting colonialism.

Take, for example, one of the central problems of the late 1960s and beyond: the provision of adequate housing for immigrants in *habitats à loyer modéré* (HLM; subsidized housing) or other dwellings, and the elimination of the *bidonvilles*. While politicians and bureaucrats struggled unsuccessfully with supplying the resources and will necessary to the task of providing adequate housing under these economic conditions, *gauchistes* and *Ordre Nouveau* adherents effectively replayed some of the battles of the French-Algerian War through employing that era's language and tropes. In particular, there was Sartre's reevocation of racism as a set of practices and a way of thinking that establishes the "subhuman" as a category of exclusion and a justification for exploitation.

Thus, when he protested an April 1972 police raid on an overcrowded building in Paris's nineteenth arrondissement during which the tenants were evicted, Sartre emphasized the objectively racist character of the system of laws and the bureaucracy governing the lodging of immigrants.[29] Effectively, uninhabitable conditions were inextricably related to racism, on his view, especially since, as he pointed out on another occasion, there were hundreds of thousands of empty apartments in Paris. *Minute*, on the other hand, dipped into the old repository of colonialist fears of native unhealthiness, dirtiness, laziness, and disease—and the best means of managing or containing them. If North Africans lived in *bidonvilles*, this logic went, it must be because they were comfortable living there, or because this was how their "nature" had fashioned them to live. The solution, then, was not to rearrange their social environment—which could have no effect, and which they did not want in any case—but rather simply to get rid of them: "Scram!"[30]

This resurgence of colonialism, decolonization, and its discursive leitmotifs and arguments in the public domain correspond to what political scientist Catherine Wihtol de Wenden has called the emergence of immigration as a "total social phenomenon" from 1968 to 1972. After having encouraged clandestine immigration in the 1960s, the French government found itself faced with a population that could no longer be considered temporary—and, hence, the recognition that immigration was related to or even causing structural changes in the economy as well as the social fabric. As the political stakes became clearer, and as *gauchistes* tried to organize immigrants, thus aiding the "awakening of a collective consciousness" among them in this period as Wihtol de Wenden describes,[31] parties on both the Left and Right began rethinking and relegislating immigration. While parties on the Right held fast to increasingly restrictive policies based on the assumption that non-European populations were unassimilable, beginning in 1972, the quickly growing *Parti Socialiste* (PS) began to develop a discourse on immigration that proclaimed a "right to difference" and a "new citizenship."[32] The question on the Left over the course of the decade was, on the one hand, whether this declaration of respect for difference would be enfolded into a politics of identity that positively valued the contributions of different cultures to democratic deliberation; or, on the other hand, whether "respect" for difference would ultimately entangle the Left in a perhaps Quixotic quest for a new form of universalism that could somehow be more broadly inclusive than the old universalism of the colonial *mission civilisatrice*.

"Internal" Colonialism: Collective Identity and Regionalist Movements

Debates on racism and immigration were not the only ones in which colonialism and decolonization figured prominently in the early 1970s, and where calls for making concrete space for culturally distinct political claims were advocated as a means of fostering more inclusive and genuinely deliberative democracy. In June 1974, linguist Robert Lafont penned an article for *Le Monde diplomatique*, "Allies in the Cultural Combat against Colonialism," whose subtitle specified a somewhat surprising union: "Worker Immigrants and Regionalist Movements in France." Indeed, for many *gauchistes*—such as *La Cause du peuple* editors Jean-Pierre Le Dantec and Michel Le Bris—activism on behalf of these issues was already well established. Lafont argued for both a practical and a conceptual link between the two. "The analysis," he wrote, "of colonial or semi-colonial situations on the territory of the metropole has been developed. It forms the basis for a new struggle in which the cultural argument plays a determining role."[33]

Lafont was one of the major left-wing French theorists of regionalism. His 1967 book *La Révolution régionaliste* popularized the concept of "internal colonialism" for the broader French public, and his 1971 book *Décoloniser en France: Les régions face à l'Europe* was an explicitly political treatise in which he argued that "regional decolonization is an important form of the global struggle against imperialism."[34] Lafont's work was symbolic of an important political trend: the shift of regionalist movements from their traditional political home on the Right to one on the Left, beginning in the early 1960s.[35] As the publication date of the first book demonstrates, the attraction of regionalist movements predated the events of 1968. Indeed, Lafont cited a rather different motive than young *gauchiste* activism for the resurgence of political contestation over regional cultures and autonomy: the French-Algerian War. Arguing that "the romantic opposition to national evolution" was no longer a viable political option for regionalists, and that they must instead "insert themselves into the center of French life," Lafont made the case that the revelation of *Algérie française* as a fiction forced people to start *"rethinking France."*

Echoing Lafont's writings, the *Gauche Proletarienne* gave regionalism significant coverage in *La Cause du peuple*—not least of all because its editors were involved in regionalist movements, but also because regionalism of Lafont's variety represented antistatist claims for broad access to and exercise of democracy. Both Le Dantec and Le Bris wrote books about regionalist movements, the latter writing a seminal work on the famed Larzac uprising, which spanned the decade and which launched the career of "alter-globalization" activist José Bové.[36] Le Bris's and Le Dantec's works were published in a Gallimard series called *La France Sauvage* (Savage France), which was under Sartre's directorship.[37]

Though Sartre's intervention in debates on regionalist claims for cultural autonomy date to the era of his involvement with the *Gauche Proletarienne*, his interest in them does not appear to be a direct consequence of that involvement. Rather, as his remarks in the preface to a 1971 book edited by Gisèle Halimi, *Le procès de Burgos*, suggest, there were strong conceptual and political continuities—in his mind—between regionalist movements and national liberation movements he had supported so strongly in the past.[38] The occasion for the text was the December 1970 trial in the Spanish town of Burgos of sixteen members of the Basque nationalist movement in

Spain, *Euzkadi Ta Askatasuna* (ETA). The trial was a major international news story, and Halimi, a lawyer who had gained fame for anticolonialist activity during the French-Algerian War, went as an observer. It was in this preface that Sartre first outlined his views on the legitimacy of ethnically based claims for autonomy and even independence in Europe, as well as the structural parallels between European regionalist movements and non-European national independence movements.

Sartre began his essay by arguing that decolonization was one of the primary spurs to nationalist movements within European countries.[39] Like Lafont, Sartre noted the possibility for an awakening of consciousness among young men from Brittany sent to fight in Algeria—against, that is, a movement for national independence—only to see that movement succeed. Sartre then shifted quickly to an explanation of events that relied heavily on his own conceptual vocabulary, and in particular the term that played a key role in his work on Flaubert: the "singular universal." Basque nationalism was, on this argument, a *collective* form of universalizing the singular. Indeed, the whole of the preface was geared toward explaining how a collectivity might be understood as a singular universal:

> I want to attempt here to oppose the abstract universality of bourgeois humanism to the singular universality of the Basque people, to show what circumstances have led it by an ineluctable dialectic to produce a revolutionary movement, and what theoretical consequences one might reasonably pull from the current situation—that is, what profound mutation that decentralization might bring today to a centralizing socialism.[40]

In making his case, Sartre privileged two arguments, both of which demonstrated strong continuities with a number of earlier writings, in particular "Black Orpheus." The first was that the basis for Basque unity and thus the proof of the legitimacy of Basque claims to independence was the historical and linguistic distinctness of the Basque language, Euzkara. The second was that group identity was reinforced through a common struggle against colonialism. The two claims were interrelated, both for Sartre and for ETA, since they took the suppression of the Basque language as the primary mode of Spanish domination and as a sign of its intent to commit "cultural genocide." Hence, and strongly echoing "Black Orpheus," Sartre held that "to speak his own language is, for a colonized person, already a revolutionary act."[41]

Sartre folded this focus on language as the carrier of the "Basque personality" into his discussion of the singular universal. Though his evocation of a "Basque personality" came perilously close to suggesting the existence of timeless group characteristics, Sartre instead wrote of the practice of being Basque, of "making oneself Basque" through the everyday act of speaking

Euzkara. Being Basque and speaking the Basque language coincided "not only because he [the speaker] recoups a past that belongs only to him, but especially because he addresses himself, even when alone, to a community of those who speak Basque."[42] It was through this practice of speaking—and speaking to one another—that Basque people might come to discern what made their culture "singular," and thus combat the homogenizing and falsely universalizing force of Spanish centralization which, especially under Franco, had targeted Euzkara for extinction. Sartre did not say why he privileged linguistic practice over other practices in the Basque struggle—it could have been because the fight to speak the Basque language was already given to Sartre as the central problem. Nonetheless, it was the specificity of the language that, for him, marked the possibility for Basque people to access their history and culture as something "concrete," thus taking a step on the road toward discovering, "not man in general, but man as Basque."[43] Once this step was taken, the nonalienated political claims of free, individual Basques might come also to express universal aims. That is, it was only through passage of the concrete singularity of one's own culture that one could hope to fully recognize not only one's own freedom but also that of other peoples.

Although Sartre's argument concerning language reaffirmed some of the key ideas of "Black Orpheus," his claims about collective identity appear to have directly contradicted a text also from that earlier period, *Antisemite and Jew*. Whereas in that essay Sartre had bracketed (or, some would argue, emptied) the contents of Jewishness for Jews themselves by averring that it is the antisemite who creates the Jew, here Sartre invoked a minority population's singular "character" and "reality"—and not others' perceptions of it—as the foundation for identity. He even made an appeal to stable somatic markers over time as a structuring force. Indeed, there are—paradoxically—commonalities not only between the Basque of Sartre's *Burgos* essay and the Jew of *Antisemite and Jew* as oppressed minorities, but also between the Basque and the antisemite: each shares an attachment to her native soil, for example, and prioritizes the given values of community over the self-created values of the individual. In many ways, then, there was something rather arbitrary about the line that Sartre and others (Le Dantec and Le Bris, specifically) wished to draw between the reactionary and the revolutionary when it came to regionalist movements. As Pierre Bourdieu would point out just a few years later, as struggles for recognition, regionalist movements should be classed as attempts to impose a legitimate scheme of "vision and di-vision" on the social world, and as attempts to define the "law" governing that scheme in order to justify the domination of one group by another.[44] A regionalist movement's attempt to gain recognition as a distinct nationality may be as much a mode of domination as a centralizing state's denial of such nationality is. This means that in terms of the desired goal—unification and autonomy/independence—there could be no easy distinction between, say, Breton regionalism and German nationalism.

Such a homology between "revolutionary" regionalism and "reactionary" nationalism cannot have been lost on Sartre and others, and one might surmise that the key to maintaining this tenuous distinction lay in situating a particular struggle in a colonialist paradigm. Reading the Burgos preface in the context of Sartre's 1964 "Rome Lecture" on ethics, which discussed at length the normative reasoning behind revolutionary action, one could plausibly argue that if the imposition of a particular set of social boundaries was unjust—if it was a "colonial" order with all of its attendant economic and social violence—one could find therein a clear cut case of a "least favored" people that would then require intellectuals' support. Moreover, in the *gauchiste* account of anticolonial struggles, the least favored held a privileged position as the suppliers of democratic innovation.

The key here is that nationalist projects that do not seek to dominate other nationalities—that seek democratic decentralization rather than undemocratic centralization—are the ones that may be legitimately supported. An anticolonialist or regionalist movement that tries to impose its own order as a matter of domination could not be considered a liberation movement. Thus, the most important, and classically Sartrean argument made in favor of regionalist movements was that their left-wing emanations claimed to represent the expansion of human freedom. In this case, Sartre's decision to use the Basque nationalist movement as his public entry into debates on regionalism was well taken since, at the time, the Basques were fighting against a reactionary dictatorship. But freedom figured as an important normative aim of political action for the *gauchistes* as well. In *Les fous du Larzac,* Le Bris stressed freedom as a goal. He argued, in a strongly Sartrean vein, that the famed mid-1970s movement of a group of the 103 farmers who defied the French government's attempt to expand a military base onto their land was guided necessarily by freedom—by the freedom of each of its members and by the recognition of freedom in others. This stress on freedom formed the cornerstone of Le Bris's concluding remarks in the book "A New Discourse on 'Revolt-Freedom,' " in which he argued that the 103 had discovered and put into action *gauchiste* aims better than the *gauchistes* themselves.[45]

Le Bris's latter point is an important one—for regionalism, *gauchisme*, and the colonial paradigm. The Larzac revolt, along with the 1973 workers' takeover and self-management (or *autogestion*) of the Lip watch factory, were the signal events marking the fact that, for Le Bris, "Marxism is at an end, and organized *gauchisme* is moribund."[46] This conclusion that *gauchiste* groups such as the *Gauche Prolétarienne* were not, in fact, driving the most innovative and significant popular movements of the early to mid-1970s forced a coming to terms with all of the old assumptions, chief among them the utility of the radical critique of colonialism for left-wing politics. Le Dantec, in his 1974 book *Bretagne: Re-naissance d'un people*, cautioned those on the Left that uncritical overuse may easily lead to misuse. Brittany, after all, was *not* Algeria. *Gauchistes*—and he criticized them explicitly in the book—should not "imagine themselves in Algeria, Vietnam, or Martinique and reinsert themselves into a model so classical as the struggle for national independence. These 'solutions' have the merit of facility; unfortunately, they do not respond in the least to the questions of a real movement."[47]

The New/Old Universalism of the Left

The cautionary note Le Dantec sounded concerning intellectuals' application of the radical critique of colonialism to situations not classically colonial was, moreover, general. By the mid-1970s, left-wing French intellectuals began a sweeping reconsideration of the meaning of colonialism and the process of decolonization—along with France's rightful role in them. Radical *gauchiste* movements were confronted with the lack of success of their own tactics for fomenting revolution and seizing state power through extraelectoral and extralegal means. At the same time, the arrival on the political scene of a consolidated and fortified Socialist Party (PS) in 1972 suddenly offered a new political option for *gauchistes* and others on the noncommunist Left who had lost enthusiasm for—and were often openly hostile to—the Communist Party. The PS quickly made the issues of the immigrant worker and the decentralization of power to regions part of their political platform, coopting two of the *gauchistes*' most significant issues.[48] This support for decentralization had immediate effects, helping the PS to extend its support in Brittany in the 1973 elections.[49] As for Larzac, it was only in 1981, with the accession to power of Socialist president François Mitterrand, that plans for the Larzac military base's expansion were canceled—in fulfillment of one of his campaign promises.[50] But this cooptation also entailed a substantial modification in the contents of political claims about identity—in effect, a shift away from a defense of cultural particularity and toward a "universal" conception of French identity that could encompass all citizens.

This shift was closely related to the late-1970s critique of Third Worldism on humanitarian grounds, which was spearheaded by Socialist intellectuals. The mistrust of the state as necessarily repressive—a suspicion that grew out of left-wing analyses of the Soviet Union under Stalin, of which Sartre's *Critique of Dialectical Reason* was among the earliest and best known in France—blossomed during the 1970s into broad support on the Left to reconcile socialism with the basic liberties guaranteed in Western democracies.

"Totalitarianism" of both the conservative authoritarian and Marxist guises was under the gun. This led to a taking stock of formerly held positions in favor of movements at one time or another deemed "progressive"—in Algeria, Cuba, Zaïre, Vietnam, and, later, Cambodia—whose outcome had been states that denied such basic freedoms. On this interpretation, the radical critique of colonialism, which had centered on a denunciation of the false premises of the *mission civilisatrice*, had acted as a cover and as a legitimating rhetoric for regimes and political movements that simply were not liberationist. Therefore, the critique itself needed to be reevaluated—and perhaps abandoned.[51]

This new debate covered some very old issues, and it marked the return of the Left to its earlier universalist position of the days of the colonial *mission civilisatrice*—albeit in a far less aggressive form than it took in the nineteenth and early twentieth centuries. Though everyone agreed emphatically that colonialism was an evil that was right to challenge, there was now marked disagreement concerning whether granting independence was the best way to end that evil. Taking the place of colonial regimes, many argued, now were simply "barbaric" regimes. On this standard, the acceptability of any particular system of governance became the guaranteeing of human rights, which became the mark of "civilization." Arguments for collective or "cultural" rights—so instrumental to the era of decolonization, and subsequently to the defenses of the worker immigrant and regionalism in France—were swept into the background as a result.

Oddly, this reevaluation of the radical critique of colonialism connected with the views expressed in the pages of *Minute* on the "barbarity" of non-European cultures in general. Indeed, one effect was to leave Socialists in a profound bind vis-à-vis those in France who were excluded from the dominant culture, and thus found it difficult to fully participate in political, social, and economic life: non-European immigrants and regional minorities. By gaining authority among members of the PS, human rights discourse would discourage thinking about the structural conditions of race or culture-based oppression on the grounds that remedies for such oppression would be available simply through guaranteeing individual rights. That is, as long as there were formal political assurances that everyone could become "French"—assurances that everyone could participate in the dominant culture—the problems associated with integration of minorities would disappear. While this belief may have held true for some immigrants and regional minorities, it has not proven true for everyone, particularly for a large portion of France's citizens of North African and West African descent.

Another effect of this reevaluation of the radical critique of colonialism was, I have suggested in my opening anecdote, on the level of a summary judgment of Sartre and others who still held fast to its now-suspect mode of analysis. Liberation and the self-determination of peoples could not be expected to go hand in hand. It is perhaps for this reason that Sartre's attempt to apply his concept of the "singular universal"—which was invented to describe how an individual could be an incarnation of the world—to collectivities such as the Basques raised more questions than it answered. As we have seen, his arguments in the preface to the *Procès de Burgos* were unclear: did Basques together represent a collective "person," which could be described as a singular universal, or was each individual Basque, as Basque, a singular universal whose universality was expressed in his free choice and exercise of the practices of his culture, such as speaking his own language? Indeed, were the rights of peoples and the rights of man incompatible? Back in 1953, Sartre did not think so; he argued for the recognition of both. In his interview from that year to *La République Algérienne*, he declared, "Neither the 'right of peoples to decide their own fate' nor the 'rights of man' formulated in 1789 have been recognized for the colonized by the colonizers. Nowhere is the exploitation of man by man more apparent; the colonizers can only justify themselves—even in their own eyes—by a racism that will finish by infecting the 'metropole' itself."[52]

By the mid-1970s, as Sartre's interventions in favor of immigrants and regional movements indicate, he had not moved appreciably away from this position. The French political context in which he took this position had, however, changed markedly. Against Sartre's argument that living fully one's own cultural identity was a basic freedom that ought to be defended, culture-based arguments for rights were increasingly treated as incompatible with the universalist-based arguments once more in vogue on the Left. Moreover, Sartre's insistence that "race" and other forms of identity be taken seriously as factors in systemic oppression that could not easily be solved through political means—a key claim of the radical critique of colonialism—was rejected in favor of appeals to a "new citizenship" based on human rights. Sartre's adaptation of the radical critique of colonialism to new social struggles in the early 1970s may not have always been convincing or unproblematic, yet it demonstrated a concern with the limits of the purely formal or human rights approach that the Socialists would once again champion.

The legacy of this shift is now only too apparent. Reconciling minority cultures remains one of the French republic's great challenges, and racism one of its growing threats. With recognition of the policies of integration and assimilation as failures, Sartre's engagements with antiracist activism and regionalist movements in the early 1970s may offer some interesting insights for thinking through new relationships between identity and democracy in the age of globalization.

Notes

1. N.a., "Poursuivi par huit journalistes de *Minute*, M. Jean-Paul Sartre est condamné à 400 francs d'amende," *Le Monde*, November 8, 1973. See also Simone de Beauvoir's account in *Adieux: A Farewell to Sartre*, trans. Patrick O'Brian (New York: Pantheon, 1984), 56–58. *Minute* was among the most important organs of the extreme right, as it was under the direction of the founding members of the *Front National*. Its tabloid style attracted a broader reader base than the other well-known right-wing publication *Rivarol*.
2. Francis Cornu, "*Minute* poursuit M. Jean-Paul Sartre en correctionelle: L'accusateur accusé," *Le Monde*, October 10, 1973.
3. N.a., "Poursuivi par huit journalistes de *Minute*."
4. N.a., "Sartre malade? Ce serait la raison de son étrange silence," *Minute* 598, September 26–October 2, 1973, 3.
5. N.a., "En prison Sartre!" *Minute* 479, June 16–22, 1971, 1, 6–9.
6. In fact, Sartre was charged shortly after the appearance of *Minute*'s accusations, which led Contat and Rybalka to imply a link between the two events. Substantiating such a link is, however, very difficult. See Michael Contat and Michel Rybalka, eds., *The Writings of Jean-Paul Sartre*, vol. 1, *A Bibliographical Life*, trans. Richard C. McCleary (Evanstan, Ill.: Northwestern University Press, 1974), 579.
7. Cornu, "L'accusateur accusé."
8. Michel Wieviorka et al., *La France raciste* (Paris: Editions du Seuil, 1992), 25.
9. Catherine Lloyd, *Discourses of Antiracism in France* (Aldershot, UK: Ashgate, 1998), 169–70.
10. Jean-Paul Sartre, "Le Nouveau racisme," *Le Nouvel Observateur*, December 18–22, 1972.
11. For a classic historiographical work using the model of internal colonialism, see Michael Hechter, *Internal Colonialism: The Celtic Fringe in British National Development* (Berkeley: University of California Press, 1975), esp. chap. 2.
12. The number of Algerians in France doubled between 1958 and 1968; by 1972, Algerians had overtaken the Portuguese, Spanish, and Italians as the largest immigrant population, at 20 percent of all immigrants. Vincent Viet, *La France immigré: Construction d'une politique, 1914–1997* (Paris: Fayard, 1998), 262, 265.
13. "Algérie ça suffit! Ils nous chassent ... chassons les!" *Minute* 470, April 14–20, 1971, 1 (cover line); see in the same issue, François Brigneau, "Algérie ça suffit!" 11.
14. J.-P. Mefret, "Les Algériens chez nous," *Minute* 458, January 21–27, 1971, 12–13.
15. Alain Gillette and Abdelmalek Sayad, *L'immigration algérienne en France* (Paris: Editions Entente, 1976), 97.
16. See the edition, *Minute* 595, September 5–11, 1973, in which the cover lines read, "Arretez l'invasion algérienne, maintenant la cote d'alerte est dépassée" and "Ceux qui vont nous amener la guerre raciale."
17. See "L'autre guerre qui commence: Le chantage arabe au pétrole," *Minute* 602, October 24–30, 1973, 1; and "La riposte aux arabes: Oui, elle est possible! Ils veulent nous mettre à genoux avec le pétrole," *Minute* 608, December 5–11, 1973, 1.
18. Gérard Noiriel, *The French Melting Pot: Immigration, Citizenship, and National Identity*, trans. Geoffroy de Laforcade (Minneapolis: University of Minnesota Press, 1996), 24.

19. See, among many others, n.a., "La guerre au racisme," *La Cause du peuple* 6, June 28, 1971, 16; and n.a., "Frapper le criminel raciste," *La Cause du peuple* 9, September 23, 1971, 14.
20. Union générale des travailleurs sénégalais en France, *Livre des travailleurs africains en France* (Paris: Maspero, 1970).
21. Reprinted as Jean-Paul Sartre, "Le Tiers Monde commence en banlieue," *Situations VIII* (Paris: Gallimard, 1972).
22. Roland Castro, Leiris, and Genet were all arrested when they occupied the offices of the French employers' organization as part of their protest. Castro was later prosecuted, and both Sartre and Genet testified at his trial. See "De la mort de cinq Maliens à l'occupation du CNPF: Une peine de prison ferme est requise contre un architecte inculpé de violences et rébellion," *Le Monde*, February 25, 1970; see also Beauvoir, *Adieux*, 4, 26.
23. Indeed, in their published conversations, Sartre, Pierre Victor (Benny Lévy), and Philippe Gavi talked of the difficulties of combating racism among French workers. Gavi pressed Victor on what role marginal politics (homosexual rights, immigrant rights, feminism) played in the Maoist conception of revolution, asking, "What kind of society do you want? A society in which those who control production continue to think 'filthy nigger' or 'fairy' does not interest me. I am not fighting for that." Philippe Gavi, Jean-Paul Sartre, Pierre Victor, *On a raison de se révolter* (Paris: Gallimard, 1974), 111.
24. Sartre, "Le Nouveau Racisme."
25. Their defense was mounted in the editorial "A ceux qui parlent de racisme," *Minute* 595, September 5–11, 1973, 2.
26. N.a., "Ce qui, un jour, amènera l'explosion: Ces casbahs au coeur de nos villes," *Minute* 595, September 5–11, 1973, 6–7.
27. See n.a., "On ne peut plus supporter cette invasion," 3–5; J.-P. M." 'Carta Toubib Choléra,' " 5; and n.a., "Dans le medina de la Goutte d'Or, le FNL [sic] est encore le patron," 6; in *Minute* 595, September 5–11, 1973.
28. See Maxim Silverman, *Deconstructing the Nation: Immigration, Racism and Citizenship in Modern France* (London: Routledge, 1992), 52.
29. See Mauriac, *Et comme l'espérance est violente*, 362; Contat and Rybalka, *The Writings of Jean-Paul Sartre*, vol. 1, 590; and Beauvoir, *Adieux*, 30.
30. "La France sans algériens: Chiche! En attendant, ils continuent à arriver à pleins bateaux" [cover line], *Minute* 598, September 26–October 2, 1973, 1.
31. Catherine Wihtol de Wenden, *Les immigrés et la politique* (Paris: Presses de la fondation nationale des sciences politiques, 1988), 147.
32. D. S. Bell and Byron Criddle, *The French Socialist Party: The Emergence of a Party of Government*, second ed. (Oxford: Clarendon, 1988), 172.
33. Robert Lafont, "Alliés dans un combat culturel contre le colonialisme intérieur," *Le Monde diplomatique* (June 1975).
34. Robert Lafont, *Décoloniser en France: Les régions face à l'Europe* (Paris: Gallimard, 1971), 287.
35. For a brief history of this shift, see Maryon McDonald, *"We Are Not French!": Language, Culture, and Identity in Brittany* (London: Routledge, 1989), esp. chap. 5.
36. See Herman Lebovics, *Bringing the Empire Back Home: France in the Age of Globalism* (Durham, N.C.: Duke University Press, 2004).
37. The idea for the series was Le Bris and Le Dantec's. See Beauvoir, *Adieux*, 67–68, 96.
38. Jean-Paul Sartre, "Préface," in Gisèle Halimi, *Le procès de Burgos* (Paris: Gallimard, 1971), vii–xxx. Sartre's preface was also excerpted in *Le Nouvel Observateur*, May 24–30, 1971.

39. Marianne Heiberg confirms that Sartre's interpretation as applied to ETA was well founded. Although only a handful of ETA's leaders were Marxist, she writes that "one factor above all the others was instrumental in pushing ETA to the extreme Left—the model of the revolutionary struggle of national liberation as exemplified by Cuba, Algeria and Vietnam." Marianne Heiberg, *The Making of the Basque Nation* (Cambridge: Cambridge University Press, 1989), 111.
40. Sartre, "Préface," in Halimi, *Le procès de Burgos*, xi.
41. Ibid., xix.
42. Ibid.
43. Ibid., xx.
44. Pierre Bourdieu, "Identity and Representation: Elements for a Critical Reflection on the Idea of Region," in *Language and Symbolic Power*, trans. Matthew Adamson (Cambridge: Polity, 1991). Bourdieu's goal was to caution sociologists against taking too seriously the representations made by regionalist movements themselves.
45. See Michel Le Bris, *Les fous du Larzac* (Paris: Les Presses d'aujourd'hui, 1975).
46. Ibid., 359.
47. Jean-Pierre Le Dantec, *Bretagne: Re-naissance d'un peuple* (Paris: Gallimard, 1974), 294.
48. See the party platform written by PS secretary Pierre Joxe: "The Socialist Party proposes to effect a profound decentralization at the level of communes, departments, and regions," and "Decent living conditions will be assured for immigrant workers; parity in wages and rights between foreign workers and French workers will be established" as part of a "struggle against all forms of discrimination." Pierre Joxe, *Parti Socialiste* (Paris: Epi Editeurs, 1973), 79, 85.
49. Yves Rocaute, *Le Parti Socialiste* (Paris: Editions Bruno Huisman, 1983), 88.
50. Mitterrand had a troubled history with the Larzac movement—he was roughed up by *gauchiste* activists when he showed up in 1974 to lend support to the cause. See Brown, *Socialism of a Different Kind*, 114.
51. For more on this point, see Susan Paige Arthur, "Decolonization on Trial, 1970–1980," in *Unfinished Projects: Decolonization and the Philosophy of Jean-Paul Sartre* (PhD dissertation, University of California, Berkeley, 2004).
52. Interview with Jean-Paul Sartre, "Jean-Paul Sartre: 'Le problème colonial et celui de la démocratie sociale en France sont indissolublement liées,'" *La République algérienne*, January 16, 1953, 1.

Part II

Sartre and Antiracist Theory

Chapter 4

Race

From Philosophy to History

Christian Delacampagne

"Race after Sartre": The subject matter of the present book illustrates, interestingly, cultural differences underlying the way we write the genealogy of concepts in France and the United States, and, more generally, the way we write or read texts, whatever texts they are. As I have spent part of my academic life traveling between France (where I studied philosophy during the 1970s and later taught in various institutions) and the United States (where I used to teach between 1998 and 2006, mostly at Johns Hopkins University), I would like, at the beginning of this chapter, to expand a little more on this particular, often misunderstood, and wrongly underestimated *gap* between our two cultures.

For the majority of American people, "race" refers to a familiar sociological reality: American citizens come or their ancestors came (out of their free will or not, that is another issue) from all over the world. This is why they actually may be white, or Hispanic, or Native American, or African American, or Asian American, or whatever categories the latest United States census designates. And such diversity, far from being an unpleasant surprise, is generally accepted by all—everybody being perfectly aware of how old and complicated the history of immigration in the United States has been. Accordingly, the word "race" may be freely used as a kind of "administrative" category (including on many U.S. official documents) without any feeling of insult, shame, or guilt.

On the other hand, for French people or, to be more precise, for educated French people, nature may allow the existence of races among dogs, cats, or cows, but the concept of a racial group within the "human race" is nothing but a pure fantasy since all human beings proceed from the same genetic stock and share the same genes. Of course, men and women may occasionally differ by the color of their skin; but this difference in color does not correspond to a difference in "race" since it does not entail, by itself, any hereditary mental or psychological difference. In addition to this purely scientific consideration, using the word "race" in colloquial French may sound shocking or, at least, inappropriate, because this word sadly reminds every educated French citizen of the racial policies that were advocated by Fascist groups in France and the rest of Europe during the 1930s, and actively put into practice by the Vichy government in German-occupied France between 1940 and 1944. Taken together, those two reasons explain why, in practice, the word "race," in the sense of subgroups within the "human race," amounts to a forbidden word in contemporary France.

Let me illustrate that point by a quick example: An African American student who wanted to complain about discrimination on his/her U.S. campus would probably say: "I am discriminated against because of my race," while a black French student, if he/she was in the same unpleasant situation on a French campus, would normally say: "I am discriminated against because of the color of my skin." Some readers may say that this is not a big deal, indeed! And, nevertheless, the gap such a small difference makes *on a scholarly level* can be spectacular.

Within the American higher education system, for instance, the concept of "race studies" has referred, for decades now, to a well-defined field of investigation, whose academic legitimacy no longer needs to be demonstrated: the study of interactions between social groups that, for historical reasons, wrongly view each other as biological groups (i.e., as "races"). For French scholars, on the other hand, there are no racial groups since racial groups are only social ones. For that reason, the study of racism (i.e., of the hatred that certain social groups can feel for other social groups, not because of what the latter *do* but because of who they *are*, either by birth or by collective choice) enjoys a different status. It still constitutes a field of investigation, of course. But this field has no specific autonomy. It simply finds its place within historical studies in the broad sense of the term, and more specifically within cultural history, or within that subdiscipline that was first called, by Philippe Ariès and other French historians in the 1960s, "histoire des mentalités" (history of mentalities, i.e., systems of thought).

And that is not all. While the question of knowing how the concept of "race" has evolved (since Jean-Paul Sartre, or since the 1900s, or since 1850) is both understandable and legitimate for an American researcher, it can only appear incongruous to a French scholar. Indeed, for this latter scholar, the concept of "race" *cannot* have evolved, since it has definitively been disqualified as an objective notion some sixty years ago, something that happened largely under the influence of philosophers like Sartre himself! This is why the present book, if it happens to be translated into French, will have to bear a new, different title: "La Race après Sartre" would not be, for a French audience, an understandable phrase.

By chance, if we know the existence of such risks of misunderstanding between our two cultures, we can find a way of giving, in French, a rational meaning to the issue of "race after Sartre." It would then consist (and this is what I will undertake in this chapter) in studying *how our representations of race have evolved*—in other words, in asking *to what extent our approach to racism and antisemitism has changed* since Sartre published his landmark book *Réflexions sur la question juive* (*Antisemite and Jew*) in 1946.

Let me recall, to start with, that Sartre was not the first philosopher who attempted to reflect on *racism* in general. The absurdity and the dangers of racism have been condemned—at the same time as the superiority of tolerance has been praised—by many European intellectuals over the past five hundred years. This started, in fact, with Bartolomé de Las Casas and Michel de Montaigne, two sixteenth-century authors who wrote in defense of Native American populations in the aftermath of the discovery of the New World.

And Sartre was not even the first one who attempted to reflect on this particular form of racism we have come to call *antisemitism*. Without forgetting that Karl Jaspers's masterpiece on *The Question of German Guilt* came out the same year as Sartre's work, it is clear that the first members of the Frankfurt School, who were forced into exile because of the nomination of Adolf Hitler as Chancellor of the Reich (1933), had many occasions to ponder the nature of antisemitism. In fact, Max Horkheimer and Theodor W. Adorno dealt with this immense and tragic issue in the last part of their major opus *Dialectic of Enlightenment*, which was published in 1947 although the manuscript was completed as early as 1944.

Yet Sartre (and this is why he remains so important for me and, I hope, for my readers) was the first one who initiated a systematic and rational approach to the irrational conception of a "Jewish race." Furthermore, he was the first one to offer, with so much force and clarity, a complex series of theoretical statements on antisemitism that not only had deep, widespread influence both in Europe and the United States, but that still remain—as we shall see—valid today. As for me, every time I am interrogated about those statements, I answer that the most important ones amount to *four*, that may be summed up in the following way:

(1) "Race" (reference to human sub-groups) is a social *construct*, not a biological *datum*.
(2) Although "race" has no denotation in the real world, this fact does not prevent racism from being a form of hatred that is felt and expressed by real social groups. In fact, racism starts as soon as somebody starts *believing* in the objective reality of "human races" (while antisemitism, accordingly, begins whenever somebody starts *believing* into the reality of a "Jewish race").

(3) This is why *racism* (or *antisemitism*) *is not an opinion among others*. In fact, it is not an opinion at all. It is a global attitude possessing its own internal coherence, a way of perceiving the world as such, an "ideology" in the Marxist sense of the word, a secular religion that is based exclusively on forgeries, lies, and errors. For that reason, it is not amenable to rational disputation—which entails, if we really want to make it disappear, psychoanalysis, education, and preventive action on a social level that will have to be complemented by faster and more effective means, such as legal repression.
(4) Finally, the fight against racism must be a challenge for any civic community as a whole, and not only for the unfortunate victims of racial hatred.

Although most reasonable people agree, today, with such assumptions (with a significant exception regarding the third thesis, which is still rejected by most in the United States who think that freedom of speech should not be restricted), we simultaneously have to acknowledge that there were also some blinders in Sartre's analysis. No surprise: Those blinders were connected to ways of thinking that were shared by lots of people in his generation—a generation that grew up in the atmosphere saturated with racism which bathed the whole of European culture in the 1920s and the 1930s. And we also have to recognize that there were some serious limitations (not to say deficiencies) in his knowledge of the history of racism, Judaism, and antisemitism.

In order to understand what I mean by "ways of thinking that were shared by lots of people in his generation," it will be sufficient to go back to the first pages of *Réflexions sur la question juive*. The word "race," for instance, appears for the first time on page 24 (in the French version): "Here is a fishmonger who, in 1942, annoyed by the competition between two Jewish fishmongers who were hiding their race, one day took a pen in order to denounce them."[1] Nobody, nowadays, would dare write such a sentence. One would resort to a periphrasis ("hiding the fact that they were Jewish") or a more appropriate formula ("were hiding their Jewishness"). But one would certainly not write a sentence insinuating the existence of a "Jewish race" so naturally and objectively that one might be tempted to want to "hide" it.

The oddest thing is, as everyone knows, that Sartre devoted most of his book to demonstrating that a Jewish race simply did not exist. Then, why did he use here the word "race"? Probably because of sloppiness, and because everyone around him, in 1946, used it in the same way. The developments that made the expression "Jewish race" disappear had not yet occurred. One can and should deplore this. But one would be mistaken to blame it on Sartre, as if he were the only one or the last one to express it in such a controversial way. After all, the leftist daily newspaper *El País* and most Spanish media still called Albert Cohen "un escritor de raza ebrea" ("a writer of Hebraic race") during the 1990s; and this expression, as well as the expressions "raza negra" (referring to blacks) and "raza gitana" (referring to the Gypsies) are still commonly heard in colloquial Spanish.

There are however, in Sartre's book, more disturbing passages than the one I just quoted. Let's go back a few pages and let's reread the third paragraph of the text. "The Jew that the antisemite wants to reach," Sartre writes, "is not a schematic being, defined only through his position as in administrative law; through his position or through his actions as within the Code. He's a Jew, a son of Jews, recognizable through his physical features, his hair color, his clothes and perhaps, as they say, his character."[2] This passage read in its context is honorable: the following sentence, destined to conclude an analysis according to which it is unacceptable to try to deny any social group its rights, is a courageous statement according to which "antisemitism does not enter into the category of thoughts protected by the right of freedom of opinion." However, Sartre does not hesitate to write that a Jew can be recognized thanks to his physical features, his hair color, or his clothes, which reveals in itself a regrettable lack of intellectual rigor. And, as if this were not enough, he adds: "and, as they say, to his character."

This "as they say" is a terrifying slip of the tongue. It means that Sartre, since he quoted this cliché without condemning it, did not totally reject the hypothesis according to which a Jewish "character"—that is to say, some kind of Jewish race—might indeed exist. How come Sartre did not realize that? Partly because he always wrote too quickly, never taking enough time to give his own manuscripts enough critical attention. But also because, once again, he did not manage to clearly break with some of the social prejudices that were still dominant within educated circles in France in the immediate aftermath of World War II (some prejudices which I remember fairly well, since I was a child at the time).

Added to these weaknesses in the Sartrean analysis (there are others of the same type, which fortunately are not very numerous, in the next pages),[3] was another type of shortcoming that should be linked, this time, to the insufficient knowledge that Sartre had of the history of racism, Judaism, and antisemitism.

His lack of knowledge about Judaism, for instance, has been often and justifiably denounced. Sartre himself later recognized that, in order to speak about the Jews in 1946, he had simply evoked the image he had of his old friend and comrade Raymond Aron, an eminent representative of what was called in France "assimilated Judaism." It is clear that before writing a book about Judaism and antisemitism, he should have gone to the trouble of getting informed in a much more serious and scientific manner.

Without wanting to exonerate him, I would like to recall nevertheless that Sartre never wanted to be a university researcher (he did not even accept the position at the prestigious Collège de France that was offered to him by the Collège itself). He did not want to be bound by the rules of his profession to minute verifications. He viewed himself as an independent writer, who was freely elaborating philosophical essays that were intended to reach and move a wide audience. I would also like to recall that, before the massive return in France of French Jews from North Africa (which essentially took place between 1956 and 1962, at the time Morocco, Algeria, and Tunisia became independent states), assimilated Judaism constituted the only ideological trend existing within the French Jewish community, a fact which contributes to explain that the available studies about Jewish culture were not very numerous yet. Lastly, as far as the history of antisemitism was concerned, the shortcomings in the 1946 book were to a large extent due to the fact that no Western scholar had started, before that date, to seriously write this complex history.

There were a few authors who had, indeed, begun writing the history of antisemitism before 1946 (in fact, they were three)—but they had done so primarily out of a spirit of philosophical propaganda or religious anxiety, rather than out of a strictly scientific interest. Let us start with *L'Antisémitisme, son histoire et ses causes* (Paris, 1894), a book by the Dreyfusard polemist Bernard Lazare, an assimilated French Jew who wanted to demonstrate that the very nature of the Jewish religion was the single and direct cause of all the forms of hostility against the Jews through the centuries. The brutal partiality of such a statement is so shocking that it makes it impossible to discuss it as a serious historical enterprise. For similar motives, the same thing might be said of Anatole Leroy-Beaulieu's book on *Israël chez les nations* (Paris, 1893). As for the third one, James Parkes's book on *The Conflict of the Church and the Synagogue: A Study in the Origins of Antisemitism* (London: 1934), it is slightly more stimulating than the previous two, but it is definitely not a great work of history.

For many reasons, therefore, most of them being largely obvious, the first rigorous investigations into the social and cultural origins of antisemitism did not start until the aftermath of World War II, when French historian Jules Isaac (himself an assimilated Jew) published successively *Jésus et Israël* (Paris: Fasquelle, 1946), *Genèse de l'antisémitisme: essai historique* (Paris: Calmann-Lévy, 1956), *L'Antisémitisme a-t-il des racines chrétiennes ?* (Paris: Fasquelle, 1960), and *L'Enseignement du mépris: vérité historique et mythes théologiques* (Paris: Fasquelle, 1962). Almost simultaneously, Fadiey Lovsky's *Antisémitisme et mystère d'Israël* came out in 1955, and Marcel Simon's *Verus Israël: étude sur les relations entre chrétiens et juifs dans l'Empire romain (135–425)* in 1964.[4]

These three authors (and especially Simon) made major contributions to the issue of the historical origins of the hatred against the Jews. They were the first ones who asked with clarity the appropriate question: *To what extent did nineteenth- and twentieth-century racial (i.e., pseudo-biological) antisemitism take its roots from the Catholic Church's anti-Judaism*, especially in the polemical anti-Jewish writings of the Fathers of the Church and the Christian theologians of the first centuries CE? Yet, they did not have enough historical knowledge to answer that big question and were unable to put some twenty centuries of European antisemitism into a *global* perspective. In addition to that, the historical knowledge they had was almost always *second-hand* knowledge: none of them (except Simon, whose book did not come out before 1964) had really worked on original archives or unpublished documents.

In fact, the first two writers who really attempted to write a *global* history of antisemitism, and who did so by conducting *first-hand* research, did it shortly after—and not before—the almost simultaneous publication, in 1946, of *Jésus et Israël* and *Réflexions sur la question juive*. They were Hannah Arendt, in the first part of her *Origins of Totalitarianism* (1951), and Léon Poliakov, in the five volumes of his huge *Histoire de l'antisémitisme*, of which the first came out in 1955 and the last in 1994.⁵ Both of them had read Sartre's *Réflexions* as soon as it had come out (we should remember that Arendt greatly helped introduce French Existentialism into the United States)—and, for them, the concepts of a "Jewish race," as well as of "human races" in general, were evidently stripped of any objective reality. At the same time, they were serious scholars who wanted to be read by other scholars: this is why their work no longer presented the same lapses as Sartre's had.

Arendt, a great political philosopher but not a professional historian, made remarkable efforts in order to address, in the first part of her inquiry into totalitarianism ("Part One: Antisemitism"), vast historical material. Nevertheless, her undertaking was severely marred by the fact that she decided (as many assimilated German Jews would have done at the time) *to disconnect nineteenth-century racial antisemitism from Christian medieval anti-Judaism*. Instead of following the path that had been opened by Jules Isaac's 1946 book, she chose a paradoxical line of demonstration: She argued that antisemitism had been born in Germany at the beginning of the nineteenth century, as a kind of mostly political, "nationalist" reaction against the progressive integration of the Jewish elite into German society. In other words, she wrote as if the horrific consequences of anti-Judaism (discrimination, expulsions, pogroms, etc.) that had happened to the European Jews before 1800 were totally separable from antisemitism—or as if the concept of "race" was inseparable from a pseudo-biological elaboration that was unthinkable before the birth of natural sciences, that is, before the Enlightenment. Today, such a disconnection would be untenable. Although some authors, and not only Catholic ones, still deny the very possibility of a Christian antisemitism in prescientific ages, it is becoming more and more evident that medieval anti-Judaism, far from being purely "theological" as it has long been assumed, already included a well-developed antisemitic dimension.[6]

As for the French historian of Russian origin, Léon Poliakov (1910–1997), by training he was no more a professional historian than Arendt. Educated as a jurist and, by virtue of his personal contacts made head of research at the newly organized Centre de documentation juive contemporaine just after the war, he got the opportunity to attend the Nuremberg trials, which gave him the idea to write, in the wake of the war, the first overarching historical study of the Final Solution, *Bréviaire de la haine* (*Harvest of Hate*, 1951). *Bréviaire*, which was published in France thanks to the help of Raymond Aron, got an excellent review by Hannah Arendt in the March 1952 issue of the American journal *Commentary*, and still remains, in spite of its limitations, the founding act of what has been called since then: "Holocaust studies"—a phrase that, paradoxically, we never use in French, since we prefer the Hebrew word "Shoah," which means "catastrophe," without any religious connotation, rather than the American word (of Greek origin) "Holocaust," which implies the historically and metaphysically disputable idea of a self-accepted *sacrifice*.

After completing that first book, and partly under the influence of Jules Isaac (who had been the first one to denounce the "teaching of contempt," i.e., the anti-Jewish content of the Christian doctrine conveyed for centuries by Catholic iconography and liturgy), Poliakov felt the need to go back in time as far as possible. He wanted to throw light on the deepest roots of this monstrous attitude, antisemitism, of which the Holocaust had been the direct consequence. His *Histoire de l'antisémitisme* was the result of the long years of solitary research that started then. It constituted the first scientific work on the multiple aspects of antisemitism in the world over the past two millennia—and remains, to this day, a major reference.

As an independent adept of Fernand Braudel's theory of the "longue durée," Poliakov established the opposite conclusion to that of Arendt (whom he nevertheless greatly respected). He demonstrated in a convincing manner (although against Braudel's wishes, in this particular case)[7] that antisemitism was a relatively stable object (in spite of the fact that it had endured some transformations) from the beginning of the Christian era to the second half of the twentieth century. In other words, Poliakov was the first one to assume that the concept of a "Jewish race" was at the very heart of antisemitism many centuries before the first pseudo-biological elaborations of the Enlightenment started explicitly. In fact, this concept of a "Jewish race" began to exist from the very moment the Jews were attributed permanent psychological and moral features supposedly transmitted by heredity—which was unquestionably the case as soon as the Christian era began.

In fact, it was even the case *before* the Christian era began—as was soon to be discovered by younger researchers. Some twenty years after the publication of the first volume of Poliakov's *Histoire de l'antisémitisme*, two European scholars who were experts in Late Antiquity, the Dutch historian J. N. Sevenster (*The Roots of the Pagan Antisemitism in the Ancient World*, Leiden: Brill, 1975), and the French papyrologist Joseph Mélèze Modrzejewski ("Sur l'antisémitisme païen," in *Le Racisme: mythes et sciences*, edited by Maurice Olender, Brussels: Editions Complexe, 1981, pp. 411–39), completed Poliakov's work, which dealt only briefly with the Ancient Greco-Roman world. Both of them showed that the attribution of hereditarily fixed mental and moral features to the Jews, in other words antisemitism, was much older than the Middle Ages, without being the consequence of some mysterious "eternal" and "unchanging" phenomenon. It precisely started, in fact, in a determined time and place: *within the Greek community in the city of Alexandria (Egypt) during the Hellenistic period, that is, somewhere between the end of the third and the beginning of the second century BC*, when Judeophobic tales began to circulate, asserting that the Jews were hereditarily *leprous, disabled,* and *impure*.

Poliakov—who like Marcel Simon and Jules Isaac tended until then to look within Christianity (and especially Eastern Christianity) for the first origins of antisemitism—had some initial difficulties in admitting these revolutionary findings relating to a Hellenistic antisemitism (although Eastern Christianity itself was, in part, a direct offspring of Ancient Greek culture). He ended up being convinced, nevertheless, by the proofs offered by the two experts on antiquity, as he acknowledged himself in the important (although little known and almost never read) preface he wrote in 1981 for a republication of his *Histoire de l'antisémitisme* in the French paperback edition "Pluriel."[8]

Simultaneously, during the 1970s, Poliakov moved toward investigations into the history of other forms of racism (mostly antiblack racism), and dedicated a lot of work to the study of the construction of systems of racial classification in the works of seventeenth- and eighteenth-century European naturalists (the Count of Buffon, Carl Linné, Peter Camper, Johann Blumenbach, etc.). Starting in the 1980s, it then became obvious for Poliakov and his first Jewish or non-Jewish disciples[9] that racism and antisemitism were not phenomena that were foreign to each other or completely separate in their histories. On the contrary, racism and antisemitism were closely related attitudes, which proceeded from similar sources and had gone through distinct yet comparable evolutions over the past two millennia (a conclusion which, of course, does not prevent antisemitism and racism of possessing their own specific histories).

Nevertheless, in the United States at the same time, most scholars, far from being familiar with the investigations their European colleagues were leading (on both sides of the Atlantic, translation has always been a problem!), still separated antisemitism from racism, and, within their own study of racism, separated the study of slavery in America from all other forms of racism in other cultures. As for me, I frankly disagree with this academic way of separating things: More than ever, I remain convinced that these complex phenomena share common structural properties and cannot be properly understood as long as their similarities are not meticulously put into light.

By chance, that situation is slowly evolving, and English-speaking research on these issues is currently getting closer to the work that has previously been done by continental scholars, as is clear by Benjamin Isaac's latest book *The Invention of Racism in Classical Antiquity* and George Frederickson's *Racism: A Short History*.[10]

In the case of Isaac, an Israeli historian of Dutch origin, one of his greatest merits has been to demonstrate, against many of his colleagues and better than anybody else had previously done, that racism was not an unknown attitude in the ancient greek world in the classical age. It was, on the contrary, such a common attitude at the time that it is not a surprise at all to observe that antisemitism too developed in the Greek-speaking area in the immediate postclassical age, that is, during the Hellenistic age. Yet, in spite of this current and important evolution of scholarship in the English-speaking world, we should not rejoice too quickly. Lots of academic efforts still have to be exerted on both sides of the Atlantic, and not only in the United States, if we want to fully appreciate, some day, the global impact of racism and antisemitism on world history.

In any case, if scholarly research has made significant advances over the past sixty years, it is unquestionable that such advances were primarily the work of philosophers with a historical turn of mind, whose theoretical insights were later empirically grounded by the efforts of professional historians. And at this stage, if we want to be fair, we should recognize that Sartre's basic axioms on those topics were not only helpful and inspiring; they still remain, indeed, *the philosophical foundation of our current understanding of "race" and racism.*

Do I need to make this last claim regarding Sartre more convincing? If that is the case, I would like—and this will be my conclusion—to stress one single, major fact. If any researcher wants to understand how the roots of modern, racial antisemitism may be located within Christian, Medieval anti-Judaism and, beyond that, within the culture of Greek communities in Hellenistic Egypt, that researcher will have first to understand that "racial antisemitism," "theological anti-Judaism," "Greek Judaeophobia," and so on, were neither "opinions" nor basically different, unrelated attitudes: They simply were different expressions of one singular attitude—the one we call "antisemitism" tout court. And this is precisely what Sartre helped us understand.

Sartre was the first one to understand (and make us understand) that antisemitism *was not an opinion* but, as I said previously, a global attitude possessing its own internal coherence, a way of perceiving the world as such, an "ideology" in the Marxist sense of the word, a secular religion (Thesis number 3). Thanks to this and his other important insights, Arendt, Poliakov, and the younger disciples of the latter became capable of demonstrating *the continuity of antisemitism through the ages* and, as a consequence, shed a new light on its origins as well as its historical transformations.

And this is why, although seventy years have passed and Sartre is perhaps not as fashionable as he once was, I still regard *Réflexions sur la question juive* as a landmark book—in fact, one of the major books that came out in the twentieth century, and one that future generations, especially if they are interested in the issue of race, will still read with profit.

Notes

1. Jean-Paul Sartre, *Réflexions sur la question juive* (1946), Paris: Gallimard, "Folio Essais' Collection, no. 10, 1985, p. 24. The translation is mine.
2. Sartre, *Réflexions*, 10. Two remarks about this passage: (a) The practice of writing the substantive "Jewish" with a capital letter, as Sartre did in the French edition of his book, was common in his time. It has disappeared in France today, since Judaism, in the strict sense of the term, cannot be considered as something other than a religion. And, in French, the name of the followers of such and such religion ("un chrétien" for "a Christian," "un hindouiste" for "a Hindu," etc.) is never capitalized, as it is in English for instance; (b) The reference to the "Code" is not, in this sentence, entirely clear. Sartre probably used the word "Code" (which was evocative of the so called Civil Code) as a metaphor to designate law or administrative regulations in general.
3. I do not intend to make an inventory of those weaknesses, since it has already been done by Jonathan Judaken in chapter 4 of his own remarkable book *Jean-Paul Sartre and the Jewish Question: Anti-antisemitism and the Politics of the French Intellectual* (Lincoln: University of Nebraska Press, 2006).
4. In fact, Marcel Simon's book of 1964 was the republication of his doctoral thesis, which had been published for the first time in 1948, although under an extremely confidential form, since it constituted the volume no. 166 of a scholarly collection, the *Bibliothèque des Ecoles Françaises d'Athènes et de Rome*. According to the foreword of the book, Simon had completed his work by 1939, but, due the Vichy Regime, had to wait until 1948 to see it published for the first time.

5. Unfortunately, the fifth and last volume of the *Histoire de l'antisémitisme* by Léon Poliakov (covering the period from 1945 to 1993) was published much later than the first four, and by a different publisher (Le Seuil instead of Calmann-Lévy, who had previously published most of Poliakov's books, but rejected this one). It is also, contrary to the first four volumes, a collective work: Poliakov did in fact direct it and also wrote some of the most important chapters himself but, judging that his competence could not be universal, entrusted other chapters to other researchers. Be it for these or for other reasons, this fifth volume, contrary to the other four volumes, has never been translated into English; consequently, many English-speaking researchers who are working on the history of antisemitism are still unaware of its existence. And yet, no English book, as far as I know, has covered the field of investigation that is covered by this fifth volume, which deals with antisemitism in the whole world since the end of World War II, and especially with antisemitism in the contemporary Arab world, a subject that was almost untouched in 1994 and which is obviously more relevant today than ever before—although many Western researchers, be it for ignorance of the Arabic language, "political correctness," or other motives, are often reluctant to address it.
6. A recognized historian of antisemitism, Gavin I. Langmuir affirms that antisemitism properly understood was born only in the twelfth and thirteenth centuries, in the aftermath of the 1096 pogroms that accompanied the first Crusade: see for instance one of his latest books, *History, Religion and Antisemitism* (Berkeley and Los Angeles: University of California Press, 1990), chapter 14. In spite of all my respect for Langmuir, I cannot agree—and, to my mind, few historians would agree today—with the idea that there was nothing antisemitic about the violent anti-Judaism of the first Fathers of the Church. As soon as 386–387, Saint John Chrysostomus delivered in Antiochus eight sermons against the Jews (*Adversus Judaeos*), in which he called the Jews "a people of dogs": such a collective condemnation of a human group to an animal species is precisely, by our presentday standards, a typically racist attitude. I admit that it is possible, as Langmuir puts it, that this early Christian anti-Judaism was limited to educated circles and did not penetrate the illiterate mob until the twelfth century; but it is unquestionable that it was already, in its essence, antisemitic.
7. It is an open secret (Poliakov himself told the story at the end of his *L'Envers du destin: entretiens avec Georges Elia Sarfati*, Paris: Editions de Fallois, 1989, pp. 79–80, and more details on it can be found in the republication of Léon Poliakov's *Mémoires* (Paris: Jacques Grancher Editeur, 1999, p. 257, note 11) that Fernand Braudel (who was an old-fashioned conservative after the war exactly as he had been before it) did not want to hear about antisemitism, that he did not want the latter to become the subject of a historical study, and that he initially denied Poliakov the possibility of transforming his *Histoire de l'antisémitisme* into a PhD dissertation under his direction.
8. Basically, those proofs (which, of course, do not exonerate the Catholic religion of its own responsibility in the later aggravation of the situation of the European Jews) consisted in recently deciphered *papyri* and other texts. Fifteen years ago, Joseph Mélèze Modrzejewski, a longtime professor at the University Paris I (Sorbonne) and at the Ecole pratique des hautes études (fourth section), presented an exhaustive and detailed view of the situation of the Jews in ancient Egypt in his excellent (although very little known) book on *Les Juifs d'Egypte de Ramsès II à Hadrien* (Paris: Editions Errance, 1991). As for Poliakov's preface of 1981 to his *Histoire de l'antisémitisme*, that was reedited in 1991 in the paperback "Points" collection (Paris: Editions du Seuil), it is to be

noted that this text has never been added to the English translation of his book, which may explain why the conception of a Hellenistic antisemitism still seems unfamiliar to many English-speaking readers or researchers.

9. If I can include myself in this latter group, I will take this opportunity to emphasize here that this vision of things (considering the history of racism and antisemitism as the history of two parallel phenomena that have always been, to a large extent, intricately linked and even inseparable), although it still does not enjoy the favors of the conservative academic establishment in France, has always been the one that governed my own research. The reader who would like to check this point may turn to my doctoral thesis *L'Invention du racisme: Antiquité et Moyen Age* (Paris: Fayard, 1983), which I defended in December of 1982 at the University Paris I-Sorbonne in front of a jury presided by Léon Poliakov, or to my more recent and more elaborate *Histoire du racisme: des origines à nos jours* (Paris: Le Livre de Poche, 2000). A new, augmented, and revised edition of this last book, which will probably be my last word on the issue, has been translated into German under the title *Die Geschichte des Rassismus* (Düsseldorf and Zurich: Artemis and Winkler Verlag, 2005).

10. Benjamin Isaac, *The Invention of Racism in Classical Antiquity* (Princeton: Princeton University Press, 2004). The fact that this book carries the same title as my own doctoral dissertation (published in 1983 and quoted in the preceding note) is a mere coincidence, to the extent that Benjamin Isaac, who teaches at the University of Tel Aviv, did not know me and was unaware of the existence of my work when he published his own—which, in fact, does not exactly cover the same historical field as mine. Contrary to me, Benjamin Isaac decided to put a (temporary?) end to his inquiry at the end of the classical age, and did not tackle the literature of the Hellenistic period (as soon as he discovered it, Benjamin Isaac mentioned this uncommon coincidence of titles in the paperback re-edition of his own book, 2006, as well as in the excellent review of the German version of my *Histoire du racisme* he published in the Israeli journal *Scripta Classica Israelica*, volume 25, 2006). See also, George Frederickson, *Racism: A Short History* (Princeton: Princeton University Press, 2003).

Chapter 5

Sartre and Levinas
Philosophers against Racism and Antisemitism

Robert Bernasconi

Recent historical research has highlighted how deeply implicated a number of the canonical figures of modern European philosophy are in the history of racism: Locke, Kant, and Hegel particularly.[1] The sad truth is that there is a great deal more evidence of Enlightenment philosophers who championed racist views than there is of Enlightenment philosophers who opposed racist practices. The abolition of slavery, for example, owed more to a rereading of the Bible than to arguments proposed by philosophers, even philosophers appealing to the Bible, and those philosophers who did argue against slavery, like Granville Sharp, are, in any event, largely forgotten by mainstream philosophy today. Things are not much better when we move to more recent history, or even the present: Philosophy has lagged behind other disciplines in reconceiving its canon in an effort to address its own racist history. What does this tell us about reason as it has been developed within the Western philosophical tradition? What resources does philosophy bring to the continuing fight against racism?

Jean-Paul Sartre and Emmanuel Levinas are two of the more prominent of recent philosophers who offer help in answering these questions. Sartre, of course, is famous for championing the cause of the oppressed: *Réflexions sur la question juive* (*Antisemite and Jew*), "Orphée noir" ("Black Orpheus"), and his prefaces to Albert Memmi's *Portrait du colonisé précédé du portrait du colonisateur* (*The Colonizer and the Colonized*) and to Frantz Fanon's *Les damnés de la terre* (*The Wretched of the Earth*) are regarded as classic. Levinas is among the most prominent contributors to what is sometimes called "postholocaust ethics." He described his life and work as dominated by the presentiment and memory of the Nazi horror.[2] To be sure, he was not as clearly focused specifically on racism as was Sartre. Moreover, as I will show, there seems to me to be some confusion as to how his work operates as a resource in the battle against racism. Indeed, on occasion he made remarks that are clear evidence of a certain antiblack prejudice.[3] Nevertheless, the experience of having been persecuted as a Jew was so central to the formation of his philosophy, as was his effort to develop intellectual resources to battle against antisemitism, that it is impossible not to include him among philosophers who have cultivated resources that combat racism. Most prominent among those resources are his concept of responsibility.

The perpetuation of the effects of centuries of racism relies on the fact that whites are all too eager to accept the advantages and privileges that they have inherited on account of their "race," while they at the same time try to limit their responsibilities to those actions for which they can be held directly accountable in a legal or quasi-legal way. Hence the significance of the fact that both Sartre and Levinas developed the idea of a responsibility without limits, a "hyperbolic responsibility," that is radically distinct from the more restricted legalistic notion of accountability.

For Sartre, responsibility means being without excuse. My responsibility arises from my freedom.[4] My choice of myself is a choice of the world, so I am responsible for it and for all human beings. As he explains in *L'existentialisme est un humanisme* ("Existentialism is a Humanism"), none is free unless all are free, so my quest for freedom implicates me in the conditions of everyone else's freedom.[5] My freedom also leaves me having to answer for the past, even the past before I was born, insofar as my actions contribute to the meaning ascribed to that past.

A few years later, Levinas similarly proclaimed "my responsibility" for everything and everybody, including those who persecute me. However, he did so on different grounds from Sartre. Indeed, in a relatively late work, Levinas explicitly rejected Sartre's starting point in the freedom of the for-itself, electing instead to locate the basis of my responsibility in an absolute passivity to which he gave the name "substitution."[6] Even before that, Levinas's account of my asymmetrical experience in the face of the Other, of the ethical demand he or she makes on me, a demand to which I am obliged to respond without concern for myself, was markedly different from Sartre's approach, which highlighted the conflictual character of the gaze of the Other, whereby the one deprives the other of his or her freedom by reducing him or her to a form of thinghood.

In contrast to my focus on responsibility here, the best discussions of Sartre's and Levinas's analyses of racial oppression have hitherto dwelled on their rival accounts of the relation to the Other.[7] Racism in Levinas's account is a denial of the ethical relation to the absolute Other, whereas in Sartre it is a denial of freedom, not only the Other's freedom but, insofar as Sartre held that none are free until all are free, my own freedom as well. The contrast between the positions of Sartre and Levinas thus readily, and with some legitimacy, comes to be viewed as a question of whether politics or ethics comes first. Whereas Levinas looks to the ethical to interrupt the political order, Sartre postpones ethics until everyone is ethical, that is to say, until a just political order has been established.[8]

However, I shall argue here that Levinas and Sartre do not represent an antinomy. There are undoubtedly fundamental differences between these two thinkers when it comes to the fight against racism, but one should not underestimate what they share, any more than Levinas himself did when, in an interview from 1980, he responded to Benny Lévy's conversations with Sartre published as *L'Espoir maintenant* (*Hope Now*) and highlighted certain points of convergence between them, while at the same time insisting that Sartre had not in the process, contrary to some critics, abandoned his general philosophical positions.[9] This lends indirect support to my claim that their contributions on this issue are in certain important respects complementary.

In order to show this, I need to address the current tendency to understand Sartre and Levinas as presenting opposed viewpoints on this issue. This tendency relies on the important insight that Levinas's account of alterity does not address specific differences: It is not because the Other is other than me in some determinate sense that there is ethics. Levinas believes that an ethical encounter with the Other in the face-to-face relation takes place only when I welcome the Other without reference to any social characteristics. Contrary to a widespread usage that associates alterity with cultural difference, the face of the Other in Levinas is "abstract or naked," without identity, "with no cultural ornament."[10] It is in this spirit that Levinas declares in "Language and Proximity" that language, "like a battering ram," is "the power to break through the limits of culture, body, and race (*espèce*)."[11] The alterity of the Other is such that, as Levinas says, I do not notice the color of his or her eyes.[12] One can presumably add that the same applies to the color of the skin.[13] It is because Judaism is, unlike paganism on Levinas's account, open to alterity that he could write in a short piece on antisemitism in 1938: Judaism is antipaganism and thus the opposite of racism.[14]

However, this important insight into Levinas's account of alterity has led interpreters like Alain Finkielkraut to associate it with the notion of colorblindness and the Enlightenment tradition, the tradition of the Declaration of the Rights of Man, and thus directly in contrast with Sartre's approach.[15] To be sure, one could object that the Enlightenment *philosophes* never sought to abandon racial identities in spite of their universal principles: This was a myth proposed by opponents of assimilation, such as Leopold de Saussure, author of *Psychologie de la colonization française dans ses rapports avec les sociétés indigenes*, who, for his own purposes, presented the *philosophes* as entirely ignorant of the science of race.[16] But it is the interpretation of Levinas that I am primarily concerned with here. Finkielkraut correctly opposes Levinas to German conceptions of the *Volksgeist* in the sense of a spirit with ethnic roots, as well as to multiculturalism, but he falsely concludes that that leaves Levinas embracing a France that cannot be reduced to Frenchness, the France of universalistic principles.[17] For one thing, Levinas did not even try to hide his ethnocentrism behind the universalistic principles of the Enlightenment: He was committed to the indefensible position that "humanity consists of the Bible and the Greeks. All the rest can be translated: all the rest—all the exotic—is dance."[18] For another, Levinas's humanism of the Other is ultimately not a kind of abstract universalism, as I shall explain.

From the fact that Sartre in *Antisemite and Jew* rejects the universalist answer to antisemitism in terms of "a sort of *universal and rationalized body*"[19] and proposes instead a concrete synthesis for which man does not exist (RJ 175; AJ 144), Finkielkraut concludes that Levinas and Sartre have opposed positions on how to combat racism: color-blindness versus "antiracist racism," overcoming racism by appealing at once to the universality of "man" in the Enlightenment tradition versus positive discrimination, which necessitates continuing use of the categories under which the oppressed have been identified. If this was the last word, then Levinas and Sartre would, as Finkielkraut maintains, be offering diametrically opposed responses to racism.

However, matters are more complex, even for Sartre, who, in his essay on the negritude poets, "Black Orpheus," calls for the eventual renunciation of race identity on the part of blacks for the sake of a raceless and ultimately classless society, even though he nevertheless supports in the meanwhile what he called provocatively "an anti-racist racism."[20] Affirmative action or so-called positive discrimination are forms of what Sartre calls antiracist racism, and it is worth remembering that, although these approaches are now widespread, at the time Sartre was heavily criticized for proposing them. Nevertheless, it is the interpretation of Levinas as an abstract universalist, rather than of Sartre, that I want to challenge here.

The problem with casting Levinas as an opponent of Sartre emerges most clearly in the context of Levinas's "Existentialism and Antisemitism," his response to a lecture Sartre gave to the Alliance Israélite Universelle in 1947 under the title "Reflections on the Jewish Question," the same title as the book that he had just published. However, rather than simply paraphrasing the earlier discussion, Sartre reworked his ideas in part in response to criticisms and in part to clarify his earlier discussion, which he believed had been misunderstood.[21] For example, the central thesis of the book, that the antisemite makes the Jew (RJ 84; AJ 69), is asserted only in the more nuanced and defensible form that antisemites, "having constructed from scratch a Jew who is simply the replica of their hatred of analytical spirit, of negation, of nuance, have created a portrait of the Jew that ends up being the image we encountered during the period of the Occupation" (R 89; O 42).

This formulation highlights a further point. Although Sartre in *Antisemite and Jew* rehearses the usual objection of existential phenomenology against analytical reason that it breaks up what it cannot subsequently reconstitute, he seems to favor synthetic thought, even though it is the kind of thought employed by the antisemite. Not yet in possession of the dialectic that incorporates a role for analytic thinking—or at least operating with only the crudest conception of it as revealed by his treatment in "Black Orpheus" of a racism sublated through antiracist racism into universalism—Sartre operates with the somewhat crude opposition of analysis and synthesis that had been at the heart also of some of the methodological problems of *Being and Nothingness*. Nevertheless, in an important concession, Sartre in the lecture stresses that analytic reason had played a productive role as a weapon against privilege and that employing an analytical conception of society and of man had helped to establish a bourgeois society (R 82–83; O 34–35).

Levinas did not use the occasion of Sartre's lecture to contribute to the rising tide of objections against his position, other than to acknowledge in passing the legitimacy of the complaint that Sartre linked Jewish destiny to antisemitism, a criticism that arose from Sartre's failure to take any account of the inherent character of Judaism as revealed in its history.[22] Instead, Levinas applauds "the wholly new" weapons that Sartre employs against antisemitism, and he specifies first and foremost Sartre's attack on the analytical vision of society according to which the human being is conceived as "independent of his milieu, birth, religion, social condition" (IH 120; UH 74). Levinas identifies as outmoded the discourses inspired by the Judeo-Christian tradition but "reformulated in our times in terms of seventeenth- and eighteenth-century rationalism" (IH 121; UH 74). Furthermore, he celebrates existentialism as a philosophy that recognizes that "the mind is tied by commitments that are not structured as knowledge" (IH 122; UH 75).

Levinas sees Sartre as providing an indication of how one can surpass a situation—social, historical, and material—not in terms of consciousness but from elsewhere. Until Sartre's existentialism, it seemed that there was no way to offer a philosophy of the situation without denying the rights of man and thereby giving up the defense against antisemitism. Yet the ideas of the rights of man had proved inadequate to protect the Jews. According to Levinas, the ease with which the followers of Nietzsche had been able to articulate a philosophy of blood and soil could be explained by the absence of a rigorously developed alternative. Levinas illustrates that inadequacy by rehearsing an antinomy that he had found documented by a UNESCO circular: "The freedom of the individual is inconceivable without economic liberation, but the organization of economic freedom is not possible without the temporary but temporarily unlimited enslavement of the individual" (IH 121; UH 74). Even though Sartre himself acknowledged in his talk he had been criticized in his appraisal of antisemitism for treating it on the psychological and physical level and not on the level of economics, Levinas seems to have seen its potential for taking the broader view.

The fact that Levinas praises Sartre's critique of the Enlightenment tradition, the very tradition to which Levinas was assimilated by Finkielkraut, will come as no surprise to careful readers of "Quelques réflexions sur la philosophie de l'hitlerisme," ("Reflections on the Philosophy of Hitlerism"), Levinas's 1934 essay. Particularly when read in conjunction with "De l'évasion" ("Of Escape") from 1935, this essay already anticipates Sartre in suggesting a new way of surpassing the alternatives thought has inherited for addressing racism. At the outset Levinas rejects the attempt to judge concrete events in terms of the logical contradiction between Christian universalism and racist particularism, the very contradiction on which Finkielkraut insists.[23] Levinas proposes to go deeper. He concludes that universalism and racist particularism are not opposed when the latter turns into the former by pursuing expansion through war and conquest (RPH 207; RH 70). To be sure, Levinas identifies another form of universalization that does not employ racist particularism, universalization by the propagation of ideas, whereby the idea detaches itself from its point of departure to become a common heritage. As we shall see, Levinas thinks of Judaism in these terms and is able to do so because he preeminently thinks of Jews as strangers on the earth in perpetual exile and thus as predisposed, as it were, to present ideas that are "fundamentally anonymous" in the sense that they are not tied to a specific soil or source.

However, it is Levinas's analysis of National Socialism and the resources available to combat it in "Reflections on the Philosophy of Hitlerism" that is of most significance here. Levinas presents Judaism, through its notion of repentance and pardon, and Christianity, through its idea of salvation secured by the crucifixion, as both overcoming the irreversibility of time and history that is characteristic of Greek notions of destiny. By allowing for a true beginning in the present, both traditions establish an idea of freedom of which the liberal idea of a sovereign freedom of autonomous reason is but a pale shadow. Furthermore, liberalism is in danger of championing the skepticism that prides itself on the possibility of going back on one's choice, so that freedom degenerates into not chaining oneself to a truth. This reveals itself in a lack of commitment to "the creation of spiritual values" (RPH 206; RH 69–70).

Levinas believes that the idea that the body is an obstacle to be overcome, an idea which liberalism inherited from Christianity, disregards that feeling of identity between our bodies and ourselves that is experienced in physical pain. This feeling of identity is at the basis of Hitlerism's radically new conception of man (RPH 203–205; RH 67–68). Hitlerism sees man's essence not in freedom but in bondage to the body, to the biological, blood, and heredity (RPH 205; RH 69). Levinas here and in his subsequent works formulates a philosophy that, in contrast with the Christian tradition, acknowledges the inherent value of the body's adherence to the self as something one does not escape but to which one cannot be reduced (RPH 205; RH 68).

Such a philosophy is better equipped to combat racism. It is clear that already in 1934 Levinas was convinced that liberalism and contemporary Christian culture lacked the resources to challenge racism effectively. It is because liberal universalism lost sight of the body that it opened the door to those, like the Nazis, who wanted to assert the primacy of the biological, and of ideas of blood and race. "Reflections on the Philosophy of Hitlerism" vindicates Finkielkraut's conviction that Levinas was opposed to the German *Volksgeist*, but read in conjunction with an essay he published in Lithuanian in 1933, it is clear that Levinas was no more enamored of French universalist culture. Indeed, he refuses to say which of the two spiritual worlds is better. They both have their dangers.[24]

In "On Escape" from 1935 Levinas explores the same ideas as can be found in "Reflections on the Philosophy of Hitlerism" in a more ontological idiom. Against the bourgeois spirit that nourishes capitalism, he asks if its fostering of a self-sufficient ego is not challenged by the experience of suffering in which one feels riveted to one's body.[25] However, in keeping with "Reflections on the Philosophy of Hitlerism" Levinas also dismisses as barbaric any civilization that accepts being (DE 98; OE 73). He thereby identifies the humanity of the human with the aspiration to surpass being, coupled with the inability to do so, and this aporetic conjunction is what Levinas consistently articulates in his philosophical works, long before he finds it concretely realized in the ethical relation to the Other.[26]

This structure is exemplified by the experience of pain, where one's desire to escape is frustrated by the feeling of being riveted to one's body, and he uses the same expression to describe the facticity of being Jewish under the form of antisemitism cultivated by Hitler: "the Jew is ineluctably riveted to his Judaism."[27] Levinas would say to Francois Poirié many years later that "Of Escape" signified the human beyond the Jewish condition.[28] However, that does not mean that he arrived at the human by abstracting from the particularities of the Jewish condition to establish the universal. If the face of the Other is "abstract," it is not in logical terms but only in the sense of being absolute, that is to say, not integratable into the horizons of the world

(HH 42 and 57–58; HO 31 and 39). Hence, in "Being Jewish," a text from 1947, he says that "the human soul is perhaps naturally Jewish."[29] The Jewish condition testifies to the human. It does not represent something concrete that must be discarded on the way to the human.

This description of 'the Jew' riveted to Judaism is in certain respects paralleled by Sartre's account in *Antisemite and Jew*: "the Jew" is objectified in the gaze, reduced to an essence, a thing, in the eyes of the antisemite (RJ 93; AJ 76–77). However, 'the Jew' nevertheless escapes this facticity by virtue of the structure of consciousness: consciousness is what it is not and is not what it is (EN 103; BN 63). Nevertheless, in "Being Jewish," in an attempt to clarify some of the differences between Sartre and himself, Levinas reiterates that Jews rediscovered in Hitlerism the irremissibility of their being (EJ 103).

Yet, for all the kind words Levinas uttered in "Existentialism and Antisemitism," in "Being Jewish" he claims that Sartre cannot see the dimension in which Jewish existence is located, and so is blind to its originality, which consists in breaking with a world without origin that is simply present (EJ 105). This is reflected in their rival positions on Jewish facticity. According to Sartre, "the Jew" in an antisemitic world has no alternative but to assume his facticity, although there are an infinite number of ways of doing so, including denying that race is a collective fiction (EN 612; BN 529). According to Levinas, there is a Jewish facticity different from the "facticity of the world" which understands itself on the basis of the present (EJ 103). This objection anticipates what Fanon issued when he complained that Sartre had forgotten that the white man experiences his body in a way different from the black.[30]

In "Being Jewish" Levinas assimilates Sartre to the philosophy of idealism (EJ 102). He has in mind Sartre's tendency to highlight how it is through the gaze of another that identities are constructed. To be sure, Sartre in the *Critique de la raison Dialectique* (*Critique of Dialectical Reason*) corrected this failure: in order to make oneself a bourgeois, one must first be bourgeois.[31] This is because class—and race too, as Sartre's examples make clear—already exists as "*the crystallized practice*" of previous generations, so that individuals find an existence, a future sentence, sketched out for them at birth (CRD 289 and 302; CDR 232 and 250).

We might also recall how Levinas already in "Existentialism and Antisemitism" highlights how Sartre's achievement as an opponent of antisemitism lay in large part because not everything was reduced to thought. Sartre pursues this approach to the point where in the *Critique of Dialectical Reason* he insisted that racism is not a thought but "the colonial interest lived as a link of all the colonialists of the colony through the serial flight of alterity" (CRD 344n; CDR 300n). To belong to a collective being, such as a race or a class, is, on Sartre's provisional analysis in the *Critique*, to belong to a matrix or milieu such that this collective being is in everyone to the extent that everyone is in it (CRD 305; CDR 252).

However, Sartre offers a more refined account later in the book in terms of the notion of seriality and at the same time revises the discussion in *Antisemite and Jew*. In his earlier works Sartre had tended to highlight the ontological bond experienced by the oppressed under the gaze of the oppressor and, by contrast, reduced to the level of psychology the bond between the oppressors because they are not united by a gaze (EN 496–97; BN 424–25). This provides an excellent basis for explaining both the solidarity uniting the oppressed under a description and the somewhat looser ties that one sometimes finds among the oppressors, such as is reflected in the tendency of the bourgeois or whites to deny the saliency of class or race in a world dominated by it. They literally do not see what is sustaining them because their own identity is invisible to them, even while they see a corresponding identity in others. In *Antisemite and Jew* Sartre discusses the relations that one Jew has to another only in the case of the authentic Jew (RJ 178; AJ 147). By the time of the *Critique* Sartre has a richer ontological framework in place and so he presents "the Jew" not as a type but in a correct response of relationships that he describes as "the internal serial unity of Jewish multiplicities" (CRD 317; CDR 267).

To explain this difficult idea, Sartre offers the example of a Jewish doctor who is told that there are too many Jewish doctors and who responds by finding the other Jewish doctors dispensable. Sartre accounts for this by going beyond the way that individual Jews living in a hostile society might be directly threatened by antisemites and indirectly threatened insofar as they see other Jews being persecuted as Jews, and by introducing into his account the additional observation that in an antisemitic society Jews do not always experience themselves as bound together by the gaze of the Other, as his earlier analysis had suggested. They can also experience their own otherness as Jews precisely to the extent that they too come to see other Jews as other. When antisemites complain that there are too many Jewish doctors, then this need not necessarily bind any single Jewish doctor to all the others, but can mean that to the extent that one of them sees him- or herself as other, then that doctor also sees the other Jewish doctors as his or her others as without them there would not be many Jewish doctors at all and the problem would be solved.

Later in the volume Sartre shows that a similar structure operates among racists and antisemites following the seriality of racism: Racism and antisemitism on this model are the attitude of the Other and as such sustained by a group (CRD 622; CDR 652). So, if one beats one's slaves, one does it because everyone else does it. In keeping with these insights Sartre, according to reports of his still unpublished Rome lecture on ethics, argues that racism is a morality of repetition which obliges the colonizer to do what is necessary to sustain the results of past praxis. That is to say, racism is the way colonists freely assume the position that they are dialectically forced to by the colonial system that sustains them, independent of their individual desires and beliefs.[32]

One way in which racism perpetuates itself is by focusing almost exclusively on racist discourse as the locus of racism whereas what is important is how racism is perpetuated as a system. Racism or colonialism can maintain itself as a system by transferring responsibility elsewhere. White families might decide to move house when a black family buys a house on the same street, not because they themselves have any personal objection to a black presence there, but because they fear that its arrival might impact the price other white families would pay for a house on the street. They therefore join other residents in putting their own houses on the market and if a significant number of them do so, prices inevitably fall: It proves to be a self-fulfilling prophecy. It is striking that such thinking could perpetuate itself without there being any white family in the world that does not want to live on the same street as a black family: Each family needs only believe that there are white families who think that way for the effect to be realized. The perpetuation of racism on this account is not dependent on an individual's thoughts. Sartre presents racism as an ideology invented to perpetuate a condition that exists for the advantage of one group. It is then this condition and not the ideology that is fundamentally racist and thus whoever does not work to alter that situation is on this account racist. In this way Sartre's idea of seriality illuminates the meaning and basis of so-called institutional racism and the way we participate in it.

Levinas's analysis of institutional racism may not be as rich as Sartre's, but he offers a proposal for combating oppression at the economic level. Indeed, his whole philosophy should be understood as an attempt to insist that this must be done, in spite of a widespread suspicion to the contrary. For Levinas, one cannot approach the Other with empty hands.[33] In the 1953 essay "The Ego and the Totality" he offered concrete indications of how this might happen in a way that the wrongs done to oppressed groups might be addressed. In this essay Levinas identifies as "true violence" not the violence of the sword, but the violence of gold, of money, which is "the way of peacetime violence, exploitation, or slow death."[34] Nevertheless, he also concedes that gold can also be an instrument of justice in reparations. So long as violence is addressed only by vengeance or forgiveness then the evil persists: "evil engenders evil, and pardon extended infinitely encourages it" (MT 373; CP 45).

Nothing can better serve to disturb the standard picture of Levinas as a philosopher of transcendence who elevates the face of the Other at the expense of ontology and economics than these lines. The suggestion is not that there is a fair sum that would establish equity in the face of past injustice. It is merely that without compensation, without reparations, all efforts at reconciliation and forgiveness, however noble, are worthless.[35] In so saying, Levinas distinguishes between desire and need. Although it is only through desire that one has access to the Other as such, one cannot disregard the Other's needs. Both levels must be addressed: it is qua Other that someone who is hungry calls on me to feed them. The same goes for identities. The self is without identity and the absolute Other as such is abstract, but this does not oblige me to bypass or neglect the Other's demand to respect his or her identity. Far from it. Sartre in his lecture on the Jewish Question explains how until 1939 he had believed that there were not Jews but just men; it was only when he was being interviewed for a Swiss journal on the Jewish Question that a Jew, Arnold Mandel, made it clear to him that, "attached to his people, utterly patriotic, [he] was rather disappointed to realize that I was not ready to see in him anything but a man similar to others" (R 83; O 35). Levinas would have responded similarly. It should be remembered that Levinas, for all his insistence on absolute alterity, is committed to maintaining Jewish identity.[36]

The decisive philosophical division on the question of racism is therefore not that between Sartre and Levinas. Rather, the division is methodological: On the one hand, there are those philosophers who restrict their efforts to identifying those specific ideas that constitute racism, so as to isolate and reject them, thereby allowing for related ideas to be exonerated. And on the other hand, those philosophers who see racism as a system that is fostered by the failure to see it as a system. Levinas and Sartre both belong to the latter group, but there are differences between them. Sartre has the better account of how racism operates in a systematic way, whereas Levinas, properly understood, contributes more to the understanding of at least one way in which the targets of racism might philosophically negotiate the nonphilosophical experience of persecution from their own resources.[37] Furthermore, Sartre shows that analytic reason is subordinated to dialectical reason and serves as a moment of the latter (CRD 148; CDR 59). Levinas does not exhibit a comparable sense of the resources of analytic reason, which leaves him particularly exposed when his own failure to appreciate cultures beyond those of Greece and the Bible is at issue. Nonetheless, drawing on the resources of phenomenology, both Sartre and Levinas offer an alternative to the so-called Enlightenment universalist approach by emphasizing the positive role played by the bodily within a synthetic or holistic account of identity to which one is nevertheless not reduced.

There is a widespread view that our best resources in the fight against racism lie in an appeal to Enlightenment universalism, in drawing distinctions between the biological and the cultural or between race and ethnicity, and in the promotion of color-blindness. I do not deny the contribution that has been made by the appeal to universal rights and principles, nor the continuing necessity to do so in political argument today. Nor do I deny the desirability on occasion of drawing distinctions between the biological and the cultural or between race and ethnicity, but I question whether these should be regarded as our ultimate resources if we are no longer willing to promote the distinction between body and mind on which they are based. Finally, I acknowledge that insofar as we mean by a colorblind society a society free of discrimination, then, of course, I would support it. But if, by contrast, colorblindness means that, as Sartre proposed in "Black Orpheus," blacks should be asked to renounce their blackness, or Jews to conceal their Jewishness for the sake of creating a society free of discrimination, then a serious mistake is being made. Nobody knows what would happen to so-called racial identities in such a society, but, even if one could succeed in renouncing talk of identities without first addressing the effects of past racisms, which seems unlikely, this would be a way of hiding the problem, not moving toward its solution. That is why I think that, notwithstanding their defects, the efforts of Sartre and Levinas to promote our responsibility to address racism deserve to be central reference points in a debate on how racism can best be combated.[38]

Notes

1. See, for example, Robert Bernasconi, "Locke's Almost Random Talk of Man," *Perspektiven der Philosophie* 18 (1992): 293–318; "Kant as an Unfamiliar Source of Racism" in *Philosophers on Race*, ed. T. Lott and J. Ward (Oxford: Blackwell, 2002), 145–66; and "Hegel at the Court of the Ashanti" in *Hegel after Derrida*, ed. Stuart Barnett (London: Routledge, 1998), 41–63.
2. Emmanuel Levinas, *Difficile Liberté* (Paris, Ablin Michel, 1976), 373; trans. Seán Hand, *Difficult Freedom* (Baltimore: Johns Hopkins University Press, 1990), 291.
3. I first made this case in "Who Is My neighbor? Who Is the Other?" in *Ethics and Responsibility in the Phenomenological Tradition*, The Ninth Annual Symposium of the Simon Silverman Phenomenology Center, Pittsburgh: Duquesne University, 1992, 1–31. Now reprinted in ed. Claire Katz, *Emmanuel Levinas: Critical Assesments* (London: Routledge, 2005), vol. 4, 5–30.
4. Jean-Paul Sartre, *L'être et le néant* (Paris: Gallimard, 1943), 638–42; trans. Hazel Barnes, *Being and Nothingness* (London, Methuen, 1957), 553–56. Henceforth EN and BN respectively.
5. Jean-Paul Sartre, *L'existentialisme est un humanisme* (Paris: Nagel, 1946), 83–84; trans. Philip Mauret, *Existentialism and Humanism* (London: Methuen, 1968), 52.
6. Emmanuel Levinas, *Autrement qu'être ou au-delà de l'essence* (The Hague: Martinus Nijhoft, 1974), 131; trans. Alphonso Lingis, *Otherwise Than Being or Beyond Essence* (The Hague: Martinus Nijhoff, 1981), 103.

7. One of these, Rudi Vissker's essay entitled "The Gaze of the Big Other: Levinas and Sartre on Racism," takes me to task for being too generous to Levinas and for not seeing the virtues of Sartre's account. See *Truth and Singularity* (Dordrecht: Kluwer, 1999), 348. There is some merit to the objection that I have devoted more energy to developing the resources Levinas provides for combating racism than exposing his philosophical blindspots and his personal limitations, but it is not true that I have ignored Sartre's resources. See already "Sartre's Gaze Returned: The Transformation of the Phenomenology of Racism," *Graduate Faculty Philosophy Journal* 18.2 (1995): 201–21. Reprinted in ed. William L. McBride, *Existentialist Ethics* (New York: Garland, 1997), 359–79.
8. Emmanuel Levinas, "Politique Après," *L'au-delà du verset* (Paris: Minuit, 1982), 221–28; trans. Gary D. Mole, *Beyond the Verse* (Bloomington: Indiana University Press, 1994), 188–95. Jean-Paul Sartre, *Cahiers pour une morale* (Paris, Gallimard, 1983), 16; trans. David Pellauer, *Notebooks for an Ethics* (Chicago, University of Chicago Press, 1992), 9.
9. Emmanuel Levinas, "Quand Sartre découvre l'histoire sainte," *Les imprévus de l'histoire*, 158; trans. "When Sartre Discovers Holy History," *Unforeseen History*, 98.
10. Emmanuel Levinas, *Humanisme de l'autre homme* (Montepelier: Fata Morgana, 1972), 48; trans. Nidra Poller, *Humanism of the Other* (Urbana: University of Illinois Press, 2003), 32.
11. Emmanuel Levinas, *En découvrant l'existence avec Husserl et Heidegger* (Paris: Vrin, 1974), 232; trans. Alphonso Lingis, *Collected Philosophical Papers* (Dordrecht: Martinus Nijhoff, 1987), 122.
12. Emmanuel Levinas, *Éthique et infini* (Paris: Fayard, 1982), 89; trans. Richard Cohen, *Ethics and Infinity* (Pittsburgh: Duquesne University Press, 1985), 85.
13. Indeed, Levinas seems to have said exactly that—"to be in relation with the face means that upon seeing a black, one does not notice the color of his skin"—in an interview with J. Goud in *God als Raadsel* (Kampen: Kok. Agora, 1992), 165. Cited R. Vissker, *Truth and Singularity*, 381.
14. Emmanuel Levinas, "A propos de la mort du pape Pie XI," in *Emmanuel Levinas*, ed. Chalier and Abensour, 152. See also *Difficile Liberté*, 232; *Difficult Freedom*, 170.
15. Alain Finkielkraut, *La sagesse de l'amour* (Paris: Gallimard, 1984), 25–45; trans. Kevin O'Neill and David Suchoff, *The Wisdom of Love* (Lincoln: University of Nebraska Press, 1997), 9–24: and *L'humanité perdue* (Paris Seuil, 1996), 41–64; trans. Judith Friedlander, *In the Name of Humanity* (New York: Columbia University Press, 1999), 25–42. For Levinas's discussion of the rights of man see, for example, Emmanuel Levinas, "Les droits de l'homme et les droits d'autrui," *Hors sujet* (Montpelier: Fata Morgana, 1987), 173–87; trans. Michael B. Smith, *Outside the Subject* (Stanford: Stanford University Press, 1993), 116–25. However, to understand Finkielkraut's position in its full complexity, one must know that he had at one time adopted Sartre's position as set out in *Antisemite and Jew*. See *Le Juif imaginaire* (Paris: Seuil, 1980), 16; trans. Kevin O'Neill and David Suchoff, *The Imaginary Jew* (Lincoln: University of Nebraska Press, 1994), 9.
16. Léopold de Saussure, *Psychologie de la colonization française dans ses rapports avec les sociétés indigenes* (Paris: Felix Alcan, 1899), 294–311.
17. Alain Finkielkraut, *La défaite de la pensée* (Paris: Gallimard, 1987), 125; trans. Judith Friedlander, *The Defeat of the Mind* (New York: Columbia University Press, 1995), 102.

18. Raoul Mortley, *French Philosophers in Conversation* (London: Routledge, 1991), 18.
19. Jean-Paul Sartre, *Réflexions sur la question juive* (Paris: Gallimard, 1954), 147; trans. George J. Becker, *Antisemite and Jew* (New York: Schocken, 1976), 121. Henceforth RJ and AJ respectively.
20. Jean-Paul Sartre, "Orphée Noir," in *Anthologie de la nouvelle poésie négre et malgache*, ed. Leopold Senghor (Paris: Presses Universitaires de France, 1948), xiv; trans. John MacCombie, "Black Orpheus," in *Race*, ed. Robert Bernasconi (Oxford: Blackwell, 2001), 118.
21. Jean-Paul Sartre, "Réflexions sur la question juive," *Les cahiers du judaisme* 3 (Autumn 1998): 82–92; trans. Rosalind Krauss and Dennis Hollier, "Reflections on the Jewish Question. A Lecture," *October 87* (Winter 1999): 33–46. Henceforth R and O respectively. A short report on Sartre's lecture was published at the time under the title "Conférence de Jean-Paul Sartre," *Les Cahiers de l'Alliance Israelite Universelle* 14–15 (June/July 1947): 3 and 14.
22. Emmanuel Levinas, "Existentialisme et antisémitisme," *Les imprévus de l'histoire* (Montpelier: Fata Morgana, 1994), 120; trans. Nidra Poller, "Existentialism and Antisemitism," *Unforeseen History* (Urbana: University of Illinois Press, 2004), 73. Henceforth IM and UH respectively.
23. Emmanuel Levinas, "Quelques réflexions sur la philosophie de l'hitlerisme," *Esprit*, 1934), 199; trans. Seán Hand, "Reflections on the Philosophy of Hitlerism," *Critical Inquiry* 17 (1990): 64. Henceforth RPH and RH respectively. Michel Delherz cites Alain Finkielkraut when he presents "Reflections on the Philosophy of Hitlerism" as an argument in favor of a liberal universalism as opposed to a racist particularism, in "La 'Kehre' levinassienne," *Revue Philosophique de Louvain*, 2002, pp. 129 and 139.
24. Emmanuel Levinas, "The Understanding of Spirituality in French and German Culture," *Continental Philosophy Review* 31 (1998): 10.
25. Emmanuel Levinas, *De l'évasion* (Montpelier: Fata Morgana, 1982), 70; trans. Bettina Bergo, *On Escape* (Stanford: Stanford University Press, 2003), 52. Henceforth DE and OE respectively.
26. See Robert Bernasconi, "No Exit: Levinas's Aporetic Account of Transcendence," *Research in Phenomenology* 35 (2005): 101–17.
27. Emmanuel Levinas, "L'inspiration religieuse de l'Alliance," *Emmanuel Levinas*, ed. Catherine Chalier and Miguel Abernsour (Paris: Editions de l'Herne, 1991), 144.
28. François Poirié, *Emmanuel Levinas. Qui êtes-vous?* (Lyon: La Manufacture, 1987), 83; trans. Jill Robbins and Marcus Coelen, *Is It Righteous to Be?* (Stanford: Stanford University Press, 2001), 39.
29. Emmanuel Levinas, "Etre juif," *Cahier d'Etudes Lévinassiennes* 1 (2002), 103. Henceforth EJ.
30. Frantz Fanon, *Peau noire, masques blancs* (Paris: Seuil, 1952), 112; trans. Charles Lam Markmann, *Black Skin, White Masks* (New York: Grove, 1967), 138.
31. Jean-Paul Sartre, *Critique de la raison dialectique* (Paris: Gallimard, 1960), 289; trans. Alan Sheridan-Smith, *Critique of Dialectical Reason* (London: NLB, 1976), 231. Henceforth CRD and CDR respectively.
32. Robert V. Stone and Elizabeth A. Bowman, "Dialectical Ethics: A First Look at Sartre's Unpublished 1964 Rome Lecture Notes," *Social Text* 13–14 (1986): 205–206.
33. Emmanuel Levinas, *Totalité et Infini* (The Hague: Martinus Nijhoff, 1961), 21; trans. Alphonso Lingis, *Totality and Infinity* (Pittsburgh: Duquesne University Press, 1969), 50.

34. Emmanuel Levinas, "Le moi et la totalité," *Revue de Métaphysique et de Morale* 59 (1954): 367; trans. Alphonso Lingis, *Collected Philosophical Papers* (Dordrecht: Martinus Nijhoff, 1987), 39. Henceforth MT and CP respectively.
35. See, further, Robert Bernasconi, "The Third Party: Levinas on the Intersection of the Ethical and the Political," *Journal of the British Society for Phenomenology* 30.1 (January 1999): 76–87. The full version of this paper, which includes a section on racism that had to be omitted from the English version for reasons of space can be found in Antje Kapust's translation: "Wer ist der Dritte? Uberkreuzung von Ethik und Politik bei Levinas?" *Der Anspruch des Anderen*, ed. B. Waldenfels and I. Därmann (Munich: Wilhelm Fink, 1998), 87–110.
36. See Alex Klaushoper, "The Foreignness of the Other: Universalism and Cultural Identity in Levinas' Ethics," *Journal of the British Society for Phenomenology*, 31.1 (January 2000): 65.
37. I make this argument in "'Only the Persecuted...': Language of the Oppressor, Language of the Oppressed," in *Ethics as First Philosophy*, ed. Adriaan T. Pepezak (New York: Routledge, 1995), 77–86.
38. An earlier version of this paper was delivered at Rhodes University in Grahamstown, South Africa, as part of their centenary celebrations. I am grateful to them for the hospitality I received and for their comments. A German translation by Julia Scheidegger of a marginally different version of this paper was published under the title "Sartre und Levinas: Philosopher gegen Rassismus und Antisemitismus" in *Verfehlte Begegnung. Levinas und Sartre als philosophischen Zeitgenossen*, ed. Thomas Bedorf und Andreas Cremonini (Munich: Wilhelm Fink, 2005), 205–222. I am grateful to the publishers and the editors for permission to publish this text here. I would like to thank Jonathan Judaken for various suggestions that I have been happy to incorporate into the English-language version of this chapter.

Chapter 6

European Intellectuals and Colonial Difference
Césaire and Fanon beyond Sartre and Foucault

George Ciccariello-Maher

This chapter approaches the question of the long and fraught relationship between European philosophy and colonialism from a direction which is—at least at the outset—immanent to Europe itself. That is, I begin by excavating a debate *within* European philosophy in order to grasp both the *limits* of European thought and the parameters of its transcendence.[1] I set out from Foucault's critique of Sartre's assertion that the situation of the intellectual implies an imperative toward totalization with the aspiration to a universal view. Through a focus on the analyses both authors offer of the gaze, we will see that Foucault offers a critique of Sartre's abstract gaze. But Sartre's "lucidity" regarding the materiality of his own intellectual gaze—a lucidity deriving in large part from the existentialist emphasis on the situation—effectively makes his thought more sensitive to the imperatives of thinkers from the anticolonial periphery, specifically Frantz Fanon.

In this way, Sartre's self-reflexive deference to Fanon serves to indicate the limitations of Sartre's own thought while simultaneously allowing that thought to reach outwards. That is to say, it was only by coming to terms with his own situation that Sartre could best contribute to decolonial philosophy, and this contribution takes the form primarily of an understanding of the limits of European philosophy. Moreover, given the importance of this "colonial difference" at the heart of European thought, Sartre's tacit admission that Europeans are not in a position to properly understand *colonialism* implies by extension that European philosophy *cannot even understand itself*.[2]

It is from this perspective that I turn, at the end of the chapter, to a discussion of alter-humanism as it emerges in the thought of Fanon and his predecessor, Aimé Césaire, in order to sketch the parameters of "a humanism made to the measure of the world" which is simultaneously treated as a resolution of the European debate on the intellectual.[3] Put another way, since it is these alter-humanisms that serve as the material vehicle for the very transcendence of Europe, the European debate on the intellectual provides a crucial point of entry to grasp the implications for European thought of formulations of humanism arising in different contexts.

My argument as a whole might appear to take the form of a dialectic that moves backward historically: To a difficulty posed by Foucault, I reply with an answer previously provided by Sartre, only to demonstrate that behind this answer, Fanon's even earlier critique looms large. Finally, I take yet another step back to Césaire, finding in Fanon's teacher the resolution of Foucault's original problematic. But there is nothing backward about this progress, and much less is it arbitrary. Rather, it is a process that some might ironically consider "genealogical": That a racialized Caribbean thinker can provide so potent a reply to a problem formulated two decades later says much about the effectiveness with which colonial difference privileges and universalizes some voices by provincializing and thereby discrediting others.

The Sartre-Foucault Debate: The Situation of the European Intellectual

The divide between Sartre and Foucault on the status of the intellectual was a subset of a broader discussion—the so-called debate on humanism—which raged in European philosophy during the 1950s and 1960s, and whose central points of contention included the essentialization of human nature and the exaggeration of human agency generally associated with the existentialist humanist project.[4] While I will return to the question of humanism later, here I would like to focus on one central difference that separated the radical humanist (broadly existentialist) and radical antihumanist (broadly structuralist and poststructuralist) participants in the debate: that of the relationship between the situation and totalization. As we will see, the existentialist emphasis on the implications of situatedness would prove central to the disagreement between Sartre and Foucault regarding the intellectual, and this disagreement would have prodigious implications for the philosophies and political potential of both.

As it appears in Sartre's seminal *Being and Nothingness*, the situation could not be more central, as it provides the foundation for subjectivity without which there could be no such thing as human freedom. This centrality is clear in the fact that "for the for-itself, to exist and to be situated are one in the same," and already we can sense the weight of the totalizing imperative implied by the situation, since Sartre continues that "the world is the total situation of the for-itself and the measure of its existence."[5] However, this situation is not external to that subjectivity that it enables, since it "is not a pure contingent given ... [but rather] is revealed only to the extent that the for-itself surpasses it toward itself."[6] The situation is best understood, in short, as a combination of the realm of facticity with the subjective response of the for-itself to that facticity, thereby encompassing what might be deemed both structure and agency and defining the freedom of the latter only in active response to the former. This emphasis on the situation—so central to existentialist doctrine from the outset—would have momentous effects on a number of later developments, not least of which concerns Sartre's formulation of the role of the intellectual. Sartre's recognition that intellectuals, like everyone else, exist in a situation requires that they come to terms with the content of that situation. This imperative simultaneously marks Sartre's distance from Foucault's notion of the specific intellectual (since the situation requires totalization) and opens Sartre's thought toward his relation to those in radically different, colonial situations.

In *What Is Literature?* Sartre laid out his devotion to "engaged" writing, which could be interpreted as a self-criticism of the abstractness of his own early philosophy. He makes clear that the "author is in a situation," as is the largely bourgeois reading public.[7] Despite the limitations this might conceivably entail, Sartre nevertheless feels comfortable claiming that reading constitutes a movement toward "the peak of ... freedom."[8] In conjunction with this paradoxical privilege comes the seemingly less comprehensible role that Sartre ascribes to the intellectual, through whose intervention the reading public "will be led by the hand until he is made to see."[9] As Mark Poster describes it: "The writer creates the public.... Sartre proclaims himself philosopher-king, without the need to hold office."[10]

Not surprisingly given his critique of humanism more generally, Foucault takes issue with this view of intellectual production. In "Truth and Power," Foucault attacks the traditional role of the universal intellectual:

> For a long period, the "left" intellectual spoke and was acknowledged the right of speaking in the capacity of master of truth and justice. He was heard, or purported to make himself heard, as the spokesman of the universal.... Just as the proletariat, by the necessity of its historical situation, is the bearer of the universal (but ... barely conscious of itself as such), so the intellectual, through his moral, theoretical, and political choice, aspires to be the bearer of this universality in its conscious, elaborated form.[11]

In opposition to this "spokesman of the universal," Foucault proposes, or rather claims to document the historical rise of an alternative: the "specific" intellectual who works "within specific sectors, at the precise points where their own conditions of life or work situate them." This role has the advantage of providing intellectuals with "a much more immediate and concrete awareness of struggles," and moreover "makes it possible, if not to integrate, at least to rearticulate categories which were previously kept separate."[12] In both the positive claim that "intellectuals have actually been drawn closer to the proletariat and the masses" and the negative worry that such an intellectual "serves the interests of the state and capital," Foucault recognizes and encourages a "shifting [of] the level of analysis to situations in daily life in which the intellectual function is closely bound in practice to the audience."[13] While this effort to "situate" the intellectual might seem to complement the existentialist emphasis on the situation, the contours of Foucault's debate with Sartre reveal their fundamental divergence with regard to intellectual totalization.

This divergence comes into view once we recognize that, while there is an immense value in Foucault's critique, to direct it at Sartre implies the latter's ignorance to such issues, and thus the argument is a bit of a straw man. In *What Is Literature?* Sartre had indeed stressed that "Literature ... manifests the totality of the human condition," but this position was emphatically not a normative one. Rather, the imperative to speak in terms of totality is *dictated by circumstance*, as Sartre continues immediately by emphasizing that, "every day we must take sides."[14] The need to totalize—which means, for Sartre, to seek a universal view—results precisely from the existential emphasis on the need to make decisions from within given situations, and the representation of totality should be interpreted as the specifically *intellectual* imperative arising from the situation, the manner in which the situation impinges on theoretical work. The relation between the situation in which the author finds herself and the imperative to take a total view is explained by Poster, who argues that for Sartre, humans are effectively totalizing beings, whose perceptions (the unification of a field of external elements) and actions (choosing from a field of options) entail a total view. It falls to the theorist, then, to do the same in the sphere of knowledge, and such theoretical totalizations are as a result necessarily imperfect and contextual.[15] Hence totalization, for Sartre, has both an ontological and epistemological moment—pertaining to the "perceiver" and the "conscious actor"—and it is the latter that informs the imperative toward intellectual totalization.[16]

We can therefore see that Sartre approached the equation of knowledge and power *not* in ignorance (as had Heidegger), and not through evasion (as would Foucault with the specific intellectual) but rather, as Neil Levy explains, "Sartre enters into ... doubles [i.e., oppositions] lucidly." He hangs on to contradiction and refuses facile reconciliation, because it is only in this way that thought and action can move forward. For Levy, Foucault's own insistence on maintaining a distance between the transcendental or totalizing and the empirical largely explains his "inability to produce a truly political style of thought." Sartre's totalizing imperative proceeds, then, by holding the universal and the particular in tension, in full knowledge of the risks involved but equally aware of the impossibility of avoiding these risks and the political dangers that attempts to do so would entail. In Levy's words, "We must jump feet first into the doubles; there must be an unthought without possibility of total clarity."[17]

By contrast, Poster identifies a number of problems with Foucault's formulation of the specific intellectual, and two interest me here. First, Foucault failed to live up to the situatedness of the specific intellectual by refusing to accept the particularity of his own voice, manifesting instead a clear preference for anonymity. As a result, he ends up embracing universality "as a cloaked disguise" or, as Poster nicely puts it, "hiding in an epistemological closet."[18] This first difficulty links with a more serious second one, which Poster identifies as a logical contradiction: Foucault's own negation remains on the level of the universal, since it attacks in the broadest of manners any and all who invoke the universal. As a result,

> Foucault himself represents the totality when he denounces totalizing positions.... Foucault's statements about the universal intellectual are themselves universal, and his theory of the specific intellectual is a general theory of the intellectual.... Foucault is implicitly totalizing the situation. Taking a position against totalization, he incurs a totalizing statement.[19]

Put more bluntly: "One cannot avoid the problems of the universal intellectual simply by negating that figure," and it is in this difficulty that we are led to realize the degree to which Foucault's own efforts provide support for Sartre's argument for totalization.[20]

Foucault's own development, moreover, indicated his recognition of the difficulty of this position. In the essay "What is Enlightenment?" presented at Berkeley shortly before his death, Foucault signals a change of heart regarding the flight from the authorial position:

> I think that the Enlightenment, as a set of political, economic, social, institutional, and cultural events on which we still depend in large part, constitutes a privileged domain for analysis.... We must try to proceed with an analysis of ourselves as beings who are historically determined, to a certain extent, by the Enlightenment. Such an analysis [should be] ... oriented ... toward what is not or is no longer indispensable for the constitution of ourselves as autonomous subjects.[21]

Foucault's later work comes to emphasize the critical *ethos* of the Enlightenment as a positive basis for critique, thereby demonstrating the insufficiency of his own earlier positions vis-à-vis Sartre, be they that of the specific intellectual or the absent author. It is in this period—and especially with the second and third volumes of *The History of Sexuality*—that Foucault would come to emphasize the constitution of the self "as a work of art."[22] Given Foucault's return to this understanding of the subject, it is perhaps unsurprising that his aesthetic vision parallels that of Sartre, who had argued earlier that "the moral choice is comparable to the construction of a work of art" in its lack of a priori guidance.[23] This should not imply, however, that Foucault's later phase constitutes a recognition of the need for a universal intellectual. While this move may be interpreted as a gesture *in the direction of totalization*, this gesture remains purely inductive, deriving its legitimacy from "historical repetition."[24] In Foucault's words, the phenomena studied by the intellectual only "have their generality, in the sense that they have continued to recur up to our time.... [This is] the way to analyze questions of general import in their historically unique form."[25]

Before turning to an analysis of the gaze, it is necessary to briefly highlight the fact that Poster's analysis of Foucault's contradiction stops here, deeming the difficulty of the specific intellectual an "aporia" and suggesting the advantages of Sartre's schema.[26] This approach is indicative of a trend in the work of scholars of the Sartre-Foucault debate, whose approach consists of little more than folding intellectual history onto itself, analyzing Foucault's response to Sartre and then proceeding to utilize the latter in an effort to resolve the shortcomings and the aporias of the former.[27] I hope to do something different, showing that while it was Sartre (and to a lesser degree Foucault, through his reconsideration of intellectual totalization) who pointed the way toward resolution of these difficulties, Sartre's development toward a deeper understanding of the situation of the European intellectual, and thereby of the implications of totalization, was spurred on and prefigured by Fanon. Neither Sartre nor Foucault would complete the task, as probably neither was properly equipped to have done so alone. To clarify what some non-European existentialists see as the internal limits of European philosophy, and thereby what sets their view of humanism apart from the pejorative use of the term, I will first consider in detail the role played by the gaze in Sartre, Foucault, and Frantz Fanon.

From Sartre to Fanon: The Materiality of the European Gaze

For both Sartre and Foucault, the gaze or the look of the Other constitutes subjectivity, and for Sartre in *Being and Nothingness*, this alter-subjectivity constitutes objectivity. Such objectivity, however, is founded on a sort of perspectivalism, as it is impossible for me to grasp the world through the subjectivity of the other. There is a distinctly negative feel about Sartre's early formulation, as the Other represents "an object which has stolen the world from me."[28] But this negativity is not at its fullest until the Other turns her look to me, at which point I become an object at the very moment that I realize the subjectivity of the Other. Our two subjectivities slide past one another, existing in a subject/object relationship that, while not being symmetrical at any given moment, is in the words of Levy "infinitely reversible" and as such always at least *potentially symmetrical*.[29] Or put another way, there exists a diachronic symmetry between myself and the other, which is made possible by the reversibility of the subject-object relation. This reversibility is perhaps best expressed in Sartre's discussion of "the Jew" near the end of *Being and Nothingness*: "If ... it pleases me to consider the antisemites as pure *objects*, then my being-a-Jew disappears immediately to give place to the simple consciousness (of) being a free, unqualifiable transcendence."[30] "The Jew" remains—in this early formulation—free to nihilate the Other, and is thereby free in the full sense of the word.

Foucault similarly associates the gaze with a simultaneous subjectification-objectification, although his approach is historical, not ontological.[31] In *The Birth of the Clinic*, as Levy has observed, Foucault chronicles the invention of the object of medical knowledge through the disappearance of the medical subject in the autopsy: gazing upon death serves as "the concrete a priori of medical experience."[32] It was only through such a detour into absence that, in Foucault's words, "Western man could constitute himself in his own eyes as an object of science."[33] *Discipline and Punish* paints a similar picture of the creation of the criminal subject-object through the gaze, but this time it is the gaze of the Panopticon, and "it is the fact of being constantly seen ... that maintains the disciplined individual in his subjection."[34] As Levy correctly points out, Foucault concretizes and historicizes the gaze, attributing it not to an abstract Other, but to the "already 'encoded' eye" of the doctor, prison guard, or teacher, an "authorized" gaze "in which field and gaze are bound together by *codes of knowledge*."[35] Hence, "Foucault brings to the analysis of the gaze a concreteness lacking in Sartre [in *Being and Nothingness*].... The subject/object relation is a power-relation, and as such is not infinitely reversible."[36] Moreover, *Discipline and Punish* shows how the gaze can "become congealed in architecture and in the structures of certain forms of knowledge," or as Martin Jay put it in a passage which is exaggerated but illuminating: "the Panopticon, with its hidden and invisible God, was an architectural embodiment of the most paranoid of Sartrean fantasies."[37] However, this double move—to a gaze expressed through power relations, and then through the material coagulation of those relations—was twice prefigured, first by Sartre and earlier by Fanon.

Levy correctly identifies the first of these prefigurations, noting that in the move from the clinic to the Panopticon, in which the gaze is "depersonalized" and "becomes more an effect of architecture than of individual persons[,] ... Foucault follows the same trajectory as had Sartre before him," as the look of *Being and Nothingness* would give way to the "practico-inert" of *The Critique of Dialectical Reason*.[38] But such a view, concerned as it is with emphasizing the compatibility of Foucault and Sartre, remains blinkered as to the source and stimulus for that shift within the work of the latter. From the infinitely reversible gaze of 1943, Sartre's theory would undergo a long and drawn-out transformation, during the course of which Fanon's influence would be paramount.[39] Specifically, this transformation would take the form of a double shift: First, in shifting from the European gaze to the autonomy of revolutionary violence, Sartre would come to recognize the emergence of a new decolonial subject; second, in shifting from racism to colonialism, Sartre would move from the individual manifestation of that European gaze to its collective, material manifestation, thereby coming to place a proper emphasis on the structure standing opposite the newly recognized revolutionary subject.

From the European Gaze to Revolutionary Violence

The first gesture of this shift occurs between 1944 and 1946, during which time Sartre adds to his earlier discussion of "the Jew" (with reference to an abstract Third) the presence of a more concrete and ubiquitous Third: the Christian or non-Jew. He argues that "even in their most intimate gatherings the Jews could say of the non-Jew what St. John Perse said of the sun: 'He is not named but his presence is among us.'"[40] Not only is the Christian gaze ever-present, but Sartre even suggests at this point that the belief that Jews can eliminate such a gaze represents little more than a "ruse ... of flight" which is "proper to the inauthentic Jew."[41] Moreover, while the reversibility of the gaze remains central in Sartre's 1948 "Black Orpheus," it is not difficult to see how different this gaze had become since *Being and Nothingness*. While the gaze remained "reversible," it was only in the limited sense suggested in *Antisemite and Jew*: the oppressed have no power to nihilate through their gaze and can only force an ethical crisis onto the oppressors through the potential shock of reversal. That is, the gaze can be reversed, but the effects of that reversal are not material. Moreover, and relatedly, the audience remains largely white, and hence this reversal is the moment when "our gaze comes back to our own eyes": "When you removed the gag that was keeping these black mouths shut, what were you hoping for? That they would sing your praises?"[42] The revolutionary violence of the oppressed remained, for the Sartre of 1948, circumscribed in world-historic terms by the European gaze. It is therefore of little surprise that Hegel would weigh heavily upon Sartre's text, and this is where Fanon would attack most forcefully.

In *Black Skin, White Masks*, Fanon addresses Sartre's conceptualization of the gaze, offering a critique on two fronts: against the essentialism of the negritude movement, and against Sartre's simultaneous endorsement of that movement and its inscription within Eurocentric world history.[43] In "Black Orpheus," Sartre had criticized Senghor for mixing the concrete particularity of race with the universal abstract category of class, arguing that "negritude appears as the minor term of a dialectical progression ... [which is] insufficient by itself."[44] But Fanon counters that "the dialectic that brings necessity into the foundation of my freedom drives me out of myself.... I am not a potentiality of something. I am wholly what I am. I do not have to look for the universal."[45] Fanon, moreover, criticizes Sartre for attempting to "Hellenize" negritude by "making an Orpheus out of ... th[e] Negro who is looking for the universal."[46] Behind both passages lies Fanon's objection, less with the dialectic itself than with the fact that Sartre claims to know the outcome in advance, and that this outcome is European.[47]

To put it in terms of our earlier discussion, Sartre's totalization remains bound to Eurocentrism, because he had still not fully digested the implications of his own "situation." Fanon sternly reminds Sartre that all situations are not created equal: Sartre's mistake is rooted in his conception of the gaze of the Other. Fanon argues that

> Sartre had forgotten that the Negro suffers in his body quite differently from the white man.... Though Sartre's speculations on the existence of the Other may be correct ... their application to a black consciousness proves fallacious ... because the white man is not only The Other but also the master, whether real or imaginary.[48]

Hence, while Fanon's understanding of the gaze might seem compatible with Sartre's position in *Being and Nothingness*—in which oppressed groups are constituted by the gaze of a "master" or oppressor—we see the difference when we consider the black body. Black skin is "overdetermined from without" and so just as Fanon criticizes those who would conflate antisemitism with Negrophobia, this same statement can be seen as a preemptive critique of the insufficiency of Foucault's emphasis on the medical subject and the criminal, who despite being defined with relation to an imposed nature are not forced to wear that nature epidermally.[49]

Fanon emphasizes the concreteness and historical ladenness of the gaze, which is asymmetrical in terms of power, but which invokes not only a history of classification, but that of a colonial classification based on phenotype.[50] For Fanon, this historical classification—the Manicheanism of black and white—is the primary source for the rebellion of the oppressed, for "black zeal":

For once, that born Hegelian had forgotten that consciousness has to lose itself in the night of the absolute.... A consciousness committed to experience ... has to be ignorant, of the essences and determinations of its being.... *Orphée Noir* is a date in the intellectualization of the *experience* of being black.[51]

While Fanon would not fully delineate his position regarding the violence of the oppressed until later, it is already visible in embryonic form in this notion of "black zeal."

Largely as a result of Fanon's 1952 critique of his position from the perspective of both racial overdetermination and "black zeal," Sartre would revise his position on the dialectic, and he would do so with regard to the importance of the violence of the oppressed. In his 1961 preface to Fanon's *The Wretched of the Earth*, Sartre writes energetically: "Will we recover? Yes. For violence, like Achilles' lance, can heal the wounds that it has inflicted," adding crucially that *"this is the end of the dialectic."*[52] The violence of the oppressed, in accordance with Fanon's emphatic critique, was now granted full autonomy to construct a new humanism (although Sartre would refrain from identifying the latter by name, referring instead to "humanity").

Moreover, Sartre moves decisively beyond the European gaze by granting full autonomy to the revolutionary periphery as the site of this violence. The dialectic no longer relied on the ethical crisis that would befall Europe when the gaze is returned:

> Europeans, you must open this book.... After a few steps in the darkness you will see strangers gathered around a fire; come close, and listen, for they are talking of the destiny they will mete out to your trading centers and to the hired soldiers who defend them. They will see you, perhaps, but *they will go on talking among themselves, without even lowering their voices.*[53]

Sartre is not unaware of his own status as a member of the European bourgeoisie, and this recognition of his own position encourages his deference to Fanon and others; it is for this reason that he would come to be known as a preface writer.[54] That is, through Sartre's simultaneous recognition of his own situation and the need to totalize he defers—in the role of preface writer—to decolonial thought. In a striking and largely unrecognized display of self-criticism, Sartre even belies that role by emphasizing that "this book [i.e., *Wretched*] had not the slightest need of a preface."[55] Indeed, when he begins his preface, it is by correcting his earlier position on the agency of the periphery by, first, abandoning the idea that it was the Europeans who "removed the gag" for the anticolonial reality in which "the mouths opened by themselves."[56] Second, Sartre explicitly recognizes

Fanon's earlier critique of his tendency to "Hellenize" blacks by attacking Europe for having "hellenized the Asian; she had created a new breed, the Greco-Latin Negroes."[57] Put in different terms, Sartre's simultaneous recognition of the implications of his own situation and the need for intellectual totalization leads him even to the point of deferring that representation of totality to the revolutionary periphery.

If Sartre's deference to Fanon were not clear enough in his responses to the latter's 1952 critique, we can also discern a similar deference to the text in question, *The Wretched of the Earth*. The grammar of Sartre's preface makes this glaringly obvious, since at the crucial point in his essay—at which historical development collides with the present—*Sartre effectively stops talking*. And if we insist on reading Sartre's own words, focusing on the interstices between quotations, we get the same impression:

> 1961. Listen: ... The tone is new. Who dares to speak thus? It is an African, a man from the Third World.... An ex-native, French-speaking, bends that language to new requirements, makes use of it, and speaks to the colonized only.... [H]is aim is to teach them to beat us at our own game.[58]

When Sartre breaks from Fanon's words, it is only to attack those Frenchmen who point to the nation's decline in the hopes of stimulating a rebirth. This gesture is then followed through by a critique of the French Left which culminates in a statement which, like the rest, applies equally well to Sartre himself: While "the more farseeing among us will be, in the last resort, ready to admit this duty and this end"—that is, to eliminate colonialism—it is nevertheless the case that "our worthiest souls contain racial prejudice."[59]

Prompted explicitly by Fanon's critique, Sartre had passed from the purely idealistic capacity for the oppressed to reverse the gaze of the oppressor, to a recognition of the historically constructed limits to that reversibility that nevertheless inscribed the oppressed within the European gaze, and finally on to granting full autonomy to revolutionary violence and the alter-humanism that Fanon believed this violence would yield. In this way, Sartre's development carried him from an unrealistic idealism, to the repressive weight of materialism, and on to a properly Fanonian dialectic.

From Abstract Gaze to Colonial Structure

In parallel with this shift from the gaze of the oppressor to the violence of the oppressed, Sartre would shift his attention from racism *per se* to the structures that supported it as, "in the late 1950s ... the analysis of racism was united with that of colonialism."[60] This, again, followed largely from Fanon's critiques. Social structures—which for Fanon consisted largely of colonial administrations and the colonial imaginary they produced—force us to turn to what he called "sociogeny." In *Black Skin, White Masks*, he writes that despite the seemingly psychoanalytic character of his work, "the effective disalienation of the black man entails an immediate recognition of social and economic realities," and he adds that

> Freud insisted that the individual factor be taken into account through psychoanalysis. He substituted for a phylogenetic theory the ontogenetic perspective. It will be seen that the black man's alienation is not an individual question. *Beside phylogeny and ontogeny there stands sociogeny.*[61]

This principle is intimately related to Fanon's own reformulation and transgression of phenomenology and psychoanalysis, which he deemed insufficient to confront colonial structures, the coagulation of the racist gaze.[62] Sociogeny is the idea that in an abnormal and pathological society, one can do no good by attempting to normalize the victims, and attention needs, on the contrary, to be turned directly to the totality of social structures, to transform the latter through revolutionary activity.

Sociogeny, then, can be seen as a simultaneous rejection of Foucault's specific intellectual (who recognizes structures but fails to confront them) and Sartre's early understanding of the totalizing writer (who seems slightly oblivious to those structures): Fanon's is a rejection per se of the sufficiency of intellectualism. A shift in the revolutionary subject—from European intellectual to decolonial guerrilla—implies a concomitant shift in how we understand both the situation and the totalizing imperative. Once the situation in question is colonialism and we are divested of all idealistic hopes that the European bourgeoisie will act to end it, totalization moves from the *Salon* to the improvised battlefield of decolonial war. This element of Fanon's philosophy is perhaps best expressed in his 1956 resignation from the Algerian psychiatric clinic in Blida-Joinville to join the FLN resistance fighters:

> If psychiatry is the medical technique that aims to enable man no longer to be a stranger to his environment, I owe it to myself to affirm that the Arab, permanently an alien in his own country, lives in a state of absolute depersonalization.... The social structure existing in Algeria was hostile to any attempt to put the individual back where he belonged.... The function of a social structure is to set up institutions to serve man's needs. A society that drives its members to desperate solutions is a non-viable society, a society to be replaced.... There comes a time when silence becomes dishonesty.... And the conclusion is the determination not to despair of man, in other words, of myself.[63]

Once again, Sartre would take his cues largely from Fanon—cues that were certainly reinforced by other thinkers and by Sartre's general intellectual-political context—but would do so in line with his own views regarding the imperative for intellectual totalization.[64]

In his introduction to Albert Memmi's 1957 *The Colonizer and the Colonized*, Sartre critiques Memmi (as well as Sartre's own former self) for failing to recognize that "racism is ingrained in actions, institutions, and the nature of colonialist methods of production and exchange."[65] This argument foreshadowed the elaboration of seriality and the practico-inert in Sartre's *Critique of Dialectical Reason*, in which the link between colonialism and racism would be formulated in the following terms:

> [C]olonialism, as a material system in the practico-inert field of colonisation ... produced its own Idea in its very development.... Colonialism defines the exploited as eternal because it constitutes itself as an eternity of exploitation.... In this form of alterity, it becomes racism. The essence of racism ... is that it is not a system of thoughts which might be false or pernicious.... *It is not a thought at all*. It can never be formulated.... In reality, racism is the colonial interest lived as a link of all the colonialists of the colony through the serial flight of alterity.[66]

Here, in accordance with Fanon's turn to sociogeny, the primary object of inquiry is no longer the racist *attitude*—as had arguably been the case in *Antisemite and Jew*—but rather the coagulation of prior praxis (what Sartre deems the "practico-inert") in colonial structures which only then "produc[es] itself in the language of the colonists."[67] The causality is reversed, and the racism of the individual comes to be seen as the result rather than the basis of colonialism. Finally, perhaps, the Fanonian problematic is most clearly manifested in Sartre's 1964 Rome lecture, in which what had earlier been conceptualized as "simply a form of bad faith attributable in that instance to the slaveholder, was twenty-five years later analyzed in terms of the inevitable violence of the colonial system," and the question of racism had become "the resolution of the contradiction embodied in colonial practice."[68]

While Robert Bernasconi offers a nuanced reading of Sartre's development that follows the broad contours outlined above, it is important to emphasize that his account requires supplementation in one crucial aspect, which is directly relevant to my argument: Bernasconi is at pains to indicate Fanon's reverence for Sartre, yet he presents Sartre's intellectual development (*toward* Fanon) as though it occurred autonomously.[69] While Fanon was certainly not Sartre's *only* influence, Bernasconi's argument has the effect of obscuring all influences, both individual and contextual. His argument that

Sartre's position in the preface was "less vulnerable to Fanon's criticism" and that "Sartre and Fanon were in closer agreement in 1961 than they had been some ten years earlier" prevents Fanon's influence on Sartre from being visible.[70] Moreover, Bernasconi recognizes the importance of Sartre qua preface writer, emphasizing Sartre's deference to Richard Wright's capacity to "complete Sartre's project of showing the oppressor to himself," but the difference with respect to the present argument is twofold: first, in his view the project conspicuously remains "Sartre's," and second (and more importantly), this deference to Wright remains within Sartre's earlier phase of "returning the gaze," prior to his granting autonomy to revolutionary violence. Bernasconi neglects Sartre's deference to Fanon during this latter phase.[71]

This neglect is reproduced in an essay which is ostensibly both more focused on and more sympathetic to Fanon, as Bernasconi suggests that Sartre's preface was "faithful to Fanon" before immediately and suggestively reversing this formulation by predicating this faith upon the fact that "Fanon's brief analysis was itself in full agreement with Sartre's own account."[72] Here, Bernasconi claims that "Fanon's decisive insight was *borrowed explicitly from Sartre*."[73] The question is not whether or not Fanon cites Sartre on the "insight" that colonialists paradoxically cannot eliminate the colonized (he does), nor even whether or not this point was "decisive" within Fanon's framework (which is dubious).[74] What is crucial is that Bernasconi misses *Fanon's influence on Sartre*, erasing the possibility that Fanon's 1952 critique (which Sartre read closely) had *any impact* on the later *Critique of Dialectical Reason*.[75]

Though Bernasconi raises the possibility that Fanon influenced Sartre's reformulation of the dialectic, he discounts his influence, arguing that "it is clear from some of Sartre's other writings that he already understood the unifying aspect of violence."[76] But, I think this too readily equates the end of the dialectic with the "unifying aspect of violence," an error compounded by a quick reference to the *Critique* (which appears too late to prove Bernasconi's point), and further by his reference to a 1952 essay which equates violence and humanism, but does so with reference to a strike by French workers (thereby revealing the degree to which this essay remained within the frame of "black Orpheus," in which the *Western working class* owned the "end of the dialectic"). Despite Bernasconi's "deference to Fanon" regarding the *content* of new humanism, it appears that Bernasconi's Fanon would only be able to provide that content by having drawn upon the pages of Sartre's *Critique*.[77] Instead, I have emphasized that Fanon's influence on Sartre was significant, rather than only the other way around.

This discussion of Sartre's development toward a more Fanonian sociogenic perspective brings us back full circle to Foucault and the evasion of totalization embodied by his specific intellectual. While we have seen that Foucault shifted drastically away from his earlier emphasis on the "specific" intellectual, his later approach remained purely inductive, and so while the intellectual was able to totalize, this could only be the totalization of the Owl of Minerva. We are left, then, to wonder about the political implications of this gesture. In a passage too often overlooked, Edward Said addresses the counterposition of Fanon and Foucault, "both of whom stress the unavoidable problematic of immobilization and confinement at the centre of the Western system of knowledge and discipline," but whose responses to that problematic could not differ more starkly:

> Fanon's work programmatically seeks to treat colonial and metropolitan societies together, as discrepant but related identities, while Foucault's work moves further and further away from serious consideration of social wholes, focusing instead upon the individual.... [I]gnoring the imperial context of his own theories, Foucault seems actually to represent an irresistible colonizing movement that paradoxically fortifies the prestige of both the lonely individual scholar and the system that contains him. Both ... have Hegel, Marx, Freud, Nietzsche, Canguihelm, and Sartre in their heritage, yet only Fanon presses that formidable arsenal into antiauthoritarian service. Foucault ... swerves away from politics entirely.[78]

For Said, Fanon's insistent totalization makes him a profoundly radical thinker, while Foucault's rejection of the intellectual need to address such "social wholes" allows his own situation—his "imperial context"—to intervene and outweigh the critical potential of his philosophy.

Foucault, then, succumbs to the "unavoidable problematic of immobilization," neglecting the fact that anything said from Europe, or more specifically anything said by an influential European philosopher, inevitably runs the risk of being filtered through colonial difference, and is thereby self-totalizing, to be applied to such "social wholes" regardless of Foucault's intent. Foucault's fear of the negative effects of the totalizing gaze blinds him to the fact that, once inversely totalized, this fear would manifest as a supremely dismissive European gaze that would imperially erase other histories and other humanisms. In his oft-repeated clarification—"I am speaking here only of Western intellectuals"—Foucault wrongly assumes, first, that one can speak of Western intellectuals in a vacuum (that is, outside a history of colonialism), and second, that his statements will actually be interpreted as provincially as he would hope.[79] Ironically, then, while Foucault would emphasize the materiality of the panoptical gaze, he would fail to effectively portray the materiality of *his own gaze*—his own situation and his own perspective—due to his denial of the totalizing imperative.

Sartre, on the other hand, by taking his cues from Fanon and the revolutionary periphery—even to the point of *altering his position on the dialectic of world history*—was able to move forward convincingly. This is not meant to imply that this divergence between Sartre and Foucault was at all accidental: to the contrary, Sartre's openness to Fanon derives directly from the "lucidity" with which he approached the totalizing imperative of the intellectual, a position that was in turn rooted in the existentialist emphasis on the situation. It was in the painful recognition of the *double materiality* of the abstract and intellectual gaze that Sartre would excel and, spurred by Fanon, provide significant insights into the limits of European thought. More precisely, while the Sartre of *Being and Nothingness* failed to recognize the materiality of the gaze *per se*, by 1947 (*What Is Literature?*) Sartre had explicitly recognized the materiality of *his own* intellectual gaze, and this recognition was arguably rooted in the basic assumptions of existentialism itself regarding the situation. Sartre's position on the intellectual would then serve as the vital conduit through which Fanon's influence would manifest itself, dragging the former beyond Europe.

In acknowledging the importance of Sartre's thought in this manner, we are immediately led to interrogate the implications of such a gesture. If Sartre could follow in the footsteps of Fanon, what does this tell us about the limits of European philosophy? In the next section, I look anew at the pathways of an alter-humanism opened by the work of Fanon, Sartre, and Césaire, pathways that no longer reinscribe philosophical agency within its traditional European locus.

Césaire, Fanon, and Alter-Humanism

As mentioned earlier, the disagreement between Sartre and Foucault on the subject of intellectual totalization was embedded within a broader debate on the merits of humanism, and it is therefore unsurprising that many critiques of intellectual Eurocentrism—especially those of an existentialist bent—are couched in terms of the purported humanist/antihumanist opposition. As will be seen, both Fanon and his teacher, the negritude poet Aimé Césaire, take European critiques of traditional humanism—such as those offered by Foucault—as an occasion to critique formulations like that of the specific intellectual, showing its complicity with both the classical humanism it opposes and the fascism from which it draws its prime examples.

Sartre's own later strategic repudiation of the term notwithstanding, he offers a crucial distinction between two *types* of humanism. The classical version, which "upholds man as the end-in-itself and as the supreme value ... according to the most distinguished deeds of certain men," is thereby "absurd ... since man is still to be determined." Moreover, beyond mere absurdity, Sartre sees a clear danger in such notions, as "the cult of humanity ends in Comtian humanism, shut-in upon itself, and—this must be said— in Fascism." Despite this, and in accordance with the importance we have seen Sartre place on the need to seek a total view, he rejects any suggestion that classical humanism exhausts the potential for humanism more generally, since "there is another sense of the word, of which the fundamental meaning is this: Man is all the time outside of himself: it is in projecting and losing himself beyond himself that he makes man exist."[80] Sartre's distinction points in the direction also pursued by Césaire, who seconds the link to fascism but does so more explicitly through a two-pronged attack on the coagulated architecture of colonialism and the specific intellectual whose raison d'être it is to uncritically philosophize from the wrong end of that architecture.

Césaire seeks to teach "the very distinguished, very humanistic, very Christian bourgeois of the twentieth century that without his being aware of it, he has a Hitler inside of him, that Hitler *inhabits him*, that Hitler is his *demon.*"[81] Like Sartre, Césaire deems this "sordidly racist" ideology "pseudo-humanism" and distinguishes it from the potential for a substantive humanism, noting that, "at the very time when it most often mouths the word, the West has never been further from being able to live a true humanism—a humanism made to the measure of the world."[82] This is because it is precisely when faced with historical adversity that the existential condition makes itself known, and despite correctly diagnosing the ills of humanism, Europeans are still on the winning end of history—having only recently tasted for themselves the dangers of pseudo-humanism—and can therefore take comfort in critique itself. In a strikingly prescient passage, Césaire issues a denunciation that can be productively interpreted as a preemptive critique of Foucault's simultaneous rejection of humanism and intellectual totalization:

> Therefore, comrade, you will hold as enemies—loftily, lucidly, consistently— not only sadistic governors and greedy bankers, not only prefects who torture and colonists who flog ... but likewise and for the same reason ... goitrous academics, wreathed in dollars and stupidity, ethnographers who go in for metaphysics ... chattering intellectuals born stinking out of the thigh of Nietzsche ... the hoodwinkers, the hoaxers, the hot-air artists, the humbugs, and in general, all those who ... try in diverse ways and by infamous diversions to split up the forces of Progress—even if it means denying the very possibility of Progress ... all of them responsible, all hateful, all slave-traders, all henceforth answerable for the violence of revolutionary action.[83]

Is this metaphysical ethnographer Lévi-Strauss? Is this chattering Nietzschean Foucault himself? If so, Césaire does more than criticize their passivity: He condemns them as collaborators.

This collaboration appears most unmistakably in Césaire's argument that, "at the end of formal humanism and philosophical renunciation, there is Hitler."[84] Aside from the straightforward attempt to reorient interpretations of Nazism and fascism, what is most crucial in this passage for our purposes is the explicit coupling of classical humanism with the "philosophical renunciation" of the specific intellectual. Césaire, then, fully recognizes the errors of what would most famously become the Foucauldian formulation of the intellectual by emphasizing the implications of occupying the situation of the European philosopher, and he adds the political charge of collaboration with the colonial system to drive the point home. Moreover, as we see in the passage above, the philosophical renunciation of the specific intellectual is but a particular moment of a broader attack on progress, in which the specific intellectual overlaps directly with the rejection of humanism.

For Césaire, the denial of the potential for progress and philosophical renunciation are more than collaboration through ignorance; they represent an *inversion of pseudo-humanism itself*, and it is here that complicity is most apparent. Those who deny progress, through their denial of an alternative humanism, are performing the same universalizing move as the pseudo-humanists and *doing so from the same location*: Europe. Such a denial is intimately related to Foucault's specific intellectual, since his aversion to totalization made him unwilling or incapable of recognizing the universalizing implications of his privileged position as an influential European philosopher. Just as empirical arguments for the specific intellectual are generated in the core (Foucault, after all, consciously limited himself to studying Western history) toward the end of dismissing all totalization, so too are such arguments deployed to issue a universal dismissal of humanism.

Such a gesture, moreover, reveals a reliance on a Eurocentric notion of "universal" that is derived in the history of Western philosophy precisely through its opposition to the particular. According to Césaire, this notion of the universal is ill-fitting for a humanity defined by particulars, and his formulation of humanism rejects any zero-sum tradeoff between particularity and the aspiration to a total understanding:

> I'm not going to confine myself to some narrow particularism. But I don't intend either to become lost in a disembodied universalism.... I have a different idea of a universal. It is a universal rich with all that is particular, rich with all the particulars there are, the deepening of each particular, the coexistence of them all.[85]

Césaire's alter-humanism, then, can be productively interpreted as embodying the resolution of the debate between Sartre and Foucault regarding the role of the intellectual—one that emphasizes more than either thinker the degree to which the situation of the European intellectual is a dangerously blinkered one.

Fanon—whom we have already seen to be the central impetus for Sartre's own theoretical radicalization—speaks of pseudo-humanism in the same terms as Césaire, but is more blunt regarding the inability of Europe to solve its own problems: "Leave this Europe where they are never done talking of Man, yet murder men wherever they find them.... Come, then, comrades, the European game has finally ended; we must find something different."[86] Humanism is formulated by Fanon as having been *identified* by Europe as a goal, but is a goal which *by definition cannot be resolved from within Europe*:

> It is the question of the Third World starting a new history of Man, a history which will have regard to the sometimes prodigious theses which Europe has put forward, but which will also not forget Europe's crimes, of which the most horrible was committed in the heart of man, and consisted of the pathological tearing away of his functions and the crumbling away of his unity.[87]

Europe had indeed discovered the question of universal humanism, but in doing so had raised barriers to the resolution of that very problematic, chief among which are colonialism and the superexploitation of the periphery, not to mention the "crumbling" of the totalizing humanist project through the uncritical celebration of the specific intellectual. By failing to confront these issues directly, by failing to come to terms with his own situation as a European philosopher, Foucault imposed an insurmountable limitation on himself, and this self-imposed limitation is the same limit that is internal to European thought as a whole.

The humanism that emerges from Fanon's oeuvre is, as has been often noted, one which is self-consciously (and self-critically) open and undefined, an empty space to be filled by radical thought and politics. But this is not to imply that it lacks content: Quite to the contrary, we have seen the axes along which Fanon's critique of Sartre—and, by extension, of European philosophy—coalesced, and it is precisely those axes that (inversely) constitute humanism. That is to say, Fanon's humanism is not a fixed concept to be thrust forward into history, but rather an idea, negatively defined through critique of *what it is not*. First and foremost, Fanon's humanism is neither classical humanism nor radical antihumanism, but it takes its coordinates largely from the shortcomings of both. Like the latter, it is resolutely antiessentialist (the faulty translation of the title of the fifth chapter of *Black*

Skin, White Masks notwithstanding), and this is precisely the root of Fanon's struggle with Senghor's negritude.[88] However, against radical antihumanism, *Black Skin, White Masks* eventually endorses a certain strategic essentialism in the guise of "black zeal," the strategic relevance of which would expire by the time Fanon engaged in a harsher critique of negritude a few years later.[89]

Fanon's humanism retains a link between agency and situation, but agency cannot be reduced to ontogenesis. The appeal to sociogeny is thus a direct reply to the crimes of classical humanism (i.e., colonialism), one that breaks equally with radical antihumanism and its crippling allergy to totalization. However, these coordinates—adopted through Fanon's engagement with European thought—are then radically transposed, and it is here that we see the precise distinction between Sartre and Fanon. While Sartre's thought on the subject of colonialism was largely inspired and encouraged by Fanon's critiques—to paraphrase, he was led by the hand until he was made to see—there was a clear limit beyond which Sartre *could not* progress. While this limit is suggested in Sartre's deference to Fanon, it effectively exceeds that gesture: remember, after all, that Sartre remains silent on humanism in his preface. Sartre *could not will himself beyond the colonial difference*. It was not merely the case that Sartre had recognized his own inability to formulate a new humanism: He was, until the very end, unable to admit that such a thing could exist without the risk of a return to classical humanism.[90] The difference between Sartre's radical European humanism and Fanon's alter-humanism of the periphery is most visible at the moment when the former refuses to recognize its own existence, disavows itself.

Fanon's position vis-à-vis colonial difference, on the other hand, bestowed a significance on the autonomy of the revolutionary periphery which, while *nominally* recognized by Sartre, was not in the end recognized for what it was: a new, alter-humanism.[91] Humanism, for Fanon, was to be approached asymptotically through liberatory activity: historical struggles are the "oxygen which creates and shapes a new humanity," and hence Fanonian humanism is perhaps most elaborately delineated in his discussions of the Algerian Revolution, in which the veil, radio and medical technology, and the family structure were all radically transformed in accordance with the strategic needs of liberation, as a result of the fact that "independence produces the spiritual and material conditions for the reconversion of man."[92] In this way, Fanon's "new humanism … is *prefigured in the objectives and methods of the conflict*," and these "objectives and methods" arose, in Fanon's context, as the two stages of the liberation: "During the colonial period the people are called upon to fight against oppression; after national liberation, they are called upon to fight against poverty, illiteracy, and underdevelopment."[93]

In an era in which this second stage is far from complete, it is more crucial than ever before to retain these negative coordinates of Fanonian humanism in order to effectively combat the various mystifications that threaten our understanding of the course of liberation.[94] This analysis should be interpreted as a reminder that, above all, Fanonian humanism entails an epistemological recognition of the situation of the intellectual that simultaneously recognizes the materiality of the European gaze and the need to totalize and that, above all, remains open to correction both from Fanon himself and from the demands of political struggles in the revolutionary periphery.

Conclusion

We have seen that the European debate between Sartre and Foucault on the intellectual offers especially potent insights into the foundations of European thought and the limits that those foundations impose. In this chapter I have sought to show, first, that a central point of contention between Sartre and Foucault—that of the totalizing imperative of the intellectual—is crucial to the interpretation of these thinkers, due to both the fact that Foucault would later admit the shortcomings of his earlier position and, more importantly, because Sartre's position on the intellectual would make him more receptive to the influence of radical decolonial thought. Second, I have shown that Sartre's deference to Fanon then manifested as a reconceptualization of the gaze, which came to recognize both the material coagulation of the gaze in colonial structures and the concomitant imperative to defer to those on the other end of the colonial difference, both philosophically and politically. Finally, I have considered the insights that Césaire and Fanon offer on the subject of the European intellectual, insights that draw us into their respective formulations of an alter-humanism, formulations that can be seen as resolving the aporias of the European intellectual. Coming to terms with the epistemological implications of the Sartre-Foucault debate on the intellectual thereby puts us in a better position to reenter into a discussion of alter-humanism—which has increasingly become a central reference point for contemporary radical and revolutionary movements—without falling into the kindred errors of classical humanism and radical antihumanism, and moreover without the temptation to neglect our own situation as privileged intellectuals whose gaze carries a certain material weight. The "European game" is certainly as consequential as it has always been, but its importance now—as it has been historically—is largely measured in terms of its capacity to do harm, and while we must be mindful of the situations it creates, we will get nowhere by remaining trapped within it or mesmerized by it.

Notes

1. While I speak of "European" philosophy, my conclusions might equally apply, with necessary adjustments, to much of what is commonly referred to as the "West," i.e., to former and present colonizers in opposition to the colonized.
2. On the colonial difference, see Walter D. Mignolo, "The Geopolitics of Knowledge and the Colonial Difference," *The South Atlantic Quarterly* 101.1 (Winter 2002): 57–96. While some thinkers—most notably Enrique Dussel—argue that it is both *possible* and *ethically necessary* to begin from the perspective of exteriority, this study implies that this necessity is equally *epistemological*.
3. Aimé Césaire, *Discourse on Colonialism*, trans. J. Pinkham (New York: Monthly Review, 2000), 73.
4. This debate was not won by the merits of poststructuralism alone, and thinkers like Foucault would eventually return to existentialist themes once Sartre had been dispensed with.
5. Jean-Paul Sartre, *Being and Nothingness: A Phenomenological Essay on Ontology*, trans. H. Barnes (New York: Washington Square, 1956 [1943]), 408–409.
6. Ibid., 409.
7. Jean-Paul Sartre, *What Is Literature?* trans. B. Frechtman (New York: Washington Square, 1966 [1947]), 101.
8. Ibid., 187.
9. Ibid., 197.
10. Mark Poster, *Critical Theory and Poststructuralism: In Search of a Context* (Ithaca: Cornell University Press, 1989), 45.
11. Foucault, "Truth and Power" [1976], in Paul Rabinow, ed., *The Foucault Reader* (New York: Pantheon, 1984 [1983]), 67. We should bear in mind that in this interview, Foucault makes clear that "I am speaking here only of Western intellectuals" (69). I will discuss the importance of this clarification later.
12. Ibid., 68.
13. Ibid., 68; 72. Poster, *Critical Theory and Poststructuralism*, 48.
14. Sartre, *What Is Literature?* 192.
15. Mark Poster, *Foucault, Marxism, and History: Mode of Production versus Mode of Information* (Cambridge: Polity, 1984), 22.
16. Ibid., 21.
17. Neil Levy, *Being Up-To-Date: Foucault, Sartre, and Postmodernity* (New York: Peter Lang, 2001), 73–74, first emphasis added.
18. Poster, *Foucault, Marxism, and History*, 24. Poster, *Critical Theory and Poststructuralism*, 51.
19. Poster, *Critical Theory and Poststructuralism*, 49.
20. Ibid., 50.
21. Michel Foucault, "What Is Enlightenment?" [1984] in Rabinow, *The Foucault Reader*, 42–43.
22. Foucault, "On a Genealogy of Ethics: An Overview of Work in Progress," in Rabinow, *The Foucault Reader*, 351.
23. Jean-Paul Sartre, *Existentialism and Humanism*, trans. P. Mairet (London: Methuen, 1948 [1946]), 48–49.
24. Poster, *Critical Theory and Poststructuralism*, 64–65.
25. Foucault, "What Is Enlightenment?" 49.
26. To his credit, however, Poster adds that such an aporia "cannot be dismissed as a logical oddity without material effects." Poster, *Critical Theory and Poststructuralism*, 49, cf. 65.

27. This is equally the case with Neil Levy, and in a different way with Robert Bernasconi. I will explore the implications of such undertakings later.
28. Sartre, *Being and Nothingness*, 343.
29. Levy, *Being Up-To-Date*, 78.
30. Sartre, *Being and Nothingness*, 674–75.
31. Levy, *Being Up-To-Date*, 79–80.
32. Ibid., 81–82. Michel Foucault, *The Birth of the Clinic: An Archaeology of Medical Perception*, trans. A. M. Sheridan Smith (New York: Vintage, 1973), 196.
33. Foucault, *The Birth of the Clinic*, 197.
34. Michel Foucault, *Discipline and Punish: The Birth of the Prison*, trans. Alan Sheridan (London: Penguin, 1986 [1975]), 187.
35. Michel Foucault, *The Order of Things: An Archaeology of the Human Sciences*, trans. Alan Sheridan (New York: Vintage, 1973 [1966]), xxi. See also Levy, *Being Up-To-Date*, 82. Foucault, *The Birth of the Clinic*, 90.
36. Levy, *Being Up-To-Date*, 82.
37. Ibid., 83. Martin Jay, *Downcast Eyes: The Denigration of Vision in Twentieth-Century French Thought* (Berkeley: University of California Press, 1994), 410.
38. Ibid., 178 n.9.
39. See Robert Bernasconi, "Sartre's Gaze Returned: The Transforming of the Phenomenology of Racism," *Graduate Faculty Philosophy Journal* 18.2 (1995): 201–21.
40. Jean-Paul Sartre, *Antisemite and Jew*, trans. G. Becker (New York: Schocken, 1948 [1946]), 102.
41. Ibid.
42. Jean-Paul Sartre, "Black Orpheus" [1948], in *"What Is Literature?" and Other Essays*, trans. B. Frechtman (Cambridge, Mass.: Harvard University Press, 1988), 291.
43. For a discussion of both sides of this critique, see Robert Bernasconi, "The Assumption of Negritude: Aimé Césaire, Frantz Fanon, and the Vicious Circle of Racial Politics," *parallax* 8.2 (2002), 69–83.
44. Sartre, "Black Orpheus," 326. This statement should be contrasted with *Being and Nothingness*, in which Sartre analyzed both race *and* class with regard to the look. See Bernasconi, "Sartre's Gaze Returned," 218 n.54.
45. Frantz Fanon, *Black Skin, White Masks*, trans. C. L. Markmann (New York: Grove, 1962 [1952]), 135.
46. Ibid., 186.
47. This is not to imply, however, that the two had the same understanding of the dialectic. See, e.g., Lou Turner, "On the Difference between the Fanonian and Hegelian Dialectic of Lordship and Bondage," in L. Gordon, T. D. Sharpley-Whiting, and R. White, eds., *Fanon: A Critical Reader* (Malden, Mass.: Blackwell, 1996), 134–51.
48. Fanon, *Black Skin, White Masks*, 138. However, as Bernasconi makes clear, this seeming critique is based upon a Sartrean understanding of race. Bernasconi, "The Assumption of Negritude," 75.
49. Ibid., 116; 157.
50. On this, see Aníbal Quijano, "The Coloniality of Power and Social Classification," trans. G. Ciccariello-Maher, forthcoming in R. Grosfoguel, N. Maldonado-Torres, and J. David Saldivar, eds., *Coloniality, Transmodernity, and Border Thinking*. Spanish original available in *Journal of World-Systems Research* 11.2 (2000): 342–86. Available online at http://jwsr.ucr.edu.
51. Fanon, *Black Skin, White Masks*, 133–34.

52. Jean-Paul Sartre, "Preface," in Frantz Fanon, *The Wretched of the Earth*, trans. C. Farrington (New York: Grove, 1963 [1961]), 30–31, my emphasis.
53. Ibid., 13, emphasis added.
54. Bernasconi, "Sartre's Gaze Returned," 207. As I will discuss later, Bernasconi underestimates the importance of this turn to preface writing by reading it through Sartre's early problematic of reversing the gaze.
55. Sartre, "Preface," 24.
56. Sartre, "Black Orpheus," 291. Sartre, "Preface," 7.
57. Sartre, "Preface," 8.
58. Ibid., 9–10.
59. Ibid., 21.
60. Bernasconi, "Sartre's Gaze Returned," 211.
61. Fanon, *Black Skin, White Masks*, 10–11, emphasis added.
62. See Lewis R. Gordon, "The Black and the Body Politic: Fanon's Existential Phenomenological Critique of Psychoanalysis," in Gordon, Sharpley-Whiting, and White, eds., *Fanon*, 83.
63. Frantz Fanon, "Letter to the Resident Minister (1956)," in *Toward the African Revolution*, trans. H. Chevalier (New York: Grove, 1988 [1964]), 53–54.
64. Accordingly, I would agree at least in part that "his letter of resignation signaled a rupture with Sartrean existentialism," but such a view wrongly portrays the latter as a monolithic and hermetically sealed unity. Turner, "On the Difference between the Fanonian and Hegelian Dialectic of Lordship and Bondage," 135.
65. Jean-Paul Sartre, "Introduction," in Albert Memmi, *The Colonizer and the Colonized*, trans. H. Greenfeld (Boston: Beacon, 1967 [1957]), xxiv.
66. Jean-Paul Sartre, *Critique of Dialectical Reason*, trans. A. Sheridan-Smith (London: Verso, 1976 [1960]), 300 n.88.
67. Bernasconi, "Sartre's Gaze Returned," 212.
68. Ibid., 213.
69. Ibid., 217 n.46.
70. Ibid., 210.
71. Bernasconi, "Sartre's Gaze Returned," 207.
72. Robert Bernasconi, "Casting the Slough: Fanon's New Humanism for a New Humanity," in Gordon, Sharpley-Whiting, and White, eds., *Fanon*, 114.
73. Bernasconi, "Casting the Slough," 119, my emphasis. Thanks to Marilyn Nissim-Sabat for bringing this passage to my attention.
74. Fanon, *The Wretched of the Earth*, 84–85 n. This paradox is of course central, but only as a sort of framework of facticity which was moreover self-evident to Fanon. The larger insight within which this passage appears is the discussion of the colonial world as Manichean, as an extension of the framework that Fanon had delineated in *Black Skin, White Masks*.
75. Macey suggests that "there is no indication that Sartre had read or even heard of Fanon until *Les Temps modernes* published the chapter from *L'An V* in May–June 1959." David Macey, *Frantz Fanon: A Biography* (New York: Picador, 2000), 452. But, my argument shows that there exist good textual reasons, most specifically in the preface, to believe that Sartre had indeed read Fanon earlier than this. While the self-criticism of the preface is compatible with Macey's historical argument, this would entail that Sartre, after having read *L'An V*, returned immediately to *Black Skin, White Masks*, digested that work (or at least the parts critical of himself), and accepted those critiques fully. Moreover, this scenario would also imply that Sartre's development up to that point had been—by mere unconscious coincidence—following the contours of those very same unknown critiques.

Textual analysis aside, Macey points out that portions of *Black Skin, White Masks* had appeared in the Parisian journal *Esprit*, which "was widely regarded as one of the great expressions of the spirit of the wartime Resistance," and even compares the small journal politically to Sartre's own *Les Temps modernes* (154). It was through *Esprit* that Fanon came into contact with Editions du Seuil, which shared an office with *Esprit* and would publish *Black Skin, White Masks*. Fanon's editor at Seuil was none other than Francis Jeanson, a radical anticolonial intellectual who would later work directly for the Algerian FLN, and whose first book was devoted entirely to Sartre. At the time, Jeanson was also editorial director at Sartre's own *Les Temps modernes*. And simultaneous to the publication of *Black Skin, White Masks*, Jeanson was embroiled in the Sartre-Camus debate due to his critical review of the latter's *L'Homme revolté* in May 1952 (Macey, 161). See also Mark Poster, *Existential Marxism in Postwar France: From Sartre to Althusser* (Princeton: Princeton University, 1975), 185–89). Jeanson would later pen a famous open letter to Sartre in 1960 and Sartre would make a number of enemies in his defense of Jeanson, who was standing trial for aiding the FLN. That Sartre would have no knowledge of Fanon's book, in which Sartre himself figured prominently, and for which Jeanson would write an extended preface, seems unlikely even if we forget for a moment the suggestive shifts in Sartre's understanding of race and colonialism (see Macey, 159). What is even more likely is that Sartre had read Fanon's anonymous editorials in *El Moudjahid*. We would be missing a large part of the picture if we were to limit our view to the question of whether or not Sartre cited Fanon's work or claimed openly to be inspired by it: That he did not may merely be part of the problem. After all, how often did Sartre cite Fanon after 1961?

76. Bernasconi, "Casting the Slough," 119.
77. Ibid., 120.
78. Edward W. Said, *Culture and Imperialism* (London: Vintage, 1993), 335–36.
79. Foucault, "Truth and Power," 69.
80. Sartre, *Existentialism and Humanism*, 54–56.
81. Césaire, *Discourse on Colonialism*, 36.
82. Ibid., 73.
83. Ibid., 54–55.
84. Ibid., 36.
85. Cited in Robin D. G. Kelley, "A Poetics of Anticolonialism," in Césaire, *Discourse on Colonialism*, 25–26.
86. Fanon, *The Wretched of the Earth*, 311–12.
87. Ibid., 315.
88. Fanon, "The Fact of Blackness," *Black Skin, White Masks*, 109–40. This translation is positively misleading, as the literal rendering is "The Lived Experience of the Black."
89. Fanon, *The Wretched of the Earth*, 215–17.
90. Such a limit is, perhaps, also visible in Sartre's position on Zionism which, at the height of the Six Day War of 1967, would lead Fanon's widow to demand the removal of Sartre's preface. Macey, *Frantz Fanon*, 467. See also Edward Said's reflections on Sartre's persistent Zionism in Edward Said, "My Encounter with Sartre," *London Review of Books* 22.11 (1 June 2000), http://www.lrb.co.uk/v22/n11/saido1_.html.
91. Accordingly, Sartre's recognition of the new "end of the dialectic" is one which remains largely at the empirical level, as a recognition of historical development, but one which bestows no additional significance on this new humanism.

92. Frantz Fanon, *A Dying Colonialism*, trans. H. Chevalier (New York: Grove, 1965 [1959]), 179; 181.
93. Fanon, *The Wretched of the Earth*, 246, emphasis added. Fanon, *The Wretched of the Earth*, 93–94.
94. Here I refer most directly to the recently rekindled debate regarding power and the state, in which intellectuals like John Holloway and Antonio Negri/Michael Hardt advocate deterritorialization and anti-Institutionalism in the face of glaring evidence that those engaged in liberatory struggle are placing transformative demands on the state and using the state as a transformative tool (for e.g., Bolivia and Venezuela). For a coherent critique of Holloway and Negri that doesn't fall into old left reductionism, see Enrique Dussel, "From Critical Theory to the Philosophy of Liberation," trans. G. Ciccariello-Maher, forthcoming in R. Grosfoguel, N. Maldonado-Torres, and J. David Saldivar, eds., *The Decolonial Turn*.

Part III

Sartre and Africana Existentialism

Chapter 7

Sartre and Black Existentialism

Lewis R. Gordon

I would love to have had a cup of coffee with Jean-Paul Sartre. Had I the opportunity, I would first thank him for his courage. He fought not only the antihuman forces of antisemitism and antiblack racism in French and American society, but also those vices within him that always offered the seduction of an easy way out. I also wonder if his academic and political critics of today could defend their values under the threats faced by him when he defended his. Think of the five thousand war veterans marching down the Champs-Élysées in 1960 chanting, "Kill Sartre!" in response to his support of Algerian independence. Think of the death threats and assassination attempts by the Organisation de l'Armée Secrète (OAS), who bombed his apartment. Think of his refusal to tour the United States during the Vietnam War. And think of his rejection of the Nobel Prize for Literature on the avowed grounds of belonging to no institution. He stood his ground, as best he could, which, for a human being, could not have been other than imperfect. Indeed that imperfection was at the heart of his committed atheism, which insisted that the human condition demanded that we face the world without God's support.[1] His response was to live that condition, and beyond the many bad readings of his critique of social reality, to do so with concern for the lives of others. His understanding of the struggle for freedom and what it means to be historical while engaged in socially transformative projects was coterminous. This made him a constant ally of black existential thought and black liberation struggles throughout most of the twentieth century, since his emphasis on what it means to be a human being was a shared interest of people whose humanity has been denigrated in the modern world.

Sartre's involvement with black existential philosophy was, however, not as an outsider. In my introduction to *Existence in Black: An Anthology of Black Existential Philosophy*, I argued that black existential philosophy is not only existential philosophy produced by black philosophers.[2] It is also thought that addresses the intersection of problems of existence in black contexts. One does not have to be black to raise and study such concerns. Some scholars are so committed to such issues that they become lived realities for them. In their social associations and political commitments, they become organically linked to the causes of communities in which they were not born. They receive, as well, the wrath from bigoted forces for their clear allegiance. It is in this sense that Sartre is also an insider to black existential philosophy.[3] He did not relate to black existential thought in an ethnographic way but as a participant in its living debates, critical reflections, and political structure. His interest in the condition of blacks was animated by concerns for freedom and an appreciation of black aesthetic production as a leitmotif of the modern world. The question of freedom for him was straightforward. Blacks are people, which means, from the perspective of his philosophy, that they are freedom. Their bondage and the subsequent institutional limitations imposed upon them by racism lead to an antisocial world, one committed to the eradication of freedom. It also leads to a form of suffering that is a function of *unfreedom*, where a free being is either repressed through violence or denies his or her freedom. The unfree include those paralyzed in their situation because of fear and anxiety over what the unknown offers, as well as the individuals who comfort themselves in the denial of other people's freedom.

Either position requires a social world in which the meeting of human phenomena as phenomena (which, for human beings, when genuinely achieved, is also noumena) is the greatest fear. This dynamic of anxiety-riddled freedom permeates Sartre's work on what he refers to, in his early writings, as "human reality." He refers to unfreedom in *Being and Nothingness* as "*mauvaise foi*" (bad faith), a lie to ourselves in the effort to hide from our freedom, to make ourselves believe what we do not believe, to make of ourselves an unconscious "thing" in the world, or to deny that we are in a world of other human beings.[4] As early as *L'Imaginaire* (1940), Sartre had pointed out that we sometimes even try to deny the role we play in the images we construct.[5] Consider his rejection of phenomenalism, which he presents through a critique of the phenomenalist. Such a view advances the absence of a distinction between a perceived object and its imagined image. Yet if such a notion were correct, then the number of columns on, say, the actually perceived Parthenon should be identical with those on the imagined one. This is, however, not so. Its reason is not, however, simply about number but also about the *distinctness* of enumeration. The "number" of columns on the imagined Parthenon is, in other words, vague and best characterized by words such as "several" or "many." The actual columns on the Parthenon, encountered by perception, are distinct and countable. The perceived object imposes a reality on the perceiver the rejection of which would either mean that there is something wrong with his or her faculties of perception and, understanding of the act of perceiving, or an unwillingness to admit what he or she perceives. The imaging, however, is completely a function of the will or agency of individual imagination. For phenomenalists to believe what they claim to believe about perceiving and imagining they must literally present an image as that which they did not present or they must collapse their perception into a purely voluntary act. Since the contradiction of presenting something as not being presented, of denying responsibility over something for which one is responsible, or of encountering something as not being encountered requires the agent's intentions or, in this case, willful presentation of the image, Sartre, in effect, reveals phenomenalism as a malediction of belief. It is, in other words, a form of believing what one does not believe while denying the responsibility for doing so.

As late as *The Family Idiot*, Sartre explored the practices for which we deny responsibility.[6] He also explicitly connects this denial to the study of racism in his writings throughout his career. Think of *Antisemite and Jew* or of the appendix to his *Notebooks for an Ethics*.[7] In the former, he argues that the antisemite wants to make himself (and others) ascribe to a version of "the Jew" constructed by antisemitic societies. It is in this sense that the antisemite "makes" the Jew. It is not that Jews have not existed before antisemitism, but "the Jew" in this form is a function of such hatred *and* as Sartre also shows, desire. It is, as in the case of phenomenalism, a form of believing what one does not really believe but wishes to be the case. The socially constructed notions of "the Jew," then, lead, as well, to the demand on Jews to become so-called authentic Jews. But such Jews often fall short of the lived reality of Jewishness—namely, not all Jews are the same and most do not subscribe to the stereotypic constructions of Jewishness advanced by the antisemite. Yet the pressure of being authentically Jewish does impose a form of bad faith in which some Jews live in bad faith as the stereotypes prescribe. The result is a form of Jewish self-denial in antisemitic Jewishness.[8]

In the *Notebooks for an Ethics*, Sartre examined the more dialectical features of imposed identity through a look at U.S. racialized slavery, in which the masters must make themselves believe that the designation of property means that the slaves were not really people while living through the constant negotiations of language and other forms of social interchange that entail otherwise.[9] Think also of "Black Orpheus," where he points to the bad faith involved in black desire to be lost in the negative moment of antiracist struggles.[10] Even though his language is more explicitly dialectical there, the point is that even "antiracist racism," although emboldening a revolutionary consciousness, is, nevertheless, a form of racism, and since racism in the end must be overcome, so must such a view, which, in the end, is a form of false belief. Or think of his *Le Figaro* article on his visit to the

United States in 1945, where he elegantly revealed the folly of racist rationality in a Southern physician who knows that there is no difference between black people's blood and white people's blood and yet still insists that it is not safe for white people to receive blood from black donors on the ground that it is not good to have black blood flowing in the veins of white people.[11] Or "Black Presence," where he looks at the semiology of Africa in the modern world as a "black hole."[12]

In the *Critique of Dialectical Reason*, Sartre also discusses the ongoing violence and racism of colonialism.[13] The pages he dedicated in that text to analyzing and criticizing France's racist policies in Algeria, where Berbers and Arabs, in addition to other black or mixed-race Algerians and Arabic Jews, were constantly struggling against a French-enforced dehumanization of them through many legal restrictions and institutions at the level of civil society, were valuable contributions in the intellectual and political struggles against racism. Their accuracy and impact were such that, as we have already seen, they endangered Sartre's life. Then there is his foreword to Frantz Fanon's *The Wretched of the Earth*, where he advanced his controversial view of European liberal narcissistic expectations of dependency-saturated gratitude from the people of the Third World.[14] That search for gratitude, of which he warned, haunts even the present, especially in the subordinated, hungry iconography of Africa today. These texts, and the many editorials and speeches he used to rally against racism worldwide, attest to Sartre's firm place as an ally of communities fighting against racial oppression.

Sartre's black existentialism was not only as an antiracist theorist and activist, however, since Sartre also loved jazz. It and the hipsters that emerged in black communities in the 1930s and 1940s offered examples of the assertion of freedom under claustrophobic circumstances. There are moments in which jazz music and correlated hipsters punctuated *Nausea*.[15] One could literally "hear" jazz as the leitmotif of the text as Roquentin, the protagonist, goes about his daily activities. The intimate blues foundations of jazz come through in the melancholia of the text. The blues, after all, is a music premised upon lost innocence. The mature reflection of productive loss, of facing the symbiotic relationship between negation and the search for meaning as an affirmation of life, comes through in the polyrhythmic and polyphonic use of dissonance in jazz. The "cool" blackness that accompanied the beatnik culture in which Sartre's writings were major contributions, as George Cotkin recently points out in *Existential America*, was more than the black turtlenecks and berets that practitioners wore.[16] It was also the bebop walk in the night beyond the false universals coughed up by European modernity. Moreover, Sartre loved and followed closely developments in African Diasporic popular culture. I am quite sure that, if he were alive today, Sartre would also be a proponent of World Music and at least the freedom-celebrating dimensions of hip hop. The author of the preface to *The Wretched of the Earth* would have surely understood the blues that mark the negritude influenced work of Milton Nascimento in Brazil as well as the Black Nationalism of Public Enemy and the Black Feminism of Me'Shell NdegéOcello in the United States.[17]

Moreover, today there are black philosophical organizations in the United States and the Caribbean with many scholars who engage Sartre's thought. The same could be said about blacks in Africa, which I will only briefly mention since Mabogo P. More has written for this volume a more detailed discussion of Sartre's influence on South African intellectuals. Sartre's relationship with blacks in the New World is not only posthumous. The most famous examples during Sartre's lifetime were Richard Wright and Frantz Fanon. Wright and Sartre argued over foundational figures of existential thought such as Kierkegaard and Nietzsche, as Margaret Walker attests in her biography of Wright.[18] And Fanon's relationship to Sartre took several indirect forms, such as his relationship with Sartre's friend, critic, and biographer Francis Jeanson, who helped publish *Black Skin, White Masks* in 1952, and then, eventually directly, in their famous meeting in Rome several months before Fanon died in 1961.[19] Let us refuse to collapse those relationships into the familiar false roles of black dependents on white originality. "Were Wright and Fanon 'Sartrean'?" is a question that cannot account for the cross-fertilization of these thinkers. The truth is that Wright and Fanon were simply too original and historic in their own right for their egos to be crushed under the weight of Sartre's greatness. Their relationship with Sartre was more dialogical than one of tutelage. But more, Sartre did not patronize them, which meant that their relationships were also more tense and turbulent, although short since Wright died at the age of fifty-two and Fanon at the age of thirty-six.

Wright offered Sartre a healthy debate on the nihilistic dimensions of modern life. He saw, as did Sartre, that in the struggle for significance we often face situations in which losers win and winners lose. I am reminded of the famous scene in the 1990 John Duigan movie *Flirting*, where the scrawny protagonist Danny Embling is beaten senseless by a large bully while he imagines Sartre raising his pipe and cheering him on, for we know, in the end, that his courage already made him a winner, which made losing the fight irrelevant. Each time the bully struck him down, Embling revealed himself courageous and the bully a coward. He thus, at the end of the fight, got the girl, which Sartre surely would have appreciated.[20] Unlike Sartrean irony when losers win, Wright's stories were often of losers losing, that Abdul JanMohamed has aptly characterized as "death-bound subjectivity." Cross Damon, Wright's antihero in *The Outsider*, struggled to be a man through a variety of personae only to find himself, at the end of a long road that included a few murders, dying of a feared innocence.[21] Since only adults, in this case a man, can be responsible for their actions, what was Damon's innocence but an absence of his responsibility, which, in the end, is also a failure of his humanity?

Fanon, too, understood that there were some battles that simply needed to be fought, but his was without the nihilating threats that faced Wright. He admired Sartre, although with lamented moments of disappointment at Sartre's willingness to write the truth even about things such as the relativism and negative dialectical moment that was Negritude, a realization that, as Fanon pointed out in the fifth chapter of *Black Skin, White Masks*, he "*needed* not to know."[22] He lamented, "Help had been sought from a friend of the colored peoples, and that friend had found no better response than to point out the relativity of what they were doing."[23] Black anti-whiteness enables blacks to fight against white supremacy, but it is reactive, a consequence of that racism, which means that to move forward, it, too, must be transcended. The black, Fanon reminds us, needed to get lost "in the night of the absolute."[24] This realization, this loss of innocence, produces a new subjectivity, a matured melancholic one living loss. At their brief meeting in Rome, where he proceeded to engage Sartre in discussion for several hours before Sartre was rescued away by Simone de Beauvoir to the refuge of some much-needed rest, Fanon revealed his distaste for men who "hoard their resources" and challenged Sartre, and by implication the rest of us, to take on the project of building new concepts, values, and material infrastructures for a healthy world. Fanon had let go of other attachments in his commitment to an open teleology of freedom. *The Wretched of the Earth* in many ways challenged the nihilistic threat through affirming political agency. Like Wright, Fanon saw that ethics as handed down by modernity lacked its own support in the face of the lived reality of black folks. For blacks and colonized peoples, the question is which political actions would enable the framework for an ethics, not, as liberal normative theory demands, that of finding an ethics on which to build politics.

There is not enough space here to provide a list of all the works and thinkers engaging Sartre's contributions to black existential thought. But, consider this short genealogy. The negritude movement, led by Aimé Césaire, Léopold Senghor, and Léon-Gontran Damas, had a steady engagement with existential philosophy, with Sartre's arguments about the metastability of the human condition, achieving particular prominence among writers from the Caribbean. In the American academy, the first, most engaged treatment of his thought in black academic philosophy was by William R. Jones.[25] There, the familiar black existential focus on philosophical anthropology (the human question) was advanced through a careful reading of Sartre's search for an ethics that did not collapse into the spirit of seriousness (a form of bad faith). Jones then followed up with *Is God a White Racist? A Preamble to Black Theology*, in which he showed that black theology faced collapsing into a theodicy of white supremacist religiosity (which he called "whiteanity") so long as it failed to raise the question of human agency on earth *independent* of theocentric rationalization.[26] Sartre and Fanon were very influential in Jones's construction of his existential philosophy of black liberation, although Jones also appreciated Camus's treatment of struggling with absurdity.

Sartre's resolute stand on embodied freedom led to critical discussions of his thought among black liberationists. Angela Y. Davis's early thought is one instance, and others include Robert Birt, who has written articles that look at questions of black liberation and racial identity from the perspective of Sartre's existential phenomenology.[27] David Theo Goldberg, the internationally renowned race theorist, too, began his career writing on Sartre, where he emphasized the importance of Sartre's *Critique of Dialectical Reason* for the study of racism.[28] Sartre's influence extended also to the Anglophone Caribbean, where it had an impact on the recent thought of Paget Henry, the leading theoretician of Afro-Caribbean philosophy.[29] In South Africa, Sartre's treatment of the body in *Being and Nothingness* and his ideas on racism in *Antisemite and Jew* were influential in the work of Noel Manganyi, Steve Biko, and Mabogo P. More. Manganyi wrote several books on alienation and the black body.[30] There is, in Biko's writings on black consciousness and his critique of liberalism and liberal colorblindness, the clear influence of Sartre's discussion of the modern liberal antisemite who will welcome "the Jew" so long as he or she does not appear as a Jew.[31] And More has written on Sartre in the South African context over the past two decades.[32] More's dissertation, "Sartre and the Problem of Racism," is the most systematic and comprehensive statement by an indigenous African on Sartre's thought and its influence in South Africa. It offers, as well, an important critique of the most recent effort at colorblindness in race theory, namely, K. Anthony Appiah's cosmopolitanism.[33] Using Sartre's discussion of groups-in-fusion and the pledge group in the *Critique*, More points out that racists see the subjects of racial hatred in terms of groups, not individuals. "Since," concludes More, "racism is fundamentally not a phenomenon about the uniqueness of an autonomous individual but about collective groups (the superiority or inferiority of a presumed racial group), each individual person belonging to that particular collective is replaceable and changeable in the manner of each individual within a seriality. For this reason, it is impossible to fight racism as an autonomous individual. This point is given explicit expression by the African proverb that the individual cannot fight the king's troops alone even though he is designated as a target of their bullets."[34]

I, too, began my academic career by building on Sartre's thoughts on bad faith in my study of antiblack racism, which was my dissertation (1993), published in revised and expanded form as *Bad Faith and Antiblack Racism* (1995).[35] My analysis extended the concept of *mauvaise foi* by exploring its ramifications for human study and its paradoxical, social dimensions, which led to my articulation of societal forms of bad faith or institutional bad faith. And since then, a group of young scholars working on the study of race and racism and constructive work in Africana thought through engaging both Sartre's thought and Merleau-Ponty's have emerged in the academy.[36] As well, my edited volume *Existence in Black* and coedited volume *Fanon: A Critical Reader* reveal the impact of Sartre's thought on black issues in the work of several leading contemporary scholars in Africana philosophy.[37] George Yancy's work exemplifies similar interest, and his recent anthologies on the study of whiteness also reveal a set of race theorists of the existential kind who are heavily indebted to Sartre's thought.[38] And in philosophical treatments of mixed-race theory, Naomi Zack attempts to build her conception of humanism and cosmopolitanism on her reading of Sartre's thought in her book *Race and Mixed Race*.[39] In black existential philosophy of education, the work of Stephen Haymes, which includes examining the ways in which black slaves developed their own pedagogy for survival and cultural growth, stands out.[40] Sartre's writings have also had continued impact on black literary existential writers such as George Lamming, whose *Castle of My Skin* bears many thematic similarities to *Black Skin, White Masks*, and cultural critic Manthia Diawara, whose *In Search of Africa* uses Sartre's "Black Orpheus," as its organizing thematic.[41]

The only other recent European thinker that I know to garner as much interest among black existentialists and other black theorists of liberation is Michel Foucault.[42] Although Foucault's prominence in many ways eclipsed Sartre across black studies, there is a growing appreciation of Sartre's ideas as more writers, ironically, begin to see the structural limits of poststructural analysis. The antiessentialism, the focus on the epistemic conditions of social phenomena, and technologies of the self offered by Foucauldian genealogical poststructuralism often elide, for some authors, the lived reality of their condition. For them, existential phenomenology offers a way of dealing with the situations and social structures in need of change, as David Fryer recently argued in his essay, "African American Queer Studies."[43] Such concerns lead inevitably to some engagement with Sartre's thought. This is ironic, given the near oedipal relationship Foucault had with Sartre, and the clearly oedipal relationship much of post-Sartrean French thought had with Sartreanism (especially in light of both Sartre's and Foucault's critiques of oedipal relationships).[44] In Africana philosophy, the situation is, however, less divided. Sartre and Foucault both offer much, often in the work of a single thinker. For Africana philosophers, the meeting of these two thinkers is not as difficult as it may appear among more Eurocentric scholars. Fanon, for example, in his discussion of the sociogenic dimensions of race, racism, and colonial psychological maledictions in *Black Skin, White Masks* clearly portends both the archaeological and genealogical discussions of the production of subjects, but he does so in dialogue with the work of Merleau-Ponty and Sartre, as well as Césaire. Foucault wrote some on racism; Sartre wrote a lot more; and Fanon rarely failed to engage the phenomenon.[45] Given the persistence of and even rise in racism in many parts of the globe, the ongoing relevance of these thinkers for theorists engaging racial dynamics makes much sense.

As a result let me turn to the central objection often raised to black liberation and Africana engagements with Sartre's existential phenomenological thought. Many critics appeal to the supposed antisocial arguments in Part 3 of *Being and Nothingness*.[46] The Other, in their interpretation of Sartre's thought, is merely a psychological phenomenon with whom the Subject is in conflict. If racism is, as Fanon has argued, a sociogenic phenomenon—a product of the social world—Sartre's failure to construct a social world in his early thought offers nothing more than a dead end. Fruit is offered in his later work, where we find the productive engagement with Marxism in his effort to bring out the truly *practical* dimensions of dialectics in his theory of groups. It is also there that he offers a philosophy of history and a theory of the ability to transform it.

I do not, however, see Sartre's later thought as incompatible with his earlier thought. Yes, he was always working on and refining his language. But the *argument*, which involves recognizing the human role in human actions, remains throughout. I do not agree with the interpretation of his early thought as nonsocial. Such an interpretation fails to see the transcendental argument implicit in his treatment of the question of others and social reality. Sartre argued, for instance, that sadism is a form of denying one's own embodiment. Since one *is* embodied, such a denial is a form of lying to oneself; it is a form of bad faith. But the crucial next observation is that Sartre argues that the sadist denies that the Other has a point of view. The sadist tries, in other words, to deny that he or she can be seen by others through denying that there are others in the world. In effect, a condition of Sartre's ascription of bad faith to the sadist is that there is a social world, a world of intersubjectivity. This argument is crucial, even for the later work, for without it, his engagement with Marxism would collapse into a naive materialism or self-deceived avowal of objectivity as completely independent of any subjectivity. It would be a materialism without human beings.

I have found Sartre's insights into the dynamics involved in denying a social world to be useful for philosophical explorations of oppression and all aspects of human study. For example, we deny social reality by suspending the norms of evidence. Evidence is, after all, peculiarly public and, hence, social. When we suspend evidence, we enable ourselves to believe all kinds of things that we may not in fact really believe. Think, for example, of the proverbial missing cookies from the cookie jar. Parents who may be invested in their child's perfection may conclude that crumbs on the child's lips are insufficient evidence in the face of the child's insistence of not having eaten the cookies. Such parents may even go so far as to deny what others might see when faced with the same evidence by appealing to a hyperrational exception. Crumbs on their child's lips, although "suggesting" that their child has eaten cookies does not logically entail that their child has eaten the cookies that were in the jar. But more, our intersubjective relations could become saturated by forms of denial, and since our institutions depend on lived social reality to maintain them, we could create ossified realities that hide us from ourselves. One could easily claim to be the best at what one does, for example, by making oneself believe that the social forces that eliminate others from the competition are valid. Fighting such structures is tantamount to attempting to run ourselves through brick walls. But for those for whom they have been designed, such structures are as permeable as water. They see no boundaries. Sartre's discussion of the anarchic consciousness in Part 3 of *Being and Nothingness* is very insightful here.[47] That such a consciousness is also a form of bad faith reveals the error in reading Sartre as a proponent of absolute, radical freedom, which he there called a "bourgeois consciousness."

Added to all this is the theory of metastability, which enables us to understand that human subjects are incomplete phenomena and can even be unstable at the metareflective level. To study human beings involves a radically different approach than to study nature. To study human beings requires also understanding the studier, which is self-referential and metastable. This aspect of Sartre's thought places his role in phenomenology as akin to that of Kurt Gödel's in mathematics. They reveal the incompleteness of foundational discourses. I have built on that insight in my book *Fanon and the Crisis of European Man: An Essay on Philosophy and the Human Sciences* to argue for the anticolonial aspect of phenomenology.[48] Where colonization occurs at the epistemological level, even method must be subject to such a critique.

Black existential philosophy is not, however, only concerned with antiblack racism, the contexts of black culture, the genealogy of black existentialism and its concomitant epistemological framework. It is also concerned with the complexity of building on ideas germane to communities designated black, most of which are African and African diaspora communities, and also include indigenous East Indian and Australian aboriginal populations. There, Sartre's thought is akin to W. E. B. Du Bois's reflections on studying populations whose existence has been treated as a problem in the modern world. We need to study their problems instead of making them into problems. Du Bois's argument accentuates Sartre's on bad faith. For instance, the spirit of seriousness, where values are treated as material features of the world instead of expressions of human reality, is a form of bad faith. Making people into problems materializes the values imposed on them into the people themselves. They literally become, regardless of what they do, problems or objects that are functions of the spirit of seriousness. Black problems, which Du Bois shows are black people as problems, become reflections of societal bad faith, of members of the society's refusal to admit the role they play in the creation of social problems, at least with regard to black people. Such a denial requires making black people into another Sartrean expression: pure facticity.[49]

Let me close this sketch of Sartre's impact on black existentialism by returning to the blues. The blues, which are the foundations for jazz and most twentieth-century popular music, are premised on an insight in stream with Nietzsche's discussion of ancient Greek tragedy in *The Birth of Tragedy from the Spirit of Music*.[50] Nietzsche argued that tragedies took on the suffering of life in its genuine terror and absurdity. In doing so, it enabled an adult affirmation of life through facing reality as void. The blues offers suffering with ironic twists and turns that point to adult responsibility. There is wisdom, for instance, in understanding that life is not fair, that there are not material values waiting out there to support us in a nest in which we could remain permanently children. Growing up is a painful ideal. It is a form of productive loss. Our attachments are often the source of misery, and much liberation is gained in discovering how much there is in life of which we must let go. We need to learn, the blues tell us, to laugh so we can cope but also *cry* so that we can see more clearly and become actional. Sartre's love for jazz, a product of blues music, was connected to his commitment to enjoy life while not denying its travails. We are now in the wake of his hundredth birthday anniversary and the twenty-fifth anniversary of his death. Like the blues, there is in these dates celebration and lamentation.

Notes

1. For discussion of Sartre's "Religious Atheism," see Sylvain Boni, *The Self and Other in the Ontologies of Sartre and Buber* (Washington, D.C.: University Press of America, 1987), 32.
2. Lewis R. Gordon, "Introduction," *Existence in Black: An Anthology of Black Existential Philosophy*, ed. Lewis R. Gordon (New York: Routledge, 1997). This chapter focuses mostly on the Africana stream of black existential thought, although the category "black" exceeds Africa. For more discussion, especially of African Diasporic philosophy, see Lewis R. Gordon,

An Introduction to Africana Philosophy (Cambridge, UK: Cambridge University Press, 2008).

3. We could, as well, add David Theo Goldberg, the famed theorist of race and racism, to this list. Goldberg commenced his professional philosophical career with his dissertation "The Philosophical Foundations of Racism" (New York: Graduate Center, City University of New York, 1985), a work that focused on Sartre's contributions to the subject.
4. *Being and Nothingness: A Phenomenological Essay on Ontology*, trans. with an intro. by Hazel Barnes (New York: Washington Square, 1956), 87.
5. This work is available in English as *Psychology of Imagination*, trans. Bernard Frechtman (New York: Citadel, 1991). The work was the second volume of the revised version of Sartre's aggregation thesis on imagination. The first, *L'imagination*, published in 1936, is available in English as *Imagination: A Psychological Critique*, trans. Forrest Williams (Ann Arbor: University of Michigan Press, 1962).
6. Published in French in 1971, the work appears in English as: Jean-Paul Sartre, *The Family Idiot: Gustave Flaubert, 1821–1857*, vols. 1–5, trans. Carol Cosman (Chicago : University of Chicago Press, 1981–1993).
7. Jean-Paul Sartre, *Antisemite and Jew*, trans. George Becker (New York: Schocken, 1948) and *Notebooks for an Ethics*, trans. David Pellauer (Chicago: University of Chicago Press, 1992).
8. The unfortunate consequence of such pressure is the political homogenizing of European Jews into the most authentic representations of Jewishness. For the rest of Jews in the world, especially those who are also part of the African Diaspora and those who are Middle Eastern and Asiatic, the result has been European and North American imposed invisibility. For a discussion of the actual diversity of Jews, see Diane Tobin, Gary A Tobin, and Scott Rubin, *In Every Tongue: The Racial and Ethnic Diversity of the Jewish People* (San Francisco: Institute for Jewish Research and Community, 2005).
9. See Jean-Paul Sartre, *Notebooks for an Ethics*, Appendix 2.
10. Jean-Paul Sartre, "Black Orpheus," trans. John MacCombie, in *"What Is Literature?" and Other Essays*, ed. with an intro. by Steven Ungar (Cambridge, Mass.: Harvard University Press, 1988), 289–330.
11. Jean-Paul Sartre, "Return from the United States: What I Learned about the Black Problem," trans. with comparative notes in 1995 by T. Denean Sharpley-Whiting, in *Existence in Black*, ed. Lewis R. Gordon, 81–90. I was delighted when Arlette Elkaïm-Sartre, his adopted daughter, gave me permission to have T. Denean Sharpley-Whiting translate his *Le Figaro* article and include it in my anthology of black existential philosophy. I know that he, too, would have been proud to have been included in such a book. He would have been so because, white though he may have been by birth, Sartre was never afraid to exist in black, and for that, I here join company with those who proverbially give him thanks and praise.

The story of Arlette Elkaïm-Sartre is a fascinating one. Sartre left his literary estate to her instead of to Simone de Beauvoir. The latter had attempted at one point to get Sartre committed to an asylum because of his behavior among the young Maoists in the 1970s, and it became clear that he did not trust her with the legacy of his words. When I had solicited the permission to translate the *Figaro* article, Elkaïm-Sartre only requested the standard fee of a few cents each word and that she review the text to make sure it did not change what Sartre actually said, even though I had proposed a fee of more than a thousand dollars above the final $180 cost to translate the text. I take it from that experience that it was not, as Sartre publicly claimed, a matter of looking after

Elkaïm-Sartre's financial welfare that he left his estate to her. I suspect that it was, quite simply, that he trusted her.

An additional point about their relationship. It is well known that Arlette Elkaïm was a former lover of Sartre. By subsequently adopting her, Sartre managed to achieve something, at least symbolically. It is well known among his biographers that Sartre wanted to be a Jew. Arlette Elkaïm is Jewish, an Algerian Jew. Thus, through her, his legacy becomes Jewish. For commentary, with all the implications of incest and betrayal that Sartre's act of adopting Arlette Elkaïm exemplified, see Ronald Hayman, *Sartre: A Biography* (New York: Carroll and Graf, 1987), 403–405.

12. Jean-Paul Sartre, "Black Presence," in *The Writings of Jean-Paul Sartre*, vol. 2, *Selected Prose*, ed. Michel Contat and Michel Rybalka and trans. Richard McCleary (Evanston: Northwestern University Press, 1974), 187–89.
13. Jean-Paul Sartre, *Critique of Dialectical Reason*, vol. 1, *Theory of Practical Ensembles*, trans. Alan Sheridan-Smith and ed. Jonathan Rée (London: Verso, 1991), 714–34.
14. Jean-Paul Sartre, "Preface," in Frantz Fanon, *The Wretched of the Earth*, trans. Constance Farrington (New York: Grove, 1963).
15. There are many instances in the text, but see, for e.g., "Real beginnings are like a fanfare of trumpets, like the first notes of a jazz tune, cutting short tedium, making for continuity ... I am so happy when a Negress sings: what summits would I not reach if *my own life* made the subject of the melody," Jean-Paul Sartre, *Nausea*, trans. Lloyd Alexander, with an intro. by Hayden Carruth (New York: New Directions, 1964), 37–38.
16. George Cotkin, *Existential America*. Baltimore: Johns Hopkins University Press, 2003), Introduction.
17. For discussion of these artists (and many more), see Lewis R. Gordon, "The Problem of Maturity in Hip Hop," *The Review of Education, Pedagogy, and Cultural Studies* 27.4 (October–December 2005): 367–89.
18. Margaret Walker, *Daemonic Genius* (New York: Amistad, 1993). These discussions between Wright and Sartre are well known. See also Simone de Beauovoir's *After the War: Force of Circumstance, 1944–1952*, trans. Richard Howard (New York: Marlowe, 1992), and Abdul JanMohamed, *The Death-Bound-Subject: Richard Wright's Archaeology of Death* (Durham, N.C.: Duke University Press, 2005).
19. Their brief meeting in 1961 while Sartre and de Beauvoir vacationed in Rome is legendary. The ailing Fanon rarely slept and wanted to take full advantage of the only moment he had with Sartre in person. See Ronald Hayman, *Sartre: A Biography* (1987), 384 and Alice Cherki, *Frantz Fanon: A Portrait*, trans. Nadia Benabid (Ithaca: Cornell University Press, 2006).
20. And sometimes one loses much by getting too much, as in another film adaptation of Sartrean themes, the pornographic film, Gerard Damiano's *The Devil in Miss Jones* (1972). The basis of the film was Sartre's play *Huis clos* (*No Exit*, 1944).
21. Richard Wright, *The Outsider* (New York: Perennial, 1993).
22. Frantz Fanon, *Black Skin, White Masks*, trans. Charles Lamm Markmann (New York: Grove, 1967), 135.
23. Fanon, *Black Skin*, 133.
24. Fanon, *Black Skin*, 133.
25. William R. Jones, "Sartre's Philosophical Anthropology in Relation to His Ethics: A Criticism of Selected Critics" (Providence, R.I.: Brown University Philosophy of Religion Doctoral Dissertation, 1969).

26. William R. Jones, *Is God a White Racist?: A Preamble to Black Theology*, second edition (Boston: Beacon, 1998). This text was originally published in 1973.
27. Angela Y. Davis, "Unfinished Lecture on Liberation—II," in *Angela Davis: A Primary Reader*, ed. with an intro. by Joy Ann James (Oxford, UK: Blackwell, 1998), 53–60; and Robert E. Birt, "Alienation in the Later Philosophy of Jean-Paul Sartre" (Nashville: Vanderbilt University Doctoral Dissertation in Philosophy, 1985); "Existence, Identity, and Liberation," in *Existence in Black*, ed. Lewis R. Gordon, 203–14, and Robert Birt (ed.), *The Quest for Community and Identity: Critical Essays in Africana Social Philosophy* (Lanham, Md.: Rowman and Littlefield, 2002).
28. Goldberg, "The Philosophical Foundations of Racism."
29. See, Paget Henry, *Caliban's Reason: Introducing Afro-Caribbean Philosophy* (New York: Routledge, 2000).
30. See, Noel Chabani Manganyi, *Being-Black-in-the-World* (Johannesburg: Ravan, 1973); and *Alienation and the Body in Racist Society: A Study of the Society that Invented Soweto* (New York: NOK, 1977).
31. Steve Bantu Biko, *I Write What I Like: Selected Writings*, New Edition, foreword by Lewis R. Gordon; ed. with a personal memoir by Aelred Stubbs; preface by Desmond Tuto; intro. by Thoko Mpumlwana (Chicago: University of Chicago Press, 2002).
32. P. Mabogo More, "Universalism and Particularism in South Africa," *Dialogue and Universalism* 5.4 (1995): 34–51; and "Sartre and the Problem of Racism" (Pretoria: Doctoral Dissertation in Philosophy and Literature, University of South Africa, 2005).
33. See K. Anthony Appiah, *In My Father's House: Africa in the Philosophy of Culture* (New York: Oxford University Press, 1992); and *Cosmopolitanism: Ethics in a World of Strangers* (New York: Norton, 2006).
34. More, "Sartre and the Problem of Racism," 266.
35. Lewis R. Gordon, "Bad Faith and Antiblack Racism: A Study in the Philosophy of Jean-Paul Sartre" (New Haven: Yale University Dissertation in Philosophy, 1993); and *Bad Faith and Antiblack Racism* (Atlantic Highlands, NJ: Humanities International Press, 1995; Amherst, N.Y.: Humanity, 1999).
36. See some of the authors in *Existence in Black*, as well as Emily Sook-Kyung Lee, "Meaning, Creativity and the Visible Differences of the Body: A Phenomenological Reading of Race (Maurice Merleau-Ponty)" (Stony Brook: State University of New York at Stony Brook Doctoral Dissertation in Philosophy, 2005).
37. Lewis R. Gordon, T. Denean Sharlpey-Whiting, and Renée T. White (eds.), *Fanon: A Critical Reader* (Oxford: Blackwell, 1996).
38. George Yancy (ed.), *What White Looks Like?* (New York: Routledge, 2004) and *White on White/Black on Black* (Lanham, Md.: Rowman and Littlefield, 2005),
39. Naomi Zack, *Race and Mixed Race* (Philadelphia: Temple University Press, 1993).
40. "Pedagogy and the Philosophical Anthropology of African American Slave Culture," in *Not Only the Master's Tools: African American Studies in Theory and Practice*, ed. Lewis R. Gordon and Jane Anna Gordon (Boulder, Colo.: Paradigm, 2005).
41. George Lamming, *In the Castle of My Skin*, with an intro. by Richard Wright (New York: Collier, 1970); and Manthia Diawara, *In Search of Africa* (Cambridge, Mass.: Harvard University Press, 1998).

42. The indexes of *Not Only the Master's Tools* and *A Companion to African American Studies* have many references to Foucault, and discussions of his work abound in most of the theoretical work in black thought since the mid-1980s. By contrast, Derrida has been of influence in primarily literary circles, and there seems to be a decline in the avowal of deconstruction in approaches to race phenomena on the one hand, while there is a clear rise in "genealogical" approaches. Within Africana philosophy proper, the closest set of thinkers to deconstruction are those who utilize hermeneutics by way of either Martin Heidegger, Hans-Georg Gadamer, or Paul Ricoeur or the growing number of Levinasians in the study of race in "continental" circles. But the numbers of Africana scholars from those wings is very small, and they have the least influence in the field. For a critique of Euro-continental philosophy in Africana thought, see Nelson Maldonado-Torres, "Toward a Critique of Continental Reason: Africana Studies and the Decolonization of Imperial Cartographies in the Americas," in *Not Only the Master's Tools*. See also Kenneth Knies, "The Idea of Post-European Science: An Essay on Phenomenology and Africana Studies," in *Not Only the Master's Tools*.
43. David Fryer, "African American Queer Studies," in *A Companion to African American Studies*, ed. with an intro. by Lewis R. Gordon and Jane Anna Gordon (Malden, Mass.: Blackwell, 2006). Cf. also, Sara Ahmed, *Queer Phenomenology: Orientations, Objects, Others* (Durham, N.C.: Duke University Press, 2006).
44. One need not look very far to find the many stabs at Sartre, the Great Father Figure of twentieth-century French thought. See the many references here and there in anthologies on the work of Derrida and on Foucault. See also Jonathan Judaken's insightful study, *Jean-Paul Sartre and the Jewish Question: Anti-antisemitism and the Politics of the French Intellectual* (Lincoln: University of Nebraska Press, 2006).
45. For Foucault on Racism, see, for e.g., his discussion of state negotiation of racial relations in *"Society Must Be Defended": Lectures at the College de France, 1975–1976*, trans. David Macey (New York: Picador/St. Martin's, 2003). See also Ellen K. Feder, *Family Bonds: Genealogies of Race and Gender* (New York: Oxford University Press, 2007).
46. The argument is familiar to the point of banal. See its various references in *The Philosophy of Jean-Paul Sartre (Library of Living Philosophers 16)*, ed. Paul Arthur Schilpp (La Salle, Ill.: Open Court, 1981), especially the chapter by Risieri Frondizi, "Sartre's Early Ethics: A Critique," 371–91. Even Alfred Schutz, who is often more careful and offers nuance in his reading of other thinkers, interprets Sartre as advancing a psychological argument against sociality. See Alfred Schutz, *Collected Papers I: The Problem of Social Reality*, ed. and intro. by Maurice Natanson, with a preface by H. L. van Breda (The Hague: Martinus Nijhoff, 1962).
47. Sartre, *Being and Nothingness*, 545.
48. Lewis R. Gordon, *Fanon and the Crisis of European Man: An Essay on Philosophy and the Human Sciences* (New York: Routledge, 1995), chapters 2 and 3.
49. For more discussion, see Lewis R. Gordon, *Existentia Africana*, fourth chapter, "What Does It Man to Be a Problem?," (New York: Routledge, 2000), 62–95.
50. See Friedrich Nietzsche, *"The Birth of Tragedy" and Other Writings*, trans. Ronald Speirs, ed. Raymond Geuss and Ronald Speirs (Cambridge, UK: Cambridge University Press, 1999).

Chapter 8

Sartre and South African Apartheid

Mabogo P. More

Nothing rouses the anger of Sartre more than institutional racialism; had he accepted the Nobel Prize in 1964, he would have donated the money to the Anti-Apartheid Movement.
—Howard Davies, *Sartre and "Les Temps Modernes"*

Those who are confronting apartheid should know they are not alone.*
—Jean-Paul Sartre

Describing racism as *the* form of "hatred for the other ... endowed with the greatest virulence," Bernard-Henri Lévy in his controversial book: *Sartre: The Philosopher of the Twentieth Century*, concludes that "there is not, and will not be for a long time, a better counter-fire to that hatred than a return to the discourse which says in substance ... existence precedes essence; essence has no existence."[1] For Lévy, therefore, Sartre provides us with effective tools for countering racism. Indeed, Sartre's commitment to freedom and his numerous texts on colonialism, racism, and antisemitism[2] had considerable impact on many South Africans whose lives were directly impacted by the oppression of apartheid. His philosophy thus became a source of personal, philosophical, and political inspiration for South African thinkers such as Steve Biko, Noel Chabani Manganyi, and Richard Turner.[3]

The aim of this chapter is to demonstrate Sartre's impact on the philosophical and political thoughts and practices of these thinkers. My contention is that by providing the necessary conceptual tools, philosophical insights, and political vision to the antiapartheid struggle of black thinkers and activists within the Black Consciousness Movement, Sartre contributed to the ultimate demise of the apartheid system. The main focus in this chapter will be on Steve Biko, for the simple reason that he ranks next to

---

*Jean-Paul Sartre, "Those Who Are Confronting Apartheid Should Know That They Are Not Alone" (1966). Press Statement. *French Liaison Committee against Apartheid*, http:// www.anc.org.za/un/sartre.html

Nelson Mandela in popularity not only as an icon of the struggle against racism, but also because his writings exhibit explicit Sartrean existentialist influences that contain categories and political problematics that Biko reconfigured and applied to the South African situation. These included Sartre's understanding of freedom, consciousness, identity, authenticity, bad faith, the critique of liberalism, and the issue of collective moral responsibility. It is the latter issue together with its correlate notions and its applicability to the South African Truth and Reconciliation Commission (TRC) that will be the focus of this chapter. The concern here is to locate Sartre's and Biko's conceptualizations of moral responsibility within the context of the TRC's discourse.

Sartre on Moral Responsibility

Western moral philosophy has generally restricted the realm of moral appraisal to actions produced by a rational, intentional act of will. This tendency can be traced back to Aristotle's *Nichomachean Ethics* in which he discusses the conditions under which we can hold someone responsible for his or her behavior; for example, voluntary or coerced actions. Modern existentialist theories of responsibility have extended Aristotle's theory to include issues not only of individual responsibility but also collective moral responsibility in contexts of oppression and violations of human and group rights. The latter theories owe a great deal to Karl Jaspers's attempt to determine and differentiate German guilt following the crimes of the Nazi period. Jaspers distinguishes between metaphysical guilt and criminal, political, and moral responsibility. He insists, for example, that metaphysical guilt involves absolute solidarity with the human being as such, because "There exists a solidarity among men as human beings that makes each coresponsible for every wrong and every injustice in the world."[4] Different as these might be, they are all interconnected since "Every concept of guilt demonstrates (or manifests) realities, the consequence of which appear in the sphere of the other concepts of guilt."[5] Sartre acknowledged that his view on collective responsibility owes much to Jaspers's *The Question of German Guilt*.[6]

Just as was Nazism, apartheid qua colonial system was an evil to an extreme degree. Such evil systems raise, for Sartre, a whole range of moral, political, and social questions that traditional moral philosophy does not often address. How, for example, can moral responsibility for such atrocious systems be appraised? Sartre held an ontological theory of "absolute freedom" and its complement, a theory of radical responsibility. "I am absolutely free and absolutely responsible for my situation,"[7] he maintained. He argued that since we are all condemned to freedom, each one of us "carries the weight of the whole world on his shoulders; he is responsible for the world and for himself as a way of being."[8] This ontological conception of responsibility has its origin as early as *The Emotions: Outline of a Theory*, in which Sartre stated that "for human reality, to exist is always to *assume* its being, that is, to be responsible for it instead of receiving it from the outside like a stone."[9] But in the light of his explicit declaration that ontology "cannot formulate ethical precepts," that we cannot derive an *ought* (moral imperative) from an *is* (ontological indicative), Sartre accordingly proffers a somewhat value-neutral definition of responsibility as "consciousness (of) being the incontestable author of an event or of an object."[10]

The is/ought distinction has plagued the phenomenological ontology of both Heidegger and Sartre. In spite of the fact that both take this distinction seriously in their work, they fail to maintain it. For their ontologies are replete with ethical implications. As a result, even though Sartre, for example, defines "responsibility" in nonmoral terms, the concept, especially in his political essays, increasingly became an ethical concept that signified ascription of blame, accountability, or culpability. A few examples will suffice to demonstrate this point. First, in response to the charge of subjectivism, Sartre offered the essence of his concept of responsibility: "When we say that man is responsible for himself, we do not mean that he is responsible only for his own individuality, but that he is responsible for all men."[11] In other words, responsibility is here broadened to be inclusive of others. For "in choosing himself he chooses for all men."[12] Any attempt to evade our responsibility constitutes bad faith. As Ronald Santoni indicates, because human beings are free and correlatively responsible in the ontological sense of "pre-reflective ontological responsibility," they can be assumed free and responsible in the more mundane (ontic) senses of "reflective, ethical responsibility."[13] This shift from the ontological to the ontic, from the "pre-reflective" to the "reflective" sense of responsibility remains "a basic premise of Sartre's later thought, especially when he turns to political polemics."[14]

It is at the level of the political and moral that Sartre's views acquired a greater Jasperian ascription of responsibility for atrocities such as racism, colonialism, and antisemitism. Sartre's postwar writings are infused with his abhorrence of the French bourgeoisie, the antisemite, the white racist, the colonizer or settler, and liberal democrats. It is to these that his concepts of collective moral responsibility and bad faith are directed. In "The Purpose of Writing" Sartre blames French society for the tortures, murders, and rapes committed by the French soldiers during the Algerian War:

> The whole of French society is responsible for the Algerian War, and for the way it is being conducted (torture, internment camps, etc.)—the whole of the society, including the men and women who have never stopped protesting against it. We are inextricably involved ... both responsible and complicit.[15]

Positions such as these trigger a number of contentious questions about the ascription of moral responsibility. How wide can the web of responsibility be cast? To what extent, if at all, can we hold individual members of a group collectively responsible for group-based harms in situations where they did not directly participate or cause the harm? Are members of a group individually and collectively responsible in situations where, despite the fact that they knew what was happening, they nonetheless failed to do anything to stop the harm? Sartre replies in the affirmative to all these questions.

He goes against the grain of traditional Western philosophical moral sensibility by expanding the moral landscape to an all-inclusive domain that constitutes collectives into moral agents. Commenting on the violence during the Indo-Chinese war, Sartre, in *What Is Literature?* had this to say: "If you say nothing, you are necessarily for the continuation of the war; one is always responsible for what one does not try to prevent."[16] Hence, to choose to do nothing in the face of human suffering and oppression is to participate in the infliction of that suffering and oppression and therefore to be responsible for it. For, as a free being, I am required by my very freedom to demand and will the freedom of others. In other words, inaction to overthrow oppression is, for Sartre, "collaborationist" precisely because it makes it clear that one finds the status quo permissible or acceptable; "if I did not find it permissible, I would be resisting in some fashion or other."[17] Hence in his "A More Precise Characterization of Existentialism"—an explicit move from ontological responsibility to ontic responsibility—Sartre makes it clear that "*existentialism is not a mournful delectation but a humanist philosophy of action, effort, combat, and solidarity.*"[18]

The suggestion of the ontological sense of responsibility—very similar to Jaspers's "metaphysical guilt"—is that each human being bears the responsibility not only for his or her own being but also for his or her fellow human beings. The ontic consequence of this ontological position defines the width of moral responsibility cast by Sartre on matters of oppression. His response to the question of moral responsibility for oppression casts the moral complicity wide enough to include those, to use Ronald Aronson's phrase "Who Oppose Apartheid, 'But' " in addition to "those who command and act; those who carry it out; those who are actively complicit (in several ways and degrees)."[19] All these are guilty of Sartrean individual and collective bad faith and, accordingly, morally responsible for the atrocities and evil committed in their name.

Clearly, a rigorous philosophical application of the discourse of "responsibility" would require mapping out the conceptual landscape associated with it. What kind of responsibility is Sartre appealing to here? Is causality or authorship the relevant concern? What about related concepts such as "accountability," "imputability," "blame," "excuse," "taint," or "guilt"? For the Sartre of *Being and Nothingness*, freedom implies the burden of responsibility: "The peculiar character of human reality is that it is without excuse." However, Sartre also speaks of "situation" and later, of "objective possibility," "the system," "the exigency of the situation," "historical environment," or "external necessity."

Biko on Moral Responsibility

It is precisely in the ethical realm that the existentialist influence of Sartre, mediated through Karl Jaspers and Fanon, emerged in Biko's thinking. Sartre's preface to Fanon's *The Wretched of the Earth*, for example, evidently had a great impact on Biko's view of moral responsibility. For it is in that text where Sartre accuses Europeans, especially the French, for "being the accomplice in the crime of colonialism."[20] It is also here that Sartre responds to Camus's protest that he be "neither executioner nor victim":

> Very well then, if you're not victims when the government which you've voted for, when the army in which your younger brothers are serving without hesitation or remorse have undertaken race murder, you are, without a shadow of doubt, executioners.... With us [Europeans], to be a man is to be an accomplice to colonialism, since all of us without exception have profited by colonial exploitation.[21]

Biko begins his ascription of moral responsibility on this Sartrean note, directed primarily against white liberals. "It may perhaps surprise some people," he writes, "that I should talk of whites in a collective sense when in fact it is a particular section—i.e., the government—that carries out this unwarranted vendetta against blacks."[22] In his view, whites are collectively responsible for at least three reasons: First, the apartheid government's "immorality and naked cruelty [is] done in the name of white people."[23] Second, the whites are responsible for putting the apartheid regime in power:

> There are those whites who will completely disclaim responsibility for the country's inhumanity to the black man. These are the people who are governed by logic for 4¾ years but by fear at election time. The Nationalist party has perhaps many more English votes than one imagines. All whites collectively recognize in it a strong bastion against the highly played-up swart gevaar [Black peril].... Thus if whites in general do not like what is happening to the black people, they have the power in them to stop it here and now. We on the other hand, have every reason to bundle them together and blame them jointly."[24]

Finally, whites remain in the country precisely because they benefit from the oppression of black people. Hence, the very fact that even the so-called "disgruntled whites remain [in the country] to enjoy the fruits of the system would alone be enough to condemn them at Nuremberg."[25] The similarity between Biko and Sartre is here remarkable as Sartre's comment on the Algerian situation indicates:

> But we vote, we give mandates and, in any way we can, revoke them; the stirring of public opinion can bring down governments. We personally must be accomplices to the crimes that are committed in our name, since it is within our power to stop them. We have to take responsibility for this guilt which was dormant in us, inert, foreign, and demean ourselves in order to be able to bear it.[26]

The Sartrean and Bikoan broad ascription of moral responsibility raises, as we mentioned earlier, numerous questions about complicity for the evils of apartheid.

It shall be recalled that one of Sartre's main targets in the *Portrait of the Antisemite* is the liberal democrat. It is the latter's perverted Western humanism whose principle of universality provides a veiled moral, political, and economic justification for racism and pillage that Sartre denounced because it fails to recognize Jewish difference. The tendency of Western humanism to collude with colonialism and its racist practices led Sartre to conclude that "Humanism is the counterpart of racism: it is a practice of exclusion."[27]

In a similar fashion, Biko's obsession is with white liberals and Leftists,[28] "that curious bunch of nonconformists who explain their participation in negative terms; that bunch of do-gooders that goes under all sorts of names—liberals, leftists etc;"[29] those "Who Oppose Apartheid, 'But,' "[30] and in Albert Memmi's phrase, "the colonizer who refuses" or "the benevolent colonizer."[31] These, according to Biko, "are the people who argue that they are not responsible for white racism and the country's 'inhumanity to the black man.' "[32] In the process, they attempt to reduce the South African problem into a "black problem" rather than a problem of "white racism ... [which] rests squarely on the laps of the white society."[33] Putting aside the stubborn, white South African racist, it is the white liberals who consistently denied responsibility for black oppression through "deliberate evasiveness,"[34] or what Sartre famously names "bad faith."

But, such white liberals cannot escape moral responsibility for apartheid because, qua members of the white South African community, they enjoyed a privileged position and they were aware of this. Therefore, Biko argued, no white person can be absolved from this "metaphysical guilt." "Thus in the ultimate analysis," Biko concludes, "no white person can escape being part of the oppressor camp."[35] His belief in collective moral responsibility is made even more evident by his citation of Karl Jaspers:

> There exists among men, because they are men, a solidarity through which each shares responsibility for every injustice and every wrong committed in the world, and especially for crimes that are committed in his presence or of which he cannot be ignorant.[36]

How wide can or should moral responsibility be cast, given that some whites—for example, Ruth First, Bram Fisher, or Neil Aggett—paid the ultimate price fighting against apartheid? Biko's argument is premised on the fact that apartheid is systemically evil. For this reason, his moral net covers a wide range because, like Jaspers and Sartre, he contends that all those who created, planned, and ordered it are responsible for it; all those who carried it out are responsible; all those who accepted it and allowed it to happen are responsible; all those who were silent about it and pretended not to know are responsible for it; and more importantly, all those who, in whatever way, benefited from the system are responsible for the atrocities perpetrated in its name. Whether they liked it or not, all whites benefited not only from the system but also by virtue of being members of the dominant white group, "the color of his skin—[was] his passport to privilege."[37] So, despite the fact that they fought against the system, they still are responsible for it. This view finds support from even the grandchild of the architect of apartheid, Wilhelm Verwoerd. According to him, "Even those whites who opposed apartheid are beneficiaries, because they were also members of a group that was systematically, unjustly privileged in terms of access to land, capital etc."[38] Besides, if whites did not like what was happening to blacks, according to Biko, they possessed enough power collectively to stop black suffering. Since they did not, he concludes, "We ... have every reason to bundle them together and blame them jointly."[39]

Biko thus maintained that no white person in South Africa can claim that he or she did not know or was not "aware" of what was happening in the country. As he puts it, "Basically, the South African white community is a homogeneous community. It is a community of people who sit to enjoy a privileged position that they do not deserve, *are aware of this*, and therefore spend their time trying to justify why they are doing so."[40] This state of unawareness is what Sartre aptly calls "the state of false ignorance"[41] imposed on the citizens by the regime but in which the citizens themselves contribute in order to ensure their peace of mind and quell their consciences. In spite of every effort by the apartheid regime to suppress the truth from reaching the public domain, almost everybody—through the few courageous media reports—knew about the death in detentions of prisoners, torture, apartheid army occupation of the townships, and bombing of so-called terrorists in neighboring states such as Lesotho or Botswana. If some white South Africans did not read the newspapers or were illiterate, they knew people who read them. Even those who had not heard of the atrocities committed in their name, heard the accounts of white police, reservists, or soldiers—their brothers, cousins, fathers, uncles, relatives, friends, neighbors, or acquaintances—who returned home and spoke about it. The international and public attention the 1960 Sharpville Massacre, the 1976 Soweto Student Riots, the death in detention of many activists (including Biko himself), and many other incidents problematize any claim or excuse of ignorance. Debunking the French citizens' appeal to ignorance during the Algerian war, Sartre commented:

> False naiveté, flight, bad faith, solitude, silence, a complicity at once rejected and accepted, that is what we called, in 1945, collective responsibility. There was no way the German people, at the time, could feign ignorance of the camps.... We were right, they did know everything, and it is only today that we can understand because we too know everything.[42]

Similarly, many white South Africans appeal to the argument from ignorance because of the strict racial separation enforced by the apartheid regime. This excuse is the most popular form of bad faith prevalent in South Africa today.

Like the inauthentic Jews in Sartre's *Portrait of the Antisemite*,[43] Biko's moral net covers the complicity of black people who participated in their own oppression, those who were "participants in the white man's game of holding the aspirations of the black people."[44] These are the "people who deliberately allowed themselves into an unholy collusion with the enemy,"[45] black leaders who are "subconsciously siding and abetting in the total subjugation of the black people."[46] The black person who has to be constantly reminded of "his complicity in the crime of allowing himself to be misused and therefore letting evil reign supreme in the country of his birth."[47] Thus, as Hegel reminds us, to the extent that a slave acquiesces in slavery, he or she is responsible for the slavish situation. Hence, the black policeman and woman, black Special Branch Agent, black civil servant, black teacher, and particularly apartheid-created Homeland (Bantustan) leader, were all directly responsible for perpetuating and propping up the apartheid machinery. These then are the people whom Biko and his comrades contemptuously labeled as nonwhites because of their collaboration with the oppressive apartheid system. Barring those who consciously and actively collaborated with the regime, those who were at once victims and beneficiaries, Biko's net did not leave out "Those Blacks Who Suffered, 'But.' " They also were morally responsible for letting it happen.

One of the major difficulties with Biko's (and Sartre's) concept of collective responsibility is that it seems to fluctuate freely between moral or political responsibility and the existentialist conception of ontological responsibility that Jaspers refers to as "metaphysical guilt." It is this conflation of responsibility that accounts for Biko's sweeping ascription of moral responsibility and guilt for the evils of apartheid. Ontological responsibility, as Biko himself recognizes, assumes that there is a solidarity among human beings that constitutes each one of us as responsible "for every injustice and every wrong committed in the world" against humankind, because in choosing for myself I am at the same time choosing for all human beings.

Moral responsibility, on the other hand, involves blameworthiness and praise for actions performed or not performed. Put differently, moral responsibility involves answerability and accountability for one's choices and actions. To apply, therefore, criteria relating to ontological responsibility to cases of moral responsibility, as both Biko and Sartre do, entails overlooking questions concerning degrees of responsibility, which are pertinent in determining moral blame. The responsibility of persons as citizens is not, as Aronson contends, only an ontological fact, but a social and historical one as well. To that extent, human beings cannot always be equally responsible for acts performed by their leaders and rulers. Surely, those who create, plan, and order, differ in degrees of responsibility from those who execute the orders, or those who merely accept and allow it to happen and those who are silent or ignorant or merely indifferent to suffering. Ontological responsibility does not allow this moral gradation and thus is subject to the criticism that if everyone is equally responsible then no one is responsible. Despite this limitation, the next section aims at applying Sartre's and Biko's conceptualizations of moral responsibility to an actual historical event: South Africa's Truth and Reconciliation Commission.

The Truth and Reconciliation Commission (TRC)

If I have belabored the issue of moral responsibility, it is for the simple reason that it has a direct bearing on the Truth and Reconciliation Commission (TRC) that was conducted in South Africa from 1996 to 1998. In January 1996 President Nelson Mandela launched the TRC under the leadership of Archbishop Desmond Tutu. The TRC was a transitional statutory body constituted by the Promotion of National Unity and Reconciliation Act (1995) *to promote justice* through the process of uncovering past violations (from 1960 to 1994) of human rights and to create the necessary conditions for *achieving national reconciliation*. In other words, part of its brief was to promote racial reconciliation. The two operative concepts of this process were the pursuit of "justice" and the achievement of national, but more precisely, racial "reconciliation" since apartheid, to use Derrida's phrase, was "racism's last word" (1985).

More often than not, the reconciliation exercise is conducted for political purposes. The absence of a clear winner or loser in the South African conflict, for instance, led to the compromise reached at the Convention for a Democratic South Africa (CODESA), a compromise having as its direct product the "promotion of national reconciliation" at the expense of "social justice." In this compromise, the apartheid regime relinquished political power while keeping economic power in a transitional arrangement that accorded the apartheid masters and functionaries immunity from charges of torture and murder.[48] This arrangement was similar in many respects to the one reached with Pinochet in Chile where the concept of "reconciliation" become popular as a political instrument during a transitory period.

Certain obvious problems arise in an arrangement of this sort that, in my view, would have militated against its acceptance by Biko or Sartre given their insistence on the all-inclusive culpability of South African whites in the violation of human rights. First, there is a tendency in arrangements such as the TRC to individualize systems of oppression such as colonialism and apartheid to certain prominent representatives. It reduces a whole system of oppression to the representatives—for example, P. W. Botha in South Africa, or General Pinochet in Chile and their numerous functionaries. As a consequence, all those who supported it, those who allowed it to happen through their silence, those who claim ignorance of atrocities committed in their name, and all those who benefited from the system, are exonerated from responsibility for the system. But, as Sartre, in his insightful "Colonialism is a System," explains:

> When we talk of the "colonial system," we must be clear about what we mean. It is not an abstract mechanism. The system exists, it functions; the infernal cycle of colonialism is a reality. But the reality is embodied in a million colonists, children and grandchildren of colonists, who have been shaped by colonialism and who think, speak and act according to the very principle of the colonial system.[49]

The significance of the concept of "the system" in the above citation and its relation to moral responsibility should not be overlooked. For it appears with regularity in a number of Sartre's anticolonial articles published in *Situation V (Colonialism and Neocolonialism)*. As Thomas Flynn observes, Sartre's intention in these articles was "to move the stolid bourgeoisie to admit its complicity in the dirty work of colonial warfare."[50] A similar conception prompted Biko and the Black Consciousness advocates to refer to apartheid and its complex mechanisms as "the system." The point is that under such "systems" everyone defending, perpetuating, reproducing, participating in, and benefiting from the system is responsible for it and its atrocities. In other words, both the perpetrators and the beneficiaries are morally responsible for the system.

Contrary to the Bikoan thesis of metaphysical responsibility for apartheid, the TRC has tended to absolve the beneficiaries from responsibility. By focusing almost entirely on the notorious state agents who committed gross human rights violations (e.g., the Vlakplaas assassin, Eugene de Kok)[51] and the counterviolence of liberation fighters like some in the African National Congress, the TRC consciously ignored the connection between perpetrators and beneficiaries of the apartheid system. Since apartheid was a form of colonialism, in Mamdani's view, it also inevitably promoted a particular arrangement of privilege such that a link between racialized power and racialized privilege forges.[52] To repress the "privileged" status of whites in apartheid South Africa would be, as Biko constantly argued, an obvious expression of Sartrean bad faith. By concentrating on the minority of perpetrators to the total exclusion of the beneficiaries of the system is to absolve them from responsibility. Such a move denies Sartre's and Biko's ascription of moral responsibility and was explicitly railed against by both of them.

One of the consequences of the TRC hearings was that it inadvertently became a rescue operation for the beneficiaries of apartheid privileges, hence, "the harmful lack of commitment shown by many apartheid beneficiaries [read white South Africans]."[53] This "lack of commitment" is an expression of the widespread refusal by the majority of white South Africans to "face the fact of being apartheid beneficiaries," that is, the bad faith refusal to accept moral responsibility for the atrocities of apartheid and the benefits accruing there from. Bemoaning this clear expression of Sartrean bad faith, Verwoerd has this to say about white South Africans:

> Many [white South Africans] ... display a shocking lack of historical awareness. They prefer to see their own and their parents' educational achievements ("human capital"), good health, and wealth as purely the product of hard work, as something they deserve. Thus they conveniently forget or underestimate the role of a midwife called apartheid.[54]

The upshot of Verwoerd's complaint is that many whites denied and continue to deny their "responsibility arising from systematic past privileging."[55]

The second problem with the TRC is that, just as there are evident problems about its exclusion of beneficiaries from moral blame, there are also serious problems with the *meaning* of "reconciliation" and its relation to what Verwoerd calls "lack of historical awareness" by whites. Truth commissions are about what happened and who is responsible for it, morally, politically, or sometimes even legally. To most whites, however—that in Sartre's eyes would constitute a consummate case of bad faith—reconciliation has come to mean blacks pretending that history did not happen as it did: that there was no seizure of African land through colonial wars of conquest. Their understanding of reconciliation, as Mosala points out, "is based on a cold-blooded exclusion of the history of alienation."[56] Also, it means that some white organizations and institutions would proclaim their remorse about the past and the status quo would continue unhindered. In the words of a white South African *Independent Newspaper* journalist, Shaun Johnson, "Black South Africa is looking for serious signs from the White community. What they are getting is a back to business attitude."[57] Black people's perspective on reconciliation, on the contrary, is predicated on an understanding and appreciation of the history of their alienation: from the land, livestock, labor, their culture, their brothers and sisters, and themselves.

Above, we noted that for Sartre, colonialism is a system governed by its own internal logic. The main aspect of the logic of this system is the occupation and appropriation of the land by the colonizers, the exploitation of the natives at starvation rates and then, with mechanization, the taking from the natives their very right to work. Historically, black people in South Africa have been subject to systematic and brutal dispossession of their land, the basic means of production, and finally the control of their labor. It is these that have been alienated from black people. Reconciliation, from this perspective, therefore, means a transcendence of alienation by being reconciled with the land, livestock, property, and self, which was at the heart of Biko's Black Consciousness message. On the basis of these considerations, it seems reasonable that Biko would have at least demanded the restoration of land to black people, an issue he was passionate about, and reparation for certain wrongs as a means of transcending black alienation and achieving reconciliation. Without these conditions being met, Biko would consider the black condition as fundamentally still an oppressive one. The notion of reconciliation, as Mosala states, "is synonymous with the idea of liberation, if not more fundamental to it."[58]

The third problem with the TRC is the dominance of the liberal paradigm that emphasizes human rights and democracy to the exclusion of the demands for fundamental transformation. Biko would have experienced difficulties, not with the concept of human rights, but with its application prior to the leveling of the playing field involving the issue of the equitable distribution of wealth and the restoration of the appropriated land to its legitimate indigenous African owners. It is this liberal paradigm emphasizing human rights that facilitated the immediate and eager adoption of the

Freedom Charter as a model for the country's constitution before the resolution of the national question, namely the land question, for which the struggle for national liberation was in fact originally waged. In adopting a constitutional framework in which the Bill of Rights is enshrined (especially the right to property), old relations of production as well as the extant unequal structure of ownership, especially the land, was reinforced.

Another problem, as Ibbo Mandaza argues, is that reconciliation is a product of a weak petit bourgeoisie "only too content to forgive as the necessary price for attaining the class goal after so many years of struggle, imprisonment and self-denial. Reconciliation is the forgiveness of the small elite that inherits state power without the fulfillment of social justice for the majority."[59] In other words, reconciliation is the lament of the weak, the fact that it is asserted from a seemingly moral and political position of superiority and strength notwithstanding. In the long run, such reconciliatory arrangements, as the skewed power relations between the ANC and the apartheid regime in the CODESA agreement amply demonstrate, end up sacrificing the imperative of social justice in favor of "national unity." The result is that the major issue that the commission did not touch was not that between "truth" and "reconciliation" but between "justice" and "reconciliation." Reconciliation need not necessarily be the direct consequence of truth. As Mamdani problematizes it in his critique of the TRC in South Africa: "Is reconciliation an inevitable outcome of truth telling? Is it also not possible that the more truth comes to light—and the less justice is seen to be done—the more truth may breed outrage amongst the majority [oppressed] and fear in the minority?"[60]

The State of Racism after Sartre and Biko in South Africa

What then is the state of racism in South Africa after Sartre, Fanon, and Biko? For starters, there have been remarkable successes undoing apartheid but a debilitating failure on the racism front. In the "new," postapartheid South Africa, it is extremely difficult to find someone who did not oppose apartheid.[61] For most English-speaking white liberals, for example, apartheid was not of their own making; they neither introduced nor supported it. Since it was an Afrikaner invention, they find it difficult to accept responsibility for it, despite the fact that they benefited from it. For the Afrikaans-speaking and other whites, since apartheid is dead, so is racism. What both groups ignore is that one can oppose apartheid qua institutional racism as wrong while still being convinced of black inferiority. Still, one can equally regard apartheid as unfair while denying that other kinds of racial exclusion are unfair. Hence, the demise of apartheid qua institutional or legal racism does not entail the transcendence of individual or even subliminal racism. To this extent, Sartre's fight against apartheid, as our epigraphs testify, has been a success. But only to the extent that apartheid qua formal institutional racism is dead can we say that Sartre won the battle and not the war.

Germany has accepted and taken collective responsibility for the Holocaust. This responsibility is expressed by what the Germans themselves call *weidergutmaching*, meaning "making good again" or simply restitution. For this, Germany paid approximately DM100 billion to Holocaust survivors, a sum that is likely to increase for at least the coming two decades. This policy is the result of the Germans taking collective moral responsibility for their past. Unlike the Germans, most white South Africans are denying collective moral responsibility for apartheid partly because of the TRC's unwillingness to deal with the issue of white moral culpability for the system. This unwillingness has, as Chris Landsberg notes, left "an undeconstructed and unreconstructed South Africa."[62] It is undeconstructed precisely because there is a failure to realize just how much in the postapartheid era the racist order still exists. This is nicely summarized by Ali Mazrui's crisp remark in a 1998 speech in Cape Town when he said of the CODESA compromise: "You wear the crown, we'll keep the jewels." South Africa remains unreconstructed because despite black political domination (wearing the crown), the country still remains, economically, socially, culturally, intellectually, and even religiously, white dominated (keeping the jewels).

Both Biko's and Sartre's conceptions of moral responsibility provide a foundational critique of the TRC for failing to take into account the bad faith of the privileged liberals and the beneficiaries of apartheid oppression. While this may have been the correct thing to do within the adopted framework and context of a liberal constitutional arrangement such as the South African one, the release from moral responsibility is contrary to Sartre's many discussions of bad faith and Biko's discussion of white evasiveness. In their respective critiques of the liberal democrat, both Biko and Sartre expose not only the bankruptcy of liberal democratic models as enshrined in the TRC process and the constitution of the "new" South Africa, but also the dilemmas that any theory of liberation must necessarily confront. The failure to deal with the question of complicity in the crime of apartheid has left things as they used to be and still are. As President Thabo Mbeki puts it, today South Africa is still largely a society of "The Two Nations" one white and rich and the other black and poor.

This failure of the TRC process has not escaped the keen and critical eye of observers of the South African situation such as Lewis Gordon. He deplores the anti-Bikoan way in which the TRC unsurprisingly handled the complicity of white liberals in particular and the white community in general. In his view, the TRC proceedings have revealed a lived reality that is painful and bitter for blacks. These proceedings,

Reveal how desperately South Africa wanted to prevent white flight; they reveal that the global market is heavily racially inflected; lurking beneath the undercurrents of transition in South Africa is the fear that the economy is the baby that could be lost with the white bath water. Whites thus walk the streets of South Africa as a precious commodity.[63]

It is this reality, Gordon concludes, that has a devastating effect on the consciousness of black South Africans.

Although Sartre's suggested solutions (moral radical conversion, violence, socialism, or even concrete liberalism) to the problem of racism contained some ideological, moral, and political weaknesses, his philosophical theories and political concerns about racism had a tremendous impact on the thinking and actions of those greatly affected by the phenomenon. Black existential philosophers, most of whom were directly or indirectly influenced by Sartre's philosophy, have made it their philosophical project to articulate the existential realities of black people in the antiblack world in which they live. This project involves revealing the alienation of black people, bringing it to their consciousness, and thereby, hopefully, moving them to collective action and transformation of their situation. For these thinkers, psychological freedom and political freedom are inextricably bound together even though they may not be identical. There can be no true political and social liberation without a liberated consciousness, just as there can be no liberation of consciousness separate from the total struggle for social and political liberation. The work of Frantz Fanon, Lewis Gordon, Robert Birt, Lucius Outlaw, Kwame Toure (aka Stockely Carmichael), Noel Chabani Manganyi, and Steve Biko, to name just a few, bear special testimony to this project. Sartre's contribution to the destruction of apartheid, mediated through the courageous political and intellectual efforts of Biko and the Black Consciousness Movement, therefore, is beyond question, a project that has ongoing relevance in postapartheid South Africa.

Notes

1. Bernard-Henri Lévy, *Sartre: The Philosopher of the Twentieth Century*, trans. Andrew Brown (Cambridge: Polity Press, 2003), 300.
2. Jean-Paul Sartre, "Black Orpheus," trans. John MacCombie, in *"What Is Literature?" and Other Essays* (Cambridge: Harvard University Press, 1988); "Preface" in Frantz Fanon, *The Wretched of the Earth*, trans. Constance Farrington (New York: Grove, 1968); "Introduction," trans. Lawrence Hoey, in Albert Memmi, *The Colonizer and the Colonized* (New York: Orion, 1965); *The Respectful Prostitute*, trans. Loinel Abel, in *No Exit and Three Other Plays* (New York: Vintage, 1989); "Return From the United States," trans. T. Denean Sharpley-Whiting, in Lewis R. Gordon ed., *Existence in Black* (New York: Routledge, 1997); *Portrait of the Antisemite (Réflexions sur la question juive)*, trans. Erik de Mauny (London: Secker & Warburg, 1948), popularly

translated as *Antisemite and Jew*, trans. George Becker (New York: Schocken, 1948). In this chapter the Erik de Mauny translation will be used; *Colonialism and Neocolonialism*, trans. Azzedine Haddour, Steve Brewer, and Terry McWilliams (London: Routledge, 2001).
3. For a lengthy discussion of the influence of Sartre on Biko and Manganyi, see my "Biko: The Africana Existentialist Philosopher" *Alternation* 11. 1 (2004): 79–108; and my "Reaching For the Primordial: Anti-Survivalist Themes in Fanon and Gordon" in Marina Paola Banchetti-Robino and Clevis Ronald Headley, eds., *Shifting the Geography of Reason: Gender, Science, and Religion*, selected proceedings from the First Annual Meeting of the Caribbean Philosophical Association (Newcastle-Upon-Tyne: Cambridge Scholars, 2007).
4. Karl Jaspers "The Question of German Guilt," in N. J. Kritz, ed., *Transitional Justice* vol. 1 (Washington, D.C.: United States Institute of Peace Press, 1995), 159.
5. Jaspers, "The Question of German Guilt," 160.
6. For this admission, see Thomas R. Flynn, *Sartre and Marxist Existentialism* (Chicago: University of Chicago Press, 1986), 209–10, n.17.
7. Jean-Paul Sartre, *Being and Nothingness*, trans. Hazel E. Barnes (New York: Philosophical Library, 1956), 509.
8. Sartre, *Being and Nothingness*, 553.
9. Jean-Paul Sartre, *The Emotions: Outline of a Theory*, trans. Bernard Frechtman (New York: Philosophical Library, 1948), 12.
10. Sartre, *Being and Nothingness*, 553.
11. Jean-Paul Sartre, *Existentialism and Humanism*, trans. Philip Mairet (London: Methuen, 1966), 29.
12. Sartre, *Existentialism and Humanism*, 29.
13. Ronald E. Santoni, *Bad Faith, Good Faith and Authenticity in Sartre's Early Philosophy* (Philadelphia: Temple University Press, 1995), 130.
14. Flynn, *Sartre and Marxist Existentialism*, 7.
15. Jean-Paul Sartre, *Between Existentialism and Marxism*, trans. John Mathews (New York: Pantheon, 1974), 25.
16. Sartre, *"What Is Literature?" and other Essays*, 232.
17. Linda A. Bell, *Sartre's Ethics of Authenticity* (Tuscaloosa: University of Alabama Press, 1989), 66.
18. Jean-Paul Sartre, *The Writings of Jean-Paul Sartre*, volume 2, Michel Contat and Michel Rybalka, eds., trans. Richard McCleary (Evanston, Ill.: Northwestern University Press, 1974), 160.
19. Ronald Aronson, *Stay Out of Politics: A Philosopher Views South Africa* (Chicago: University of Chicago Press, 1990), 74.
20. Sartre in Fanon, *The Wretched of the Earth*, 24.
21. Sartre in Fanon, *The Wretched of the Earth*, 25.
22. Steve Biko, *I Write What I Like* (Randburg: Raven, 1996), 77.
23. Biko, *I Write What I Like*, 76.
24. Biko, *I Write What I Like*, 77, 78.
25. Biko, *I Write What I Like*, 78–79.
26. Sartre, *Colonialism and Neocolonialism*, 55.
27. Jean-Paul Sartre, *Critique of Dialectical Reason*, vol. 1, trans. Alan Sheridan-Smith (London: Verso, 1982), 752.
28. For an interesting view on the reasons why Biko devoted so much energy to critiquing liberals, see Lewis R. Gordon's "Foreword" in Steve Biko, *I Write What I Like* (Chicago: University of Chicago Press, 2002), vii. For a problematic version of this interpretation see Themba Sono, *Reflections on the Origins of Black Consciousness in South Africa* (Pretoria: HSRC, 1993), chap. 1.

29. Biko, *I Write What I Like*, 20.
30. Aronson, *Stay Out of Politics*, 74.
31. Memmi, *The Colonizer and the Colonized*, 27.
32. Biko, *I Write What I Like*, 20.
33. Biko, *I Write What I Like*, 23. Sartre also notes that since the United States, according to Richard Wright, had only a white problem and not a black problem, then "we can say, in the same way, that antisemitism is not a Jewish problem: it is *our* [French] problem." Jean-Paul Sartre, *Portrait of the Antisemite*, trans. Erik de Mauny (London: Secker & Warburg, 1948), 127.
34. Biko, *I Write What I Like*, 23. For a recent articulation of "white evasiveness" see Ruth Frankenberg, *White Women, Race Matters: The Sociological Construction of Whiteness* (Minneapolis: University of Minnesota Press, 1993). For the application of Frankenberg's concept of "race evasiveness" within the South African context, see Melissa Steyn, *Whiteness Just Isn't What It Used to Be: White Identity in a Changing South Africa* (Albany: State University of New York Press, 2001); and Mashuq Ally, "White South African Identity and an Ethnic Reconciliation: Racism, Guilt, and a Sense of Shame," *Unisa Latin American Report* 20.2 (2005).
35. Biko, *I Write What I Like*, 23.
36. Cited in Biko, *I Write What I Like*, 23.
37. Biko, *I Write What I Like*, 23.
38. Wilhelm Verwoerd, "The TRC and Apartheid Beneficiaries in a New Dispensation." Paper delivered at "Politics and Promises: Evaluating the Implementation of the TRC's Recommendations" Conference, Centre for the Study of Violence and Reconciliation, (Johannesburg: October 27, 2000).
39. Biko, *I Write What I Like*, 78.
40. Biko, *I Write What I Like*, 19. Emphasis added.
41. Sartre, *Colonialism and Neocolonialism*, 55.
42. Sartre, *Colonialism and Neocolonialism*, 60–61.
43. For an interesting discussion of this Sartrean discrepancy in the ascription of moral responsibility on Jews, see Linda A. Bell, "Different Oppressions: A Feminist Exploration of Sartre's *Antisemite and Jew*," in Julien S. Murphy, ed., *Feminist Interpretations of Jean-Paul Sartre* (University Park: Pennsylvania State University Press, 1999).
44. Biko, *I Write What I Like*, 146.
45. Biko, *I Write What I Like*, 81.
46. Biko, *I Write What I Like*, 85.
47. Biko, *I Write What I Like*, 29.
48. For the juridical issues on amnesty, see Kader Asmal, Louise Asmal, and Ronald Suresh Roberts, *Reconciliation through Truth: A Reckoning of Apartheid's Criminal Governance* (Cape Town: David Philip, 1996), especially chapter 3. The fact that the granting of amnesty to certain individuals (e.g., army generals) was part of the compromise reached at CODESA, comes from a letter Bishop Desmond Tutu wrote to the *Sunday Times* (South Africa) December 4, 1996: "Many of those now calling for justice through criminal trials supported the negotiated settlement AT Kempton Park [CODESA], and seem to forget that amnesty was a crucial ingredient of the compromise which reversed the country's inevitable descent into a bloodbath."
49. Sartre, *Colonialism and Neocolonialism*, 64.
50. Flynn, *Sartre and Marxist Existentialism*, 57.
51. Eugene de Kok belonged to an apartheid security police unit located in a farm known as Vlakplaas where they tortured, killed, and disposed of the activists' bodies by using all sorts of methods such as packing explosives around the

bodies of their victims and blowing them away, blowing them up with land mines, burning them and throwing their ashes into the river, or throwing them down mine shafts.
52. Mahmood Mamdani in *Beyond Racism: Embracing an Interdependent Future* (Atlanta, Ga.: Southern Education Foundation, 2000), 19.
53. Verwoerd, "The TRC and Apartheid Beneficiaries in a New Dispensation," 1
54. Verwoerd, "The TRC and Apartheid Beneficiaries in a New Dispensation," 2.
55. Verwoerd, "The TRC and Apartheid Beneficiaries in a New Dispensation," 2.
56. Itumeleng J. Mosala, "The meaning of Reconciliation: A Black Perspective," *Journal of Theology for Southern Africa* 59 (June 1987): 19. The idea of the relation between the concept of "reconciliation" and the concept of "alienation" is traceable to—among others—Hegel. For a thorough discussion of the two concepts in Hegel's work, see Michael O. Hardimon, *Hegel's Social Philosophy: The Project of Reconciliation* (Cambridge: Cambridge University Press, 1994), especially chapter 3. See also Richard Schacht, *Alienation* (Lanham, Md.: University Press of America, 1984).
57. Cited by Ellis Cose, "From Rodriguez to Raça," in *Beyond Racism: Embracing an Interdependent Future* (Atlanta, Ga.: Southern Education Foundation, 2000), 9.
58. Mosala, "The Meaning of Reconciliation: A Black Perspective," *Journal of Theology for Southern Africa*, 25.
59. Ibbo Mandaza, "Reconciliation and Social Justice in Southern Africa: The Zimbabwe Experience," in Malegapuru William Makgoba, ed. *African Renaissance: The New Struggle* (Sandton: Mafube, 1999), 81.
60. Mahmood Mamdani, "When Does Reconciliation Turn into a Denial of Justice?" *Sam Nolutshungu Memorial Series* 1 (Pretoria: HSRC, 1998): 13.
61. For the Afrikaner "denial phenomenon" see Pierre Hugo, "The Politics of 'Untruth': Afrikaner Academics for Apartheid," *Politikon* 25.1 (1998): 31–55. Focusing on the legal profession, the editorial of the Johannesburg-based *Mail and Guardian* (May 17–23, 1996) had this to say about the "denial phenomenon": "The age of reconciliation is characterized by a great deal of humbug. It is almost impossible in the legal profession nowadays to find a good old-fashioned Nat[ionalist]: apparently they were all against apartheid, and many claim to have been fighting it from within.... But this is not the truth."
62. Chris Landsberg, *City Press* (January 22, 2006).
63. Lewis R. Gordon, "Foreword" in Steve Biko, *I Write What I Like* (Chicago: University of Chicago Press, 2002), xii. Indeed, Mandela bent over far backward in a desperate attempt to allay white fears and curb white flight. Early in his presidency Mandela visited the racially exclusive Orania and had tea with Betsy Verwoerd, the widow of the architect of apartheid, Dr. Hendrik Verwoerd. He extended a hand of friendship to Percy Yutar, the prosecutor who made it possible for him to spend twenty-seven years on Robben Island. He even appointed his former prison guard as part of his security brief. Most of all, he wore a Springbok rugby jersey in support of the all-white national rugby team that won the Rugby World Cup in 1995.

Part IV

Sartre and the Postcolonial Turn

Chapter 9

Difference/Indifference
Sartre, Glissant, and the Race of Francophone Literature

Richard H. Watts

When considering the meaning of "race" after Sartre, an important vein to mine is the postwar interaction that the most visible public intellectual of the period maintained with black writers from the French colonies and the newly created overseas departments.[1] In his patronage of writers such as the Senegalese Léopold Senghor, the Guyanese Léon Damas, and, most passionately and extensively, the Martinican Aimé Césaire, Sartre created a compelling template for understanding "race" and its relation to cultural production in the twentieth century. But from the moment of its creation, this template was questioned, and most vociferously by some of those whose cause Sartre was ostensibly promoting. Just as Sartre was dismissed as the "total intellectual" by Pierre Bourdieu, one who establishes "asymmetric relations" with writers and "think(s) them through more ably than they could think themselves," so has Sartre's patronage of black writers been dismissed by many of his critics as a totalizing gesture that blots out the work of the very writers he is supporting.[2] Frantz Fanon, in *Peau noire, masques blancs* (*Black Skin, White Masks*), accused Sartre of sapping the enthusiasm of black writers before they had had a chance to fully develop their aesthetics and their critiques.[3] Jean Bwejeri, for his part, castigates Sartre for masking his profound nihilism regarding the place of blacks in the postwar world—that is, they have none—with superficial optimism about the power of black cultural expression.[4] What, then, is there left to salvage of Sartre's discourse on "race" and its relation to cultural production? What happens in the half century after Sartre's most substantive interventions on the subject to the category of "black writing" that he helped bring into existence? And is there an alternative to Sartre's criticism and patronage of black writers?

To answer these questions, this chapter considers the respective contributions of Jean-Paul Sartre and the Martinican novelist, poet, and theorist

Edouard Glissant to the promotion of the category belatedly known as "francophone literature," specifically in the form of prefaces or introductions that each has written. Prefaces written by one author or public intellectual for another—what Gérard Genette calls allographic prefaces—forcibly constitute a discourse on the Other.[5] With very few exceptions, the allographic preface writer occupies a position of greater status or authority in the literary mediascape than the author being prefaced, and this disparity in status necessarily creates the conditions for an "othering" discourse (e.g., established writers referring to the "youth" of the writers for whom they are prefacing). But not all othering discourses that appear in prefaces are equal: The prefaces under consideration here are fraught with profound cultural and political implications because they address—directly in one case, obliquely in the other—the racialized Otherness that has been a factor in the interest in the literary field of colonial or postcolonial francophone literature since its inception.

Fifty years separate the two prefaces that are most integral to my argument—Sartre's 1948 preface "Orphée noir" ("Black Orpheus"), the text that effectively added negritude to the mix of postwar cultural and political movements, and Glissant's interventions or "entre-dires," as they are designated, in a 1997 novel by fellow Martinican and Prix Goncourt–winning author Patrick Chamoiseau—making the apposition of their practices potentially anachronistic and tendentious.[6] But it is precisely the difference in their respective approaches to essentially the same task and the same object that justifies this rapprochement. Both intend to promote, validate, and otherwise enable the circulation of works in French from the colonies and former colonies of France. Each employs, however, such remarkably different rhetoric and tactics for doing so that each writer's prefaces raise pointed questions about the other's practice—and position—as literary patron.

Of course, the situation of the francophone post/colonial writer changes significantly in the fifty years that separate their two most important prefaces in this field, and I will necessarily account for shifts along the diachronic axis as I consider how the rhetoric and form of the preface are transformed in the passage from Sartre's omniscient patronage to Glissant's willfully partial or minor one.[7] Still, the task of the allographic preface writer remains fundamentally the same at the turn of the millennium as at mid-century, if not at any other point since the advent of "literature" as a marketable commodity: to grant some portion of the authority of the preface writer to the prefaced writer in order to create an audience for the work in question.[8] It is the means of fulfilling that mandate—and everything those means imply—that has changed. For all of Sartre's insistence on his abdication of the preface writer's authority, "Orphée noir" remains an act of panoptic and potentially totalizing analysis. Glissant's preface, for its part, takes the opposite tack, written as if hoping to pass unnoticed and in the process shift the focus to Chamoiseau, but at the risk of falling into insignificance. It is the case, I will argue, that the respective position of these writers on the question of "race" and, more broadly, difference determines in large part the rhetorical stance each strikes vis-à-vis the text in question. My objective, then, is to read Sartre's prefaces in light of Glissant's, and vice-versa, in order to show what role "race"—the preeminent marker of hierarchized difference in the post/colonial context—plays in the articulation of a discourse on francophone literature and on the form that articulation takes.

Speaking for Others: Sartre and Negritude

In this mutual interrogation of Sartre's and Glissant's prefaces, it is not the commercial utility or "success" of the patronage that is at issue; it is beyond debate that Sartre's prefaces had a far greater impact on the original consolidation of the field of francophone post/colonial literature than any of Glissant's prefaces have had in its subsequent popularization. For better or for worse, the one writer or critic to do more than any other to put francophone literature on the cultural map is Sartre. "Orphée noir," the essay/preface to the *Anthologie de la nouvelle poésie nègre et malgache de langue française*, edited by Léopold Senghor and first published in 1948, was for many the text that signaled the arrival and guaranteed the cultural importance of writers from the French colonies. Similar volumes published the previous year—the collectively edited *Les Plus beaux écrits de l'Union française et du Maghreb* and Léon-Gontran Damas's *Poètes d'expression française 1900–1945*—generated less interest and did not circulate nearly as widely, partly, it must be assumed, for lack of a metropolitan patron authorizing the endeavor.[9] As further evidence of the crucial role it played, Senghor's *Anthologie* was also the only one of these three postwar anthologies of "colonized" francophone literature to be reissued, which it now has been seven times.

The presence of Sartre's name on the cover of the *Anthologie* was sufficient to draw readers to this emerging field of cultural production. However, the preface did far more than that: It defined negritude as an aesthetic and social movement in so comprehensive and persuasive a fashion that it became the authoritative document of its time on the subject. There are many signs of the discursive reach of "Orphée noir," though perhaps none more poignant than Présence Africaine's editorial decision in 1963 to publish the preface as a stand-alone document, implying through subtraction that the *Anthologie*'s poets' own creative articulation of the concept of negritude was superceded by Sartre's essay.[10]

But the suggestion of subaltern or colonized voices having been effectively silenced by Sartre's patronage, however well intentioned, has dogged the essay almost from the moment of its publication, and this presumably informs Glissant's palpable resistance to the role of literary patron (even as he plays it). One cannot fault Sartre for the ethic of generosity on display in "Orphée noir" and in other interventions on behalf of the colonized. Many have asked, though, if "Orphée noir" might not be a poisoned gift. This is where the critical reception of "Orphée noir" seems to stand at the present. My brief consideration below of the patronage of francophone literature from the colonial period—prior to Sartre's intervention—is meant to complicate this perspective, as is my subsequent rereading of Sartre's "Orphée noir" and its antithesis, Glissant's "entre-dires."

The packaging of what was known as "indigenous literature"—the first works in French from the 1920s and 1930s written by colonial subjects—was characterized by a discourse of objectification. The preface writer was almost always positioned hypertextually, dispensing praise or, more often, criticism from an elevated vantage point. To take a representative example of the discourse of the preface from those years, Georges Hardy, a colonial administrator, referred to Paul Hazoumé's 1938 historical novel *Doguicimi* as a sign of the "conquêtes intellectuelles et morales" (intellectual and moral conquests) effected by French colonialism, while forcefully excluding it from the category of Literature, since, for him, Hazoumé's text was nothing more than a repository of ethnographic data.[11] Other ostensibly well-meaning prefaces insisted on the essential goodness and refreshing naïveté of the black writers. Although there are a few prefaces from the period that resist this discursive norm, none did so as directly and as powerfully as Sartre's "Orphée noir," which bucked this entire tradition.

As a result of the participation of colonial subjects in the Resistance and the Liberation and the emergence of a new colonial configuration known as the *Union française* based on the politics of association as opposed to the politics of assimilation, this paternalistic paratextual discourse vanished after the end of the World War II. The category of indigenous literature, largely a phenomenon of colonial publishing, was essentially dissolved and replaced by what Senghor would call "littérature négro-africaine d'expression française" (Black African literature of French expression), which he later revised to "littérature négro-africaine de langue française" (Black African literature in French). This was a predominantly metropolitan French publishing enterprise, with the quintessential instantiation being Présence Africaine, headquartered as it was (and is) on the Rue des écoles in Paris. Accordingly, it began to receive the support of important metropolitan intellectual figures: André Breton, André Gide, Jean Cocteau, Louis Aragon, and, most emphatically, Sartre. If all of these metropolitan preface writers practiced their patronage from a more sympathetic and less authoritative position than their prewar counterparts, Sartre took this the furthest, perhaps even, as Daniel Maximin has suggested, to the point of masochism.[12] The paratextual discourse of racial objectification of the interwar years became in the opening lines of "Orphée noir" a discourse of racial subjectification, and Sartre and the white world became the objects of the gaze of these newly emerging black subjects.

Unlike the patrons of indigenous literature from the interwar years, Sartre adopted a posture of humility in relation to the texts he introduced. He focused on the gulf that existed between him and the poets whose work appears in Senghor's *Anthologie*, a gulf that is the result, as he saw it, of "race" or, rather, of racial differentiation. Sartre maintained that whereas whiteness had come to be a signifier for technical mastery and domination, blackness was at its core the collective memory of slavery and of the objectification enacted by it (xxxvii). Having found themselves the inheritors of this position, black writers write to reclaim their individual and collective subjectivity, and it is this hypersubjectivity that Sartre identified as the force of black poetry. Sartre established a new, reversed hierarchy of value in which white culture was less vibrant than the black culture manifested in the *Anthologie*, and most strikingly for him in the excerpt of Aimé Césaire's *Cahier d'un retour au pays natal* (Notebook of a Return to my Native Land) that it contains.

This subject/object reversal has the effect of placing Sartre in the unusual position of the literary patron who views the object of his patronage from below. The most hyperbolic expression of this appears in a phrase paradoxically designed to bring Sartre closer to his object of study and patronage: "Our whiteness seems a strange opaque varnish that keeps our skin from breathing, a white suit, worn at the elbows and knees, under which, if it could be removed, we would find true human flesh, flesh the color of black wine."[13] This black wine ("vin noir") is in fact borrowed from the famous Senghor poem "Femme noire" ("Black woman") that Sartre had just cited, and clearly suggests, in this context, the color of black skin. Sartre's desire to peel back his white skin and reveal the authentic color of humanity—which is depicted here as blackness—constituted, at this point in the history of the reception and patronage of colonized literature, a clear epistemic break. It suggests, if we are to take Sartre at his word, that blackness constitutes the baseline of humanity, and that white skin is a dangerous supplement that, as the history of colonialism indicates to Sartre, obscures that humanity.

Sartre's desire to transform himself into his object of study also manifests itself in the form that the language of the preface takes. As Ronnie Scharfman has pointed out, there are passages in "Orphée noir" that "strain to espouse the Césairian text itself."[14] The most imitative passages in Sartre's preface are the ones that address the explicitly sexual elements of Césaire's poetry. Sartre mimics this language, I suspect, for the same reason that he expresses a desire to remove his white skin: The vivid phallic imagery, learned medical vocabulary, and percussive, repetitive language employed by Césaire is as foreign to Sartre's writing as the experience of being black. In order to be able to comment meaningfully on this Francophone poetry that is linguistically intelligible but culturally opaque, Sartre seems compelled to inhabit it.[15] In writing of the mimicry of the colonized, Homi Bhabha characterizes it as "a complex strategy of reform, regulation and discipline, which 'appropriates' the Other as it visualizes power."[16] In a complex reversal, especially for the year 1948, Sartre visualizes the power of being physically and, as it were, aesthetically black, of adopting the role of the previously subordinate term in colonial "race" relations.

Sartre's gestures of radical and perhaps even exaggerated empathy, along with his mimetic language, could be read as forms of appropriation, as hijacking the other's voice, which silences it, but such a reading is inconsistent with his broader stated goal of infusing morose capitalist Europe with the vitality of blackness, a vitality that is not an essence but the result of an anticapitalist and noninstrumental relation to the world. Perhaps "borrowing" is a term preferable to "appropriation" here: The gestures of rapprochement with the black poets give Sartre the critical authority necessary to write the preface. He has, in spite of his outsider's position, an insider's knowledge. This is necessarily an uncomfortable position for the preface writer, and Sartre acknowledges relatively late in "Orphée noir" the uneasiness that he, the white metropolitan literary figure prefacing a collection of "poésie nègre," feels:

> And what is, then, this negritude that is the sole concern of these poets and the only subject of this book? I must first answer that a white man is not capable of explaining it properly because he does not experience it internally.... But this introduction would be incomplete if [...] I did not show that this complex notion is, at its core, pure poetry.[17]

In this striking act of preterition ("It's not for me to say, but it's my conviction that ..."), Sartre concedes his unsuitability to the task of defining negritude, before proceeding to perform that very task.

This passage could serve, then, as an encapsulated version of the rhetorical strategy of the entire preface: Sartre positions himself outside of the black poet's work in one breath and comments upon it in the next. While this can be read as another instance of Sartre's confiscation of the black writers' project, is it not also possible to read it as a marker of what Daniel Maximin characterizes as Sartre's "realization [...] of the indignity of speaking for others, while continuing to speak with them"?[18] To avoid speaking for the Other, especially in the immediate postwar period when polarized difference was all there was, Sartre would have had to avoid speaking altogether.

The strongest objections to "Orphée noir" stem from its conclusion. In many cases the essay has been reduced by its critics to those few lines in which Sartre famously confines negritude to the position of antithesis in a dialectic and therefore slates it for disappearance. Although Ronnie Scharfman remains vague on exactly who indicts Sartre, she suggests that it is for its conclusion that "Orphée noir" has "gained [...], ironically, the epithet of 'racist' in black circles."[19] The central point of contention in the preface appears two paragraphs from the end when Sartre reclaims the preface writer's authority that he had spent the better part of the preface foreswearing in order to claim that "the man of color and only the man of color can be asked to renounce his racial pride" in the name of ushering in "the imminent universalism that will constitute the decline of negritude,"[20] The impetus for the accusation of racism in "Orphée noir" is still difficult to identify: Is Sartre racist because he romanticizes blackness earlier in the preface (which would make him more properly *racialist*)[21] or because he announces its demise at the end, if that is in fact what he does?

The argument between Denis Hollier and Susan Suleiman regarding Sartre's 1946 essay *Réflexions sur la question juive* is instructive for understanding the controversy aroused by some of the movements and gestures in "Orphée noir."[22] Concerning the charge of racial stereotyping, Suleiman, who has in recent years famously (or infamously, depending on one's view of the debate) argued that Sartre's passionate defense of "the Jew" paradoxically produces an "antisemitic effect." She writes that "although Sartre rejects racial determinism (in principle, if not always in 'detail'), he substitutes for it a determinism of situation," which she suggests amounts to the same thing.[23] While this tendency is certainly on display in "Orphée noir," the traits of the white working class are as "essentialized" as those of the black poets, and, in both cases, these traits are shown to be responses to a situation but not the only possibility. The hyperbolic characterization of the differences between blacks and whites in "Orphée noir" is more plausibly the result of the fact that the Sartre of this period viewed social change through the lens of the Hegelian dialectic, which requires a sharp distinction between the first two terms in order to arrive at the synthesis.

However, the problem of the synthesis, which requires the disappearance of difference in the universalizing gesture of the dialectic, remains. Suleiman and others have taken Sartre to task for asking Jews to assimilate in order to defeat antisemitism, just as he asks blacks to renounce negritude to put an end to racism. While these are important and at least partially valid critiques, Sartre's position in both instances has been reduced to a caricature, as if the postwar Sartre were articulating the same fundamentalist Republican position as Alain Finkielkraut in *La défaite de la pensée*.[24] Denis Hollier argues in response to Suleiman that Sartre's call to assimilation at the end of *Réflexions sur la question juive*

> is no longer associated with a repressive antipluralistic program, with any form of renouncing differences, with having to conform, to resemble, to be the same as everyone. Assimilation simply connotes [...] sharing the same, open, secular time. Not being the same in history, but being in the same history. Assimilation, here, simply means the pure openness of historical synchronicity. That there is one and only one time and one history. That history (as opposed to memory) is never strictly of one's own. That history means risking one's past in the other's language, in the other's time.[25]

Sartre makes this very point regarding the role of negritude within the synthesis of previously opposing forces at the end of "Orphée noir": "Race has transformed itself into historicity; the black present is exploding and entering time; negritude, with its past and its future, is inserting itself into universal history; it is no longer a *state* nor even an existential attitude, but a becoming."[26] Black cultures, having been confined to the margins of history, have reached the point of being able to assert themselves on a global historical scale. This does not mean that the concerns of the poets of the *Anthologie* will now mirror those of the white working class; it means, rather, that there will be new set of global concerns that will include those of the formerly enslaved.

This is not to deny that Sartre overstates the difference between black and white in "Orphée noir." But it is hard to imagine how he could avoid doing so while writing on the threshold of a collection of poetry that performs that very gesture. In any case, this is a different problem than the one evoked by the conclusion to the preface. If one concedes that the binary oppositions constructed by Sartre are rhetorically necessary for the preface's conclusion, then it is simply a question of gauging the meaning and importance of the "synthesis" of the dialectic. Writing very much against the grain, Nik Farrell Fox argues that, "unlike the Hegelian dialectic, Sartre's dialectic does not collapse one term into the other. It explores the ground that lies between them—the space of the conjuctive."[27] Fox positions Sartre not as the foil to postmodernism but as a transitional thinker, and, read in relation to what comes before and after it in Sartre's work, the dialectic in Sartre's "Orphée noir" can be understood as an early movement toward that transition. Reading the conclusion to the preface in this way makes "Orphée noir" less a definitive, totalizing statement on blackness than an exploration of the space between black and white. Sartre does attempt to partially bridge this space, but not at the expense of all difference as many have argued. Blackness for Sartre can no longer be, as many of the poets of the *Anthologie* would seem to have it, a self-constituting, self-sustaining movement; it must join other imagined communities (e.g., Sartre's "whites") in the broader struggle for justice.

Speaking with Others: Glissant's Utopia of Horizontality

Sartre's call for negritude to join "universal history" came perhaps too early for some (Fanon, most prominently), but it is difficult to argue that this call was not heeded by the writers and theorists of postcolonialism, or at least that Sartre's aims do not align in some way with theirs. The project of literary postcolonialism is not simply to supersede colonialism; that, in essence, was the project of decolonization. There is a generalized renouncement in the works of postcolonial authors of the illusion of transparency in language and of the stark political oppositions of the period of decolonization. There is also in these works a forsaking of the "race" politics of anticolonial movements, which lead in their extreme form into the racial absolutism of Duvalier's *noirisme* in Haiti and Mobutu's *authenticité* in Zaire.

This movement away from racial-identity politics is reflected in the postcolonial literary field in the emerging demand for prefaces from the generation of postcolonial writers who initiated their production near the beginning of the post-independence period. Léopold Senghor, who wrote a number of prefaces in the 1940s and 1950s that associated aesthetics with race, seems not to have been solicited by the younger generation of postcolonial writers. White metropolitan patrons, for their part, played hardly any role in the paratextual promotion of postcolonial literature (Sartre's last preface to the work of a black writer was to a posthumous collection of essays by Patrice Lumumba published in 1963).

Among those whose patronage was solicited by postcolonial writers and their publishers, Edouard Glissant was and remains perhaps the most sought after imprimatur. Glissant was asked to write a number of allographic prefaces during these years precisely because his patronage marked works as existing beyond the binary oppositions of the period of decolonization. Glissant's prefaces manifests an intensifying discomfort with the allographic preface writer's authority, the wielding of which contrasts sharply with Glissant's concept of *Relation*.[28] A recent paratextual intervention by Glissant stands as his most compelling reflection on the institution of patronage and constitutes a transfiguration (more precisely, a fragmenting) of the preface and, by extension, the promise of the disappearance of the last traces of colonial ideology in the presentation and marketing of francophone literatures.

But it is also symptomatic of a discourse on difference that has difficulty accounting for difference.

Glissant is in many respects both the Sartre and the anti-Sartre of his generation. He is one of the leading and most active theoreticians of the global postcolonial condition, while remaining a reluctant authority, if not quantitatively then at least qualitatively. In the patronage of francophone literature, after Léopold Senghor, it is Edouard Glissant who has written more prefaces than anyone else. However, meaningful comparison with Senghor stops at quantity. Already in his first preface written in 1959 for Kateb Yacine's trilogy of plays, *Le cercle des représailles*, Glissant reflected upon the problem of the vertical, racialized nature of the patronage of so-called Third World literature. Glissant's preface describes Kateb's plays by insisting on the poetic, allusive nature of Kateb's writing that is in part a product of its Algerian specificity. But the preface also inscribes Kateb's plays in a much broader context: "Today, more than ever before, we cannot imagine our life or our art existing outside of the remarkable efforts of people of different races and cultures who are attempting to approach and become familiar with one another. Today, the circle is closed, we are all in the same place, and it is the entire planet."[29]

Glissant addresses this text not from the perspective of racial similarity, as Senghor tended to, but that of situational similarity. In other words, Glissant is able to write "nous" and imply that he and Kateb share certain aesthetic sensibilities and are working toward the same objectives because they are both part of the collective of the colonized that Frantz Fanon would theorize two years later in *Les damnés de la terre* (*The Wretched of the Earth*). It is from this situational affinity with Kateb that Glissant derives his authority. Glissant's use of the collective personal pronoun "nous" is already different from Senghor's contemporaneous gesture of calling for a specifically black African criticism of black African literature in that it is situational rather than racialized. It is also, more significantly, a departure from Sartre's initial discourse of differentiation in "Orphée noir." Glissant seeks in this preface to undo the hierarchies that had, up to this point, governed relations between patron and author, not to mention between colonizer and colonized or between black and white.

Over time, though, Glissant, like many other philosophers of the postcolonial condition, became suspicious of the "nous" (us) and its implication of racial and cultural homogeneity within the postcolonies. In subsequent prefaces, Glissant found different ways of mitigating the problem of authority in the paratext that avoid suggesting a form of forced solidarity. In 1979, Glissant wrote an otherwise unremarkable preface to a collection of poems by the Guadeloupean Henri Corbin, which he titled not "préface" but "avant-dire" (foreword or, more literally, the "pre-speech"). Glissant did not coin a term here, the "avant-dire" having been a common name for the preface until the beginning of the twentieth century. That said, Glissant's rehabilitation of the term was a deliberate gesture to move the preface into the less vertical realm of orality. It is worth recalling that, at about the same time, Glissant qualified the oral in *Le discours antillais* (*Caribbean Discourse*) as "le geste organisé de la diversité" (the organized gesture of diversity) and the written as "la trace universalisante du Même" (the universalizing trace of Sameness).[30]

By extension, then, a preface that presents itself in form and content as a sort of transcription of the oral sidesteps the problem of authority in the paratext. In a similarly minor preface to the childhood memoirs of Maurice Roche, a white French writer, *Un petit rien-du-tout tout neuf plié dans une feuille de persil* (1997), Glissant pursues this minimally invasive form of paratextual patronage. Most of this preface is devoted to describing Maurice Roche's polymorphous aesthetics through the characteristics of his ... cats: "M.R. changes with them, he becomes multi-cat, which explains (to us) why he welcomes so many of them to his side."[31] Glissant is content in this preface to simply exchange a few words, and to do so with a white French writer in this spirit is to, once again, break down the racial binary.

Another way of diminishing the authority of the allograph is to do away with precedence. A preface comes *before*, and therefore at least symbolically dictates the meaning of the text to follow. Glissant responds by writing a short "postface" to the Franco-Peul writer Sylvie Kandé's *Lagon, lagunes* from 2000. Here too, Glissant did not invent the postface, or afterword, but it seems clear that he intends to have the placement of his paratextual intervention signify not his understanding of the work in question—and we know that for Glissant "compréhension," or understanding, equals appropriation—but a lateral appreciation when he writes "there is no point in my lecturing you here. I simply wanted, *in this place*, to share with you the unfathomable and the unpredictable."[32]

Glissant's preface "Un marqueur de paroles," ("A Word Scratcher") attached to the paratextually enriched second edition of Patrick Chamoiseau's *Chronique des sept misères* (1988; *Chronicle of the Seven Sorrows*, 1999), seemed to mark a retreat to a more conventional form of patronage. It is far more descriptive and analytical than Glissant's other prefaces, and assumes a more authoritative voice in its inscription of Chamoiseau in a cultural and intellectual movement of Glissant's invention:

> Patrick Chamoiseau belongs to a generation that did not thrill to the noble generalities of negritude but focused instead on the particulars of West Indian reality. The particulars? One should say, rather, the inextricable mass of experience, a questioning of the wellsprings of language and history, the groundwork of what I have called our *antillanité*, that Caribbeanness so much in evidence and so imperiled.[33]

This passage stands out for two reasons: First, this preface is one of the few sites where Glissant directly expresses his opposition to what he considers negritude's excessively broad ambitions. Second, it is also the only preface in which Glissant subordinates the writer he is introducing; to paraphrase Glissant, Chamoiseau belongs to a movement of his own invention. Of course, this arrangement is at least partially reciprocal since the epigraph at the beginning of the novel, just a few pages after Glissant's preface, is culled from Glissant's *Le discours antillais*. There is, nonetheless, an unacknowledged imbalance of authority in the paratext to *Chronique des sept misères*, as there is generally in the relations between Chamoiseau and Glissant, especially as it relates to epigraphs and other markers of a literary institutional hierarchy.

In a more recent allographic paratextual intervention, which is not a preface per se, Glissant, with the cooperation and encouragement of Chamoiseau, attempted to displace the power imbalance that existed in the margins of *Chronique des sept misères*.[34] He produced an interesting innovation in the paratext, but does so, as in his previous prefaces, in a minor key. A problem of residual authority exists in the prefaces to Kateb, Chamoiseau, Corbin, Kandé, and Roche, and it is the problem of distinction. Any type of preface or afterword stands outside of the text and, by extension, *supra*, thereby running the risk of constituting the sort of totalizing "compréhension" (understanding *and* appropriation) against which Glissant's critical work argues. A way out of this particular problem comes in Patrick Chamoiseau's *L'esclave vieil homme et le molosse* (1997) and can be characterized in the following way: Do not preface the author—not even in a manner that flatters through imitation, as in the case of "Orphée noir"—but share the page with him.

Esclave vieil homme et le molosse recounts, in quite linear fashion, the story of a Martinican slave who maroons and heads for the interior of the island, with the eponymous "molosse" (attack dog) and his béké master on his heals throughout. The question of the authorship and authority of the text is raised from the outset by the fact that every chapter is prefaced by a short passage from Glissant. Glissant's "entre-dires," as they are dubbed on the inside cover of the novel, are culled, as Chamoiseau informs the reader elsewhere in the paratext, from Glissant's *Intention poétique* and another text unpublished at the time, "La folie Celat." Unlike the typical preface, Glissant's "entre-dires" do not explicate or promote the texts they introduce. Rather, they are disconnected textual episodes that anticipate and run parallel to Chamoiseau's. In his "entre-dire" to the chapter titled "Eaux" (Waters), which concerns the runaway slave's communion with water during his escape, Glissant inserts a paragraph in which Marie Celat ponders the depths of the ocean (58). Later, before the chapter titled "La Pierre" (The Rock), Glissant writes allusively of the Rocher du Diamant, a large outcropping of rock off the southern tip of Martinique: "This stone is a rock. It grew in the depths of the sea, like a patina-covered cannonball."[35]

In these passages, Glissant abandons the authority of the preface writer in order to participate in the creation of the narrative or, perhaps, of a kind of hypertext within the text. Whereas a preface or afterword speaks *about* a text, the "entre-dire" speaks *with* the text. By creating resonances between his work and Chamoiseau's, and by doing so in the text rather than around or above the novel, Glissant transforms the paratext from a discourse on the text to a dialogue with it. Glissant's "entre-dires" are principally meaningful as a gesture (they do not in any way advance the narrative). By speaking briefly and obliquely of Chamoiseau's text, Glissant's intratext suggests not the "we" of the preface to Kateb or Chamoiseau's *Chronique des sept misères*, but rather two "I's" coming into contact with each other in a situation of transversality, not verticality, of horizontality, not hierarchy. These two first-person singulars are different, but they exist on the same plane. It is implied that they are equals in the francophone literary ecology. This paratext clearly aspires to bring into existence a new protocol governing the relations between author and preface writer and the inside and the outside of the text.

There is something profoundly utopian in this gesture, as there is, I would argue, in Glissant's work as a whole. It is as if the intratextuality of the "entre-dires" were enough to completely erase the historically hierarchal relationship between author and patron, as well as between Glissant and Chamoiseau. In spite of the transversality of the personal relationship between them that is averred elsewhere, the publishing context implies a hierarchy that is simply ignored in the paratext to *Esclave vieil homme et le molosse*. The existence of this hierarchy is evident in the fact that Chamoiseau inserts an epigraph from Glissant at the beginning of nearly every one of his works, indicating at the very least a debt to his predecessor, whereas, to my knowledge, Glissant mentions Chamoiseau just once in the paratext to his own works.[36]

This ostensible evacuation of the problem of authority in the paratext by Glissant evokes a broader tendency in his work identified by Celia Britton, who notes that Glissant writes "as though the values of Relation, chaos, and diversity have in fact already prevailed."[37] I would add that, in the world of literary publishing, those values have decidedly *not* prevailed. Glissant tries to move the text toward the plane of immanence, the plane of the unmediated, but it remains most evidently mediated by the French literary institution (after all, the novel is published by Gallimard).[38] Through an act of relational voluntarism, Glissant attempts to evacuate the difference in status between author and patron in a space where to do so is quite simply an act of denial.

Difference/Indifference: A Conclusion

If Sartre's "Orphée noir" was the exaggerated expression of racial *difference* (which is perhaps too quickly bridged at the end), Glissant's "entre-dires" suggest *indifference*, in both senses of the word: Indifferent, in that it seems as if Glissant sent Chamoiseau whichever scraps of texts he had close at hand (Chamoiseau has remarked that he wished that Glissant had done something more substantial with the "entre-dires"[39]); indifferent too, and more significantly, in that the "entre-dires" suggest that there is no difference between their texts, their cultural projects, and their respective places in the postcolonial literary field. Glissant's paratextual intervention certainly avoids obscuring the Other through analysis, but it is not clear what it accomplishes beyond that.

Sartre takes the risk of speaking for the Other, of naming racial and cultural difference, and this is an endeavor fraught with potential consequences, especially when viewed from our present. The generation that follows Sartre's will announce that speaking for the Other is obscene, although perhaps obscenity is preferable to extreme discretion. If one respects Glissant's "droit à l'opacité" (the right not to be understood), which finds its logical extension in all of Glissant's prefaces and especially in the "entre-dires" to Chamoiseau's novel, not very much is exchanged—there is no arguing with the "entre-dires." Sartre's "Orphée noir," which is generous but also potentially overbearing, risks saying too much and being an appropriative gesture, but—in spite of all of the voices that have paradoxically professed to the contrary—the argument continues.

Notes

1. This chapter compresses some parts and expands other parts of arguments I made in two chapters of my book *Packaging Post/Coloniality: The Manufacture of Literary Identity in the Francophone World* (Lanham, Md.: Lexington, 2005). I would like to thank those in attendance at the "Sartre and His Others/Sartre et ses autres" conference held at Harvard University in April 2005 who commented on an earlier version of the current chapter, in particular Denis Hollier, Annie Cohen-Solal, and Alice Jardine. I am also grateful to the faculty in French at UC Berkeley for their intellectual and moral support throughout my semester-long exile from New Orleans in the aftermath of Hurricane Katrina, during which time I completed this chapter. Unless otherwise noted, translations are mine.
2. Pierre Bourdieu, *The Rules of Art: Genesis and Structure of the Literary Field*, trans. Susan Emanuel (1992; Stanford: Stanford University Press, 1996), 209.
3. Frantz Fanon, *Peau noire, masques blancs* (Paris: Editions du Seuil, 1952), 187. What often gets lost in the debate, however, is that Fanon was as ambivalent as Sartre about "race" and its place in the struggle for the emancipation of the oppressed. In the same section of *Peau noire, masques blancs* in which he critiques Sartre's conclusions to "Orphée noir," Fanon also writes, "le nègre

n'est pas. Pas plus que le blanc" [the black man doesn't exist. No more than the white man].
4. Jean Bwejeri, "*Orphée noir* ou la lettre qui tue: éléments pour une évaluation du concept sartrien de négritude," *Les Lettres Romanes* 43.1–2 (1989): 97.
5. Gérard Genette, *Paratexts: Thresholds of Interpretation*, trans. Jane E. Lewin (New York: Cambridge University Press, 1997), esp. 244–47.
6. Jean-Paul Sartre, "Orphée noir," preface to *Anthologie de la nouvelle poésie nègre et malgache*, ed. Léopold Sédar (1948; Paris: Presses Universitaires de France, 1977); Edouard Glissant, "Entre-dires," prefaces to Patrick Chamoiseau, *Esclave vieil homme et le molosse* (Paris: Gallimard, 1997). Subsequent references to Sartre's "Orphée noir" and Glissant's "entre-dires" will appear in the body of the text.
7. I borrow the term "post/colonial" from Chris Bongie who uses it to signify the epistemic complicity between the colonial and postcolonial periods. See his *Islands and Exiles: The Creole Identities of Post/Colonial Literature* (Stanford: Stanford University Press, 1998), 13.
8. Gérard Genette points to a number of other functions that the allographic preface performs, such as presentation and recommendation (*op. cit.*, 244–47). But these functions can all be considered means of granting authority. I insist on the term "authority" because it is precisely what the post/colonial writer is lacking in the eyes of the metropolitan French literary institution.
9. *Les plus beaux écrits de l'Union française et du Maghreb,* ed. and pref. Mohamed El Kholti, Léopold S. Senghor, Pierre Do Dinh, A. Rakoto Ratsimamanga, and E. Ralajmihiatra (Paris: La Colombe, 1947); *Poètes d'expression française, 1900–1945,* ed. Léon Damas (Paris: Seuil, 1947). Although Damas's anthology had a modicum of success, there are, according to the WorldCat database, only eight extant copies worldwide of *Les Plus beaux écrits de l'Union française et du Maghreb.*
10. Jean-Paul Sartre, *Black Orpheus*, trans. S. W. Allen (Paris: Présence africaine, 1963). This is neither the last nor even the most famous instance of a preface by Sartre becoming a major document in its own right. Sartre had been asked in 1951 by the publisher Gallimard to contribute a preface to Jean Genet's complete works to date. This quickly became a five hundred-page chapter that Gallimard chose to publish as a stand-alone study and that was published in advance of Genet's *Oeuvres complètes.* See Jean-Paul Sartre, *Saint Genet, comédien et martyr* (Paris: Gallimard, 1952). Suggestive of the problem of Sartre's totalizing analysis is Genet's response to the "preface," as related by Sartre: "Ça le dégoûtait parce qu'il se sentait bien tel que je l'avais décrit" [It disgusted him because he liked himself as I had described him]. Simone de Beauvoir, *La Cérémonie des adieux* (Paris: Gallimard, 1981), 350.
11. Paul Hazoumé, *Doguicimi*, pref. Georges Hardy (1938; Paris: G.-P. Maisonneuve et Larose, 1978), 9–11.
12. Daniel Maximin, "Sartre et le tiers(-monde)," *Sartre: Catalogue de l'exposition à la BNF,* ed. Mauricette Berne (Paris: Bibliothèque Nationale de France/Gallimard, 2005), 124.
13. "Notre blancheur nous paraît un étrange vernis blême qui empêche notre peau de respirer, un maillot blanc, usé aux coudes et aux genoux, sous lequel, si nous pouvions l'ôter, on trouverait la vraie chair humaine, la chair couleur de vin noir" (ix).
14. Ronnie Scharfman, *Engagement and the Language of the Subject in the Poetry of Aimé Césaire* (Gainesville: University Press of Florida, 1987), 12.
15. Arlette Elkaïm-Sartre remarked on Sartre's tendency to mimic his object of analysis in a preface to her adoptive father's essay on Mallarmé, suggesting

that it is not so much racial difference but difference tout court that inspires Sartre's will to (sometimes totalizing) understanding. Jean-Paul Sartre, *Mallarmé: La lucidité et sa face d'ombre*, pref. Arlette Elkaïm-Sartre (Paris: Editions Gallimard, 1986), 9.

16. Homi Bhabha, *The Location of Culture* (London: Routledge, 1994), 86.
17. "Et qu'est-ce donc à présent que cette négritude, unique souci de ces poètes, unique sujet de ce livre? Il faut d'abord répondre qu'un blanc ne saurait en parler convenablement, puisqu'il n'en a pas l'expérience intérieure.... Mais cette introduction serait incomplète si ... je ne montrais que cette notion complexe est, en son coeur, Poésie pure" (xxix).
18. "la prise de conscience [...] de l'indignité de penser pour les autres, sans pour autant cesser de parler avec eux" (Maximin, 125).
19. Scharfman, *Engagement*, 12.
20. "à l'homme de couleur et à lui seul il peut être demandé de renoncer à la fierté de sa couleur"; "l'universalisme futur qui sera le crépuscule de sa négritude ..." (xlii).
21. In the popular understanding of this distinction (as put forward by, for instance, the NAACP), a racist argues for the supremacy of one race over the others while a racialist simply acknowledges the importance of "race" in social movements.
22. Jean-Paul Sartre, *Réflexions sur la question juive* (Paris: Gallimard, 1946).
23. Susan Suleiman, "Rereading Rereading: Further Reflections on Sartre's *Réflexions*," *October* 87 (Winter, 1999): 132.
24. Finkielkraut argues that France is the home of universal values without acknowledging, of course, that such a statement is itself an affirmation of cultural particularity and an act of differentiation. Since culture is something one *has*, Finkielkraut asks the Muslim immigrant to step out of his cultural skin without acknowledging that to become "French" he must step into a new one. Alain Finkielkraut, *La Défaite de la pensée: essai* (Paris: Gallimard, 1987), 131.
25. Denis Hollier, "Mosaic: Terminable and Interminable," *October* 87 (Winter, 1999): 159.
26. "la race s'est transmuée en *historicité*, le Présent noir explose et se temporalise, la Négritude s'insère avec son Passé et son Avenir dans l'Histoire Universelle, ce n'est plus un *état* ni même une attitude existentielle, c'est un Devenir" (xxxix).
27. Nik Farrell Fox, *The New Sartre: Explorations in Postmodernism* (New York: Continuum, 2003), 51–52.
28. Although difficult to pin down, *Relation* is probably best described in opposition to conceptions of the universal: Whereas universalism posits an underlying identity or disposition accessible to all, *Relation* sees a global totality made up of discrete, nonhierarchized individuals. It is, by extension, a theory of irreducible diversity.
29. "Aujourd'hui plus qu'hier, nous ne pouvons envisager notre vie ni notre art en dehors de l'effort terrible des hommes qui, de races et de cultures différentes, tentent de s'approcher et de se connaître. Aujourd'hui le cercle est fermé, nous voici tous dans le même lieu: et c'est la terre tout entière." Kateb Yacine, *Le cercle des représailles*, pref. Edouard Glissant (Paris: Editions du Seuil, 1959), 10–11.
30. Edouard Glissant, *Le discours antillais* (1997; Paris: Gallimard, 1981), 330–31.
31. "M.R. change avec eux, il devient multichat, c'est ce qui explique (pour nous) qu'il en accueille autant près de lui." Maurice Roche, *Un petit rien-du-tout*

tout neuf plié dans une feuille de persil, pref. Edouard Glissant (Paris: Gallimard, 1997), ii.
32. "il ne sert de rien que je vous administre ici. Je voulais seulement, *à cette place*, partager avec vous l'insondable et l'imprévisible." Sylvie Kandé, *Lagon, lagunes*, "postface" by Edouard Glissant (Paris: Gallimard, 2000), 76, emphasis mine.
33. "Patrick Chamoiseau est d'une génération qui n'a pas vibré aux généralités généreuses de la Négritude, mais qui a porté son attention sur le détail du réel antillais. Le détail ? Il faudrait plutôt dire la masse inextricable du vécu, l'interrogation des sources du langage et de l'histoire, le débroussaillage de ce que j'ai nommé notre antillanité, tellement présente et menacée." Patrick Chamoiseau, *Chronique des sept misères*, pref. Edouard Glissant (1986; Paris: Gallimard, 1988), 3; translated passage from *Chronicle of the Seven Sorrows*, trans. Linda Coverdale (Lincoln: University of Nebraska Press, 1999), vii.
34. Chamoiseau has stated that the format of the book was his idea and that he asked Glissant to participate. Personal interview with Patrick Chamoiseau, March 17, 1998.
35. "Cette pierre est une roche. Elle a grossi aux profonds de mer, comme un boulet verdi" (120).
36. In the glossary to *Tout-monde* (Paris: Gallimard, 1993).
37. Celia Britton, *Edouard Glissant and Postcolonial Theory: Strategies of Language and Resistance* (Charlottesville: University of Virginia Press, 1999), 9.
38. This critique of Glissant owes much to Peter Hallward, who argues in *Absolutely Postcolonial: Writing between the Singular and the Specific* (Manchester, UK: Manchester University Press, 2001) that Glissant's concept of "la Relation," which is indeed operative in his paratextual practice, is a singular configuration, a "self-asserting, self-constituting singular immediacy on the Deleuzian or Spinozist model—an 'already immediate' immediacy, so to speak" (67). Glissant wills Chamoiseau to this plane of nonhierarchical immediacy or relation, but this remains an act of the imagination that the Chamoiseau who wrote *Ecrire en pays dominé* (Paris: Gallimard, 1997) would find unconvincing.
39. Personal interview.

Chapter 10

Violence, Nonviolence
Sartre on Fanon

Judith Butler

What is immediately strange about Sartre's controversial preface to Fanon's *The Wretched of the Earth*[1] is its mode of address. To whom is this preface written? Sartre imagines his reader as the colonizer or the French citizen who recoils from the thought of violent acts of resistance on the part of the colonized. Minimally, his imagined reader is one who believes that his own notions of humanism and universalism suffice as norms by which to assess the war for independence in Algeria and similar efforts at decolonization. Sartre's address to his audience is direct and caustic: "What does Fanon care whether you read his work or not? It is to his brothers that he denounces our old tricks." At one point, he seems to take his implied readers aside, addressing the preface to them directly:

> Europeans, you must open this book and enter into it. After a few steps in the darkness you will see strangers gathered around a fire; come close, and listen, for they are talking of a destiny they will mete out to your trading centers and to the hired soldiers who defend them. They will see you, perhaps, but they will be talking among themselves, without even lowering their voices. This indifference strikes home: their fathers, shadowy creatures, *your* creatures, were but dead souls; you it was who allowed them glimpses of light, to you only did they dare to speak, and you did not bother to reply to such zombies.... Turn and turn about; in these shadows from whence a new dawn will break, it is you who are the zombies (*les zombies, c'est vous!*)." (13)

There are many curious aspects of this mode of address. It may well have been presumptuous of Sartre to address those living under conditions of colonization directly, since it would have put him in a position of pedagogical power over them. He has no information to impart *to them*, no advice, no explanation; and certainly no apology for European colonial dominance and, in particular, French colonial rule in Algeria. So he speaks, as it were, to his white brethren, knowing perhaps that his own name on the preface will attract such readers to this text by Fanon. So Sartre or, rather, Sartre's name, is bait for the European reader. But do we understand what "Europe" is in this context or, for that matter, the European? Sartre himself assumes that the European is white and a man. And so two separate zones of masculinity are contoured when he imagines Fanon speaking to his brothers, his colonized brothers, in the text, whereas Sartre speaks to his European brothers, collaborators with the powers of colonization in one way or another.

We might ask whether these two racially divided fraternities are being built through the modes of direct address that structure this text. Matters are made more complex by the fact that Fanon speaks to many audiences, and sometimes his lines of address interrupt each other. A European, in Sartre's view, will read this text only as a kind of eavesdropping: "Europeans, you must open this book and enter into it. After a few steps in the darkness you will see strangers gathered around a fire; come close, and listen (*approchez, ecoutez*)." So Fanon's text is a conversation figured as a conversation *among* colonized men, and Sartre's preface is less a conversation *among* the colonizers than an exhortation of one to the other, asking the European to read as one would listen to a conversation that is *not* meant for the one, the "you" addressed by Sartre. Just as Sartre's preface is not intended for the colonized population (though we might nonetheless consider it as a kind of display of Sartre's politics for them), so Fanon's text is construed as not addressed to a white, European audience. In effect, Sartre writes, "Come listen to this text that is not meant for you, that is not speaking to you, that cuts you out as its audience, and learn why this text had to be addressed instead to those living in the decolonized state of being, that is, neither fully dead nor fully living. Come and listen to the voices that are no longer petitioning you, no longer seeking inclusion in your world, no longer concerned with whether you hear and understand or not." Sartre petitions his European brothers, presumptively white, to bear up under this rejection and indifference and to come to understand the reasons why they are not the intended audience of Fanon's book. Of course, it is unclear how they could come to learn this lesson or see this truth without becoming its audience and reading the book. But that is the paradox at stake here. In the course of exhorting them to "listen in" on this book, Sartre is positioning his white audience at a curious distance where it is made at once to suffer peripheral status. The white audience can no longer presume itself to be the intended audience, equivalent to "any" reader, anonymous and implicitly universal. The paradox, as I mentioned, is that the white brethren are asked to read on nonetheless and are even exhorted to read on, though their reading on is to be construed as a listening in, instating their outside status at the moment of their comprehension. This seems another way of saying: this book is for you, you would do well to read it. The kind of displaced comprehending that Sartre proposes for the white reader is one that deconstitutes the presumptive privilege of the European reader in the act of taking in this new historical constellation. Decentering and even rejection are absorbed, undergone, and a certain undoing of the *presumption* of racial privilege is enacted between the lines or, rather, in the nonaddress that is, paradoxically, delivered through Sartre's preface to the European. The preface thus functions as a strange mode of delivery, handing the white reader the discourse not intended for him, and so handing him dislocation and rejection as the condition of possibility for his comprehension. Sartre's writing to the European reader is a way of acting upon that reader, positioning him outside the circle, and establishing that peripheral status as an epistemological requirement for understanding the condition of colonization. The European reader undergoes a loss of privilege at the same time that he is asked to submit to an empathetic enactment with the position of the socially excluded and effaced.

So Fanon's text, figured by Sartre as plurivocal and fraternal—that is, as a conversation among a group of men—undoes the notion of Fanon the singular author. Fanon is a budding movement. His writing is the speaking of several men. And when Fanon writes, a conversation takes place; the written page is a meeting, one in which strategy is being planned, and a circle is drawn tight among fellow travelers. Outside of the circle are those who understand that this speaking is indifferent to them. A "you" is being spoken around the fire, but the European no longer counts as part of that "you." He may hear the word "you" only to recognize that he is not included within its purview. If we ask how this exclusion came about for the European, Sartre claims that it follows dialectically from the way that white men suspended the humanity of the fathers of those who have lived under colonialism. The sons saw their fathers humiliated, treated with indifference, and now that very indifference has been taken up and returned to its sender in new form.

Interestingly, it is the humanity of the fathers subjugated under colonialism that is at issue here, and that implies that the dehumanization of others under colonialism follows from the erosion of paternal authority. It is this offense that mandates exclusion from the conversation that composes Fanon's text. This is a choreography of men, some forming inner circles, some cast to the periphery, and it is their manhood or, rather, the manhood of their fathers, that is at stake in the direct address. Not to be addressed as a "you" is to be treated as less than a man. And yet, as we will see, the "you" functions in at least two ways in Fanon: as the direct address that establishes human dignity through masculinization and as the direct address that establishes the question of humanity beyond the framework of masculinization and feminization alike. In either case, though, the "you" does not merely refer to the one who is addressed, but address itself is the condition of becoming a human, one who is constituted within the scene of address.[2]

If the excluded European asks *why* he is not privy to the conversation, then he must consider the implications of being treated with indifference. The problem to consider is not just that colonizers bear bad attitudes toward the colonized. If the colonized are excluded from the conversation in which humans are not only addressed but constituted through the address, the very possibility of being constituted as a human is foreclosed. To be excluded from the conversation is the unmaking of the human as such. The fathers of these men were not treated as men, certainly not addressed, directly or otherwise, as men, and so, failing that address, they were never fully constituted as human. If we seek to understand their ontology, these men who were never addressed as men, we find that no fixed determination is possible. The face-to-face address to a "you" has the capacity to confer a certain acknowledgment, to include the other in the potentially reciprocal exchange of speech; without that acknowledgment and that possibility for reciprocal address, no human may emerge. In the place of the human a specter takes form, what Sartre refers to as the "zombie," the shadow figure who is never quite human and never quite not. So if we are to tell the prehistory of this complex scene of address within Fanon's *The Wretched of the Earth*, or rather the two scenes of address that separate its traditional preface from the text itself, we would begin, according to Sartre, with the view that the colonizers had no "you" for the colonized, that they could and would not address them directly, and, as a result, withheld a certain ontological determination, one that follows only through recognition as a reciprocal exchange, a mutually constituting set of acts.

The colonizer had no "you" for the colonized, but once again, in Sartre's preface, the "you" is paradoxical, and again, *not* deployed for the colonized, but reserved exclusively for the colonizer. Who will speak to the colonized? For Fanon, the colonizer is not the "you," or so Sartre tells us, but for Sartre, the colonized is not the "you." So Sartre continues the very tradition of nonaddress that he seeks to indict. Sartre speaks as a spectral double: in the name of the European who shows how deconstituting his own privilege is apparently done, but also in a prescriptive vein, calling upon other Europeans to do the same. When Sartre effectively says "you" are not the intended reader of this text, he constitutes the group who ought to undergo the deconstitution of their privilege; in addressing them, however, he does not de-constitute them, but rather constitutes them anew. The problem, of course, is that in addressing them as the privileged, as one privileged speaker to another, he solidifies their privilege as well. And where before, in withholding address from the colonized, the colonizers imperiled an ontological determination for them, now, in Sartre's usage, the "you"—directed toward his European counterparts—is being asked to assume responsibility for this colonial condition of destitution. Sartre mobilizes the second person, strikes out with his "you" in order to accuse and demand accountability: "their fathers, shadowy creatures, *your* creatures, were but dead souls; *you* it was who allowed them glimpses of light, to you only did they dare to speak, and you did not bother to reply to such zombies."

In the stark scene of colonial subjugation that Sartre lays out, the colonized did not address each other but spoke only to *you,* the colonizer. If they could have addressed one another, they would have started to take shape within a legible social ontology, they would have risked existence through this communicative circuit. They only dared to speak to "you"—in other words, you were the exclusive audience for any direct address. You [the colonizer] did not bother to reply, for to reply would have meant to confer a certain human status on the one speaking to you. The mode of address, far from being a simple rhetorical technique, enacts the social constitution of ontology. Or let me put it more starkly: The mode of address enacts the social possibility of a livable existence. Correspondingly, refusing to reply to or address another who speaks, or requiring an asymmetrical form of address according to which the one in power is the exclusive audience for the second person—these are all ways of deconstituting ontology and orchestrating a nonlivable life. This is clearly the paradox of dying while alive, a further permutation of what Orlando Patterson, invoking Hegel in the context of describing slavery, called *social death*.[3] And there, as well as here, this social death touches fathers first, which means it leaves its legacy of shame and rage for the sons. Most importantly, social death is a not a static condition but a perpetually lived contradiction that takes shape as a particularly masculine conundrum. In the context of Algeria and the war for independence, the colonized man is left with a choice that cannot culminate in a livable life: "If he shows fight, the soldiers fire and he's a dead man; if he gives in, he degrades himself and he is no longer a man at all; shame and fear will split up his character and make his inmost self fall to pieces" (15).

Of what use is it for the European man to know of this impossible choice, of this historical formation of the life-and-death struggle within Algerian colonialism? Although Fanon's book is *not* written as a petition to the European liberal to see his complicity with the violence in Algeria, Sartre's preface clearly is. Sartre imagines his interlocutor: "In this case, you will say, let's throw away this book. Why read it if it is not written for us?" (13). Sartre offers two reasons, and they are worth drawing attention to here: The first is that the book gives those for whom it is not intended, the European elite, a chance to understand themselves. The collective subject designated by the "we" is reflected back to themselves in an objective mode through the "scars" (*blessures*) and the "chains" (*leur fers*) of our victims. What, he asks, have we made of ourselves? In a sense, Fanon's work gives the European man a chance to know himself, and so to engage in that pursuit of self-knowledge, based upon an examination of his shared practices, that is proper to the philosophical foundations of human life, as Sartre understands it.

The second reason he gives is that "Fanon is the first since Engels to bring the processes of history into the clear light of day" (apart from Georges Sorel, he claims, whose work Sartre considers to be fascist) (14). What is meant by the processes of history here? Which processes, and through what means are they brought to light? The process of history is dialectical, but the situation of the colonized is a "portrait"—to use Albert Memmi's term—of a dialectical movement at an impasse. Sartre predicts that decolonization is an historical necessity nonetheless, precisely because the effort to annihilate the other is never fully successful. Capitalism requires the labor power of the colonized. "Because," Sartre writes, "[the colonizer] can't carry massacre on to genocide, and slavery to animal-like degradation, he loses control, the machine goes into reverse, and a relentless logic leads him on to decolonization" (16).

So we can see at least two further purposes at work in Sartre's preface at this point. He is arguing, on the one hand, that the *scars* and *chains* of the colonized here brought to light reflect back the colonizer to himself, and in this way become instrumental to the European task of self-knowledge. On the other hand, he is arguing that the scars and the chains are, as it were, the motors of history, the pivotal moments; as the animating traces of a subjugation just short of death, these scars and chains mobilize an inexorable historical logic that, in turn, culminates in the demise of colonial power. In the first instance, the scars and chains reflect not only the actions of European power but also the default implications of European liberalism. For while the liberal opposes violence and considers colonial violence to be part of what happens elsewhere, the liberal also endorses a version of the state that marshals violence in the name of preserving that liberalism against a putative barbarism. I want to suggest that the scars and chains are *in this regard* considered instrumental, producing a reflection of the violence of European liberalism but only as part of the larger reflexive project of self-knowledge, self-critique, and even self-deconstitution on the part of a European elite. In the second instance, the scars and chains are understood as signs of an unfolding historical logic, one that conditions and drives the agency of the colonized as they oppose colonialism by every means possible.

These two ways of considering suffering under colonialism maintain a distance from the humanist point of view that would simply and emphatically oppose such suffering as morally wrong. Sartre openly worries about a liberal humanism that is blind to the political conditions of morally objectionable suffering, since one could oppose the suffering on moral grounds and leave unchanged the political conditions that regenerate it again and again. Suffering under colonialism thus needs to be situated politically. And within such a context, suffering of this kind, although deplorable, or precisely because it is deplorable, constitutes a resource for political movements. The scars and chains figure in at least two ways, *both* as the effects of criminal deeds *and* as the motors of history—a notion to which I will return shortly. At worst, a European liberal can oppose suffering under colonialism without necessarily engaging in a critique of the state formation that outsources its violence to preserve its spuriously humanist self-definition. If there are parallels with our contemporary political situation, especially with the outsourcing of torture, that is not by accident, since the colonial condition is by no means definitively past.

In a new introduction to *The Wretched of the Earth*, Homi Bhabha asks explicitly what this tract concerning decolonization has to say to the present circumstance of globalization (xi). He notes that whereas decolonization anticipates the "freedom" of the postcolonial, globalization is preoccupied with the "strategic denationalization of state sovereignty" (xi). And whereas decolonization sought to establish new national territories, globalization confronts a world of transnational connections and circuitry. Rightly, Bhabha rejects the historiography that would posit the succession of colonialism by postcolonialism, and then, ultimately, by globalization in the current epoch. In Bhabha's terms, colonialism persists within the postcolonial and, in his words, "the colonial shadow falls across the successes of globalization." Within globalization, dual economies are established that produce profitable circumstances for an economic elite and institute persistent "poverty, malnutrition, caste and racial injustice." This is, of course, the case that has been made concerning neoliberal strategies within globalization as well. In Bhabha's argument, though, "The critical language of duality—whether colonial or global—is part of the *spatial* imagination that seems to come so naturally to geopolitical thinking of a progressive, postcolonial cast of mind: margin and metropole, center and periphery, the global and the local, the nation and the world" (xiv).

As much as these divisions persist, it may be that Fanon offers us a way to think beyond these polarities and thus takes a certain distance from the instant binarism of Sartre's preface. Bhabha, for instance, sees in Fanon a trenchant critique of these polarities in the name of a future that will introduce a new order of things. Bhabha discerns the critique of these polarities through the specific rhetorical use of the term "third world" in Fanon. The "third" is the term that will destabilize the polarities of colonization, and it constitutes a place holder for the future itself. Thus, Bhabha cites Fanon: "The Third World must start over a new history of Man" (xiv).

Fanon's text, in Bhabha's view, creates a way of understanding moments of transition, especially in those political economies and political vocabularies that seek to get beyond the partitions bequeathed by the Cold War. What is important about these moments of transition is their "incubational" status, to use a Gramscian term. Bhabha claims that "'new' national, international, or global emergences create an unsettling sense of transition"(xvi). He maintains that Fanon, rather than remaining content with the establishment of a new nationalism, conducts a nuanced critique of ethnonationalism. In Bhabha's view, Fanon's contribution consists in supplying a picture of the "global future" as a "an ethical and political project—yes, a plan of action as well as a projected aspiration" (xvi).

Bhabha's reading implies moving beyond the established grounds of a humanism to re-pose the question of the human as one that must open up a future. We might well wonder whether humanism has had such established grounds, and this seems reasonable to ask. But let me make the point more precisely: If we object to the suffering under colonialism, even decry it, without calling for a basic transformation of the structures of colonialism, then our objection remains at that register of moral principle that can attend only to the deleterious effects of political systems without attempting a broader social transformation of those conditions that generate those effects. This does not mean that we have to retract our objections to suffering, but only that we must exchange that form of humanism for an inquiry that asks: What has happened to the very notion of the human under such conditions? Our objections to suffering then become part of an operation of critique and a way of opening up the human to a different future.

But even if we get this far with the argument, we are still left with the question of violence and what precisely its role is in the making of the human. Bhabha reads Fanon's discussion of insurrectionary violence as "part of a struggle for psychoaffective survival and a search for human agency in the midst of oppression" (xxxix). Violence holds out the possibility of acting, of agency, and it also rebels against a social death, even as it cannot escape the parameters of violence and potential death. Indeed, under these conditions of colonial subjugation, violence is a wager and a sign that there is an ongoing psychoaffective struggle to be. For Sartre, however, the matter is less equivocal, at least in these pages, about the role of violence in the making of the human, even within the horizon of posthumanism. If for Nietzsche the categorical imperative is soaked in blood, then for Sartre a certain kind of humanism surely is soaked in blood as well.

In both prefaces, Sartre's and Bhabha's, there is a question of the human to come. Their writings precede Fanon's text, but come later, and the question they pose before Fanon's text begins to be read is whether there is a future for the human opened up by this text. There is in both prefatory writings a way of thinking about the human beyond humanism, and this is part of what the Sartrean preface tries to do, in the mode and through the example of direct address. When Sartre writes "you," he is trying to bring down one version of man and bring about another. But his performative appelations do not have the force of God's, so something invariably misfires and we find ourselves in a bind. Is Sartre perhaps posing as a superhuman agent in thinking he can destroy and make man in the image he so desires? Just as the performative force of Sartre's direct address does not straightaway bring about a new man, neither do the scars and chains straightaway bring about the end of colonialism. Finally, though, we have to understand whether, for Sartre, violence is generative of a "new man"—and whether, in saying that this is also Fanon's view, Sartre is rightly citing him or making free use of his text for his own purposes.

While I will hope to show that it is a specific cultural formation of the human that Sartre traces and applauds here, one that I would call "masculinist," it seems important to keep in mind that in Fanon, and perhaps in Sartre as well, there is both a demand for a restitution of masculinism as well as an effort to query who the "you" might be beyond the strictures of gender. Sartre's effort to think the human on the far side of a certain kind of liberal humanism cannot resolve the equivocation at the heart of *homme* as both "man" and "human." But certain possibilities nevertheless emerge from that equivocal designator; interestingly, it is the "you"—the second person—that disrupts its usual signifying circuits.

Sartre clears textual space for the reflexivity of the European man—his perennial first-person task to know himself. But does the colonized have any such reflexivity? Sartre locates the mobilizing wounds of the colonized that produce decolonization as an historical inevitability, as if those wounds did not have to pass through the reflexive subjectivity of the wounded. In this way, he seems to eclipse the reflexivity of the colonized in his preface. This is evident not only in the politesse with which Sartre refuses to address the colonized, reiterating a nonaddress that he himself diagnoses as the root of their suspended humanity, but also in his treatment of counterinsurgent violence as if it were a determined or mechanized reaction and precisely *not* the deliberative or reflective decision of a set of political subjects engaged in a political movement. Indeed, when we ask about the agency of insurgent, anticolonial violence, it turns out that the only real agent of violence is that of the colonizer. Sartre says as much when he claims that the "only violence is the settler's" (17). In arguing this, Sartre seeks to derive the violence of colonial insurrection from the primacy of state violence, casting revolutionary violence as a secondary effect of a primary form of violent oppression. If the colonized respond with violence, their violence is nothing other than a transposition or transmutation of the violence done to them. Fanon's formulation differs slightly from the Sartrean account when Fanon claims, in the first chapter of *Wretched* called "Concerning Violence,"

> The violence which has ruled over the ordering of the colonial world, which has ceaselessly drummed the rhythm for the destruction of native social forms and broken up without reserve the systems of reference of the economy, the customs of dress and external life, *that same violence* will be claimed and taken over by the native at the moment when, deciding to embody history in his own person, he surges into forbidden quarters. (40, my emphasis)

The violence travels, passes hands, but can we say that it remains the settler's violence? Does it actually belong to either party if the violence remains the same as it shifts from the violence imposed by the ruler to the violence wielded by the colonized? It would seem to be fundamentally transferable. But this is not the Sartrean view. Indeed, his view makes the colonizer into the only subject of violence. And this claim seems to contradict his other claim; namely, that under these conditions, violence can be understood to bring the human into being. If we subscribe to his first thesis, we are left with the conclusion, surely faulty, that colonization is a precondition for humanization, something that civilizational justifications for colonization have always maintained, and a view which, we would have to surmise, Sartre wanted vehemently to oppose.

Sartre makes several efforts to account for violent resistance on the part of the colonized. He takes on the charge leveled by colonialists that there are simply base or animal instincts at work in these apparently precivilizational peoples. Sartre asks, "what instincts does he mean? The instincts that urge slaves to massacre their master? Can he not here recognize his own cruelty turned against himself?" (16). Anticipating his claim that "the only violence is the settler's," he remarks here that the colonizer finds in the violence of the colonized only his own violence. The colonized are said to have "absorbed" the settler's cruelty through every pore. And though the colonized are said to take in and take on the violence by which they are oppressed, as if through the inexorable force of transitivity, the colonized are also said to become who they are "by the deep-seated refusal of that which others have made of [them]" (17).

Here Sartre seems to subscribe to a theory of psychological absorption or mimeticism that would simply transfer the violence of the colonizer onto and into the violence of the colonized. In his view, the colonized absorb and recreate the violence done to them, but they also refuse to become what the colonized have made of them (17). If this is a contradiction, it is one in which the colonized are forced to live. Just as, earlier, we remarked upon the impossible choice: "if he shows fight, he will be killed; if he gives in, he degrades himself." He is made violent by the violence done to him, but this violence puts his own life at risk; if he fails to become violent, he remains its victim, and "shame and fear will split up his character and make his inmost self fall to pieces" (15). Shame because he could not or would not assume violence to counter violence, and fear since he knows how precarious and extinguishable his life finally is under violently imposed colonial rule.

The problem of violence, then, seems to appear here, in what Bhabha calls "psychoaffective survival," from a self imperiled by shame and fear, one that is internally split up and at risk of falling into pieces. The question is whether anything can stop this fatal splintering of the self and why violence appears as the route toward selfhood, agency, and even life. Note that this self is distinct from the one who simply absorbs or uncritically mimes and returns the violence done against him. There is, here, a passage through a decimated self that has to be navigated, and violence appears as one route out. Is it the only route? And did Fanon think so?

In order to answer this, we have first to understand what happens to violence when it is taken up or taken on by the colonized in the name of an insurgent resistance. It is only "at first" that violence is the settler's, and then, later, it is made into their own. Is the violence that the colonized make into their own different from the violence imposed upon them by the settler's? When Sartre endeavors to explain this secondary violence, the one derived from the settler colonialist, he remarks that it is *"the same violence* [that is] *thrown back upon us as when our reflection comes forward to meet us when we go toward a mirror"* (17). This description suggests that the insurgent violence is nothing but the reflection of the colonizer's violence, as if a symmetry exists between them, and the second follows only as the dialectical reflection of the first. But this cannot be fully true. Since, the colonizer "no longer remembers clearly that he was a man; he takes himself to be a horsewhip or a gun," (16) but violence is precisely the means through which the colonized "become men" (17). Later he remarks that the "European has only been able to become a man through creating slaves and monsters" (26). So it would appear that Sartre maintains at least two different conceptions of the human here. The colonizer forgets that he is a man when he becomes violent, but the particular sort of man that he becomes is dependent on this violence. As I mentioned earlier, Sartre uses the term *"homme"* for "human" here, and the equivocation runs deep throughout the argument. *But it would seem that the colonizer who has forgotten that he is a "man," crazed by the fear of losing his absolute power, becomes a gun or a horsewhip and seeks to attack the men he does not regard as men, who have also, by virtue of this violent encounter, become, as well, precisely a horsewhip or a gun.*

So many men seem to be forgotten in this scene. Who is this forgotten man? And who is the man to come? The colonized is said to become a "man" through violence, but we know that the violence that the colonized takes on is at first the settler's violence. But does the colonized separate from the settler's violence, and does this very separation serve as a condition of the "becoming human" of the colonized? Sartre is clear that the "hidden anger" that various forms of humanism condemn is actually the "the last refuge of their humanity." In that anger Sartre reads both the effect of colonial legacy as well as the refusal of that legacy, a knot, a contradiction, that produces a finally unlivable bind and then a demand for total change. Violence becomes a clear alternative when a life of continuing famine and oppression seems far worse than death (20). At this point, Sartre writes, "there is only one duty to be done, one end to achieve: to thrust out colonialism by *every* means in their power." Sartre's portrayal of insurgent violence is meant to provide insight into the person who lives under such oppression. As such, it serves as a reconstruction of an induced psychological state. It also reads as a fully instrumental rationalization for violence and, thus, as a normative claim. Indeed, the violent acts by which decolonization is achieved are also those by which man "recreates himself" (21). Sartre is describing a psychopolitical reality, but he is also offering, we might say, a new humanism to confound the old, one that requires, under these social conditions, violence to materialize. He writes, "no gentleness can efface the marks of violence, only violence itself can destroy them" (21).[4] Of course, we have to ask whether violence itself, said to efface the marks of violence, does not simply make more such marks, leaving new legacies of violence in its wake.

Moreover, weren't those very scars and chains necessary to motor the revolution? The scars and chains served a double purpose: First, they reflected back to the European the consequences of his failed humanism, his exported colonial domination; second, they were said to animate the inexorable logic of decolonization in history and are now precisely what stand to be "effaced" through the acts of violence that effect that decolonization. These scars and chains serve as mirrors for the European, serve as historical motors for the colonized, and are finally negated, if not fully transformed, through the act of self-creation. The existential dicta to know and to create oneself thus makes its appearance toward the end of Sartre's provocative preface, when he claims that the violent acts of the colonized finally establish him as existential subject par excellence: "When his rage boils over, he rediscovers his lost innocence and he comes to know himself in that he himself creates his self" (21). Of course, this self-making is a curious one, since the violence seems to be induced by an historically inevitable dialectical development, but this form of determinism is not yet reconciled with the theory of self-constitution in Sartre, and the tension between the two positions turns out to bear significant implications.

Sartre began this preface with an allocation of pronouns according to a strict division of labor. Fanon will speak to the colonized; Sartre will speak to the European, especially the liberal man in France who understands himself to be morally and politically at a distance from the events in Algeria and the French colonies. Sartre will not speak to the colonized, and we presume that this is so because he does not want to occupy a morally didactic position. He suggests that the Europeans listen in, and that they be made to suffer their peripheral status to the conversation at hand. And yet, Sartre will characterize through a psychological portrait the violence of the colonized and then claim that the man who engages in violent acts of overthrow fulfills his own existential Marxism. In deconstructing the social conditions of dehumanization, the colonized effects his own decolonization, and through this double negation makes himself a man: "The new man," Sartre writes, "begins his life as a man at the end of it; he considers himself a potential corpse" (23). To say that the man is potentially dead is to say that he lives this potentiality in the present, so that death is hardly risked; it functions as an epistemic certainty, if not a defining feature of his existence. Bhabha refers to this as a "life-in-death." To finally die is thus to realize what has already been mandated as true or necessary. And yet to die in the service of deconstructing these conditions of social death is done precisely in the name of future life and future men.

It is in this preface, you will remember, that Sartre debunks Camus's earlier position on nonviolence.[5] The believers in nonviolence, he quips, say that they are "neither executioners nor victims." But Sartre refuses the effort to sidestep this binary alternative, claiming instead that nonviolence and passivity is tantamount to complicity, and, entering into a direct address, remarks that "your passivity serves only to place you in the ranks of the oppressors" (25). What it requires is a deconstruction of the notion of man, especially if to be a man, as Sartre claims, is to be an accomplice to colonialism. Only through the deconstruction of this version of being a man can the history of the human unfold. We are not given much idea of what the final unfolding of the human will look like, but Sartre offers a brief remark toward the end of the essay where he imagines a history of humankind that culminates in a future state of becoming "full-grown." When human kind reaches this state, he claims, "it will not define itself as the sum total of the world's inhabitants, but as the infinite unity of their mutual needs" (27).

Here, at the end of a piece that is widely regarded as an encomium to violence, Sartre takes another turn, manifesting perhaps the fundamental ambivalence of his views on violence that have been ably demonstrated in Ronald Santoni's recent book *Sartre on Violence: Curiously Ambivalent*.[6] Obviously, this vision of the infinite unity of mutual needs that might exist among the world's inhabitants is one in which physical need and vulnerability would become matters for mutual recognition and regard. If we consider what Fanon claims about violence, we can see there as well a certain understanding that violence has its place in the overcoming of colonialism, but also a recognition that it brings with it a nihilism, a corrosive spirit of absolute negation. If he argues that it can be no other way under such conditions of oppression, he argues as well that such conditions of oppression must be fully overcome in order for violence no longer to pervade social life. What is remarkable about Fanon's view, perhaps put more strongly than Sartre is willing to replicate, is that *the body itself becomes historical precisely through an embodiment of social conditions*. The wrecked and muted body is not merely an example of the condition of colonial rule; it is its instrument and effect, and moreover, colonial rule *is not* without such instruments and effects. The destitution of the body is not only an effect of colonialism, where colonialism is understood as something prior, something separate, a "condition" both analytically and historically separate from the body at issue. On the contrary, *the body is the animated or, rather, deanimated life of that historical condition, without which colonization itself cannot exist*. Colonization is the deadening of sense, the establishment of the body in social death, as one that lives and breathes its potentiality as death, and so working and reproducing its force at the somatic and affective level.

It would seem then that any effort to reconstruct the human after humanism, that is, after humanism's complicity with colonialism, would have to include an understanding of humans as those who may suffer death in advance of the cessation of bodily function, who suffer it at the heart of life itself. If humans are those kinds of beings who depend on social conditions to breath and move and live, then it is precisely at the psychophysical level that the human is being redefined in Fanon. This is a psyche that is "crushed with inessentiality" and a body that is restricted in its fundamental mobility. There are places it may not go, first-person utterances it may not inhabit and compose, ways in which it cannot know or sustain itself as an "I." It has not come to know itself as the "you" addressed by the other, and so when it addresses itself, it misses its mark, vacillating between a certitude of its nonexistence and an inflated notion of its future power.

If there is a cult of masculinism that emerges from this situation, perhaps it is explained by Fanon's description of the fantasy of muscular power. Showing his own alliances with a European educated class and with a civilizational project, Fanon refers to the indigenous population of Algeria as "the native" and then proceeds to offer his own portrait of his psychological circumstances. He describes first the facts of spatial restriction: "the native" is hemmed in, learns that there are places he cannot go, becomes defined by this limitation on spatial motility. Consequently, the idea of himself that compensates for this restriction takes on hyperbolic forms:

> This is why the dreams of the native are always of muscular prowess; his dreams are of action and aggression. I dream I am jumping, swimming, running, climbing; I dream I burst out laughing, that I span a river in one stride, or that I am followed by a flood of motorcars which never catch up with me. (52)

Fanon regards this hypermuscularity, this superhuman capacity for action to be compensatory, impossible, fantasmatic, but fully understandable under such conditions. When he claims that the oppressed dream of becoming the persecutor, he is giving us a psychosocial description of the fantasies that take hold under such conditions. He is not necessarily arguing for them, although he will also oppose both nonviolence and compromise as political options during the War for Independence in 1961. His argument is strategic: If the decolonized decide upon violence, it is only because they are already in the midst of violence. Violence was not only done in the past, but violence is what continues to happen to them and so forms the horizon of political life. Thus, it is a matter of seizing violence and giving it a new turn. He writes, "Now the problem is to lay hold of this violence that is changing direction" (58). Violence here is not defended as a way of life, and certainly not a way of imagining the normative goal of a social movement. It is an instrumentality in the service of invention.

Of course, there is a question of whether violence as a pure instrument can remain such, or whether it comes to define, haunt, and afflict the polity that instates itself through violent means. Neither Sartre nor Fanon ask this question. Whether the aspiration is either to create man anew, or to produce a community defined as an infinite unity of mutual needs, or to achieve decolonization, we have to ask whether violence continues to play a role in what it means to create oneself, what it means to produce such a community, what it means to achieve and sustain decolonization as a goal. It seems clear that violence drops out of the picture when we imagine a community defined as an infinite unity of mutual needs. And violence would not necessarily have a role to play once an unequivocal decolonization is achieved—if that, indeed, proves possible. Where the role of violence is most difficult to understand is in the model of self-creation. It might be easy enough to say that only under the conditions of colonization does violence emerge as a key means through which man makes himself, and that without colonization self-making is no longer achieved through violent means. This position would distinguish itself from one that models self-making on violent negation, that is, the position that claims that all self-making requires violence as a matter of course. Fanon is clear at the end of *The Wretched of the Earth* that the task of decolonization is to create or invent "a new man," one that will not constitute a simple of faithful reflection of European man.

Can we think self-invention in Fanon outside the concept of violence? And if we cannot, is that because violence is necessitated under conditions of colonization, the context that limits what he himself can imagine in 1961? At the end of his book, does he leave open the possibility of a new kind of self-making yet to be imagined? Can he not supply it precisely because he is not yet historically there, in the place where it can be imagined?

What seems clear is that to be colonized is to be humiliated as a man and that this castration is unendurable. It is the wife of the colonized who is raped or disregarded, and this is for Fanon an offense to the man, the husband, more profoundly than to the woman herself. Rey Chow and others have examined the pervasive masculinism in Fanon's work, and I do not want to belabor it here.[7] But I do want to make two points that lead us toward another way of thinking. First, it strikes me that Fanon understands masculine violent fantasy as compensatory, and this suggests that he understands the fantasmatic dimension of a hypermasculinism. As such, it does not serve as a moral ideal toward which the decolonized should strive. Rather, it serves as a motivational component in the struggle toward decolonization. The distinction is important, since it would follow that, under conditions of decolonization, hypermasculinity as a fantasmatic ideal would lose its force as a compensatory motivation for conduct and as a fantasmatic model for self-making. A gendered man would have to cross a river like any other mortal: Decolonization does not promise god-like powers and, if it does, necessarily fails to make good on its word.

Although Sartre restrictively makes use of the "you" to constitute and deconstruct his European reader and to divide two different fraternities, the colonizers and the colonized, Fanon offers another version of direct address that moves beyond this rigid binary and that holds out the possibility of thinking the human apart from "man." When, for instance, Fanon prays to his body at the end of *Black Skins, White Masks*, "O my body, make of me always a man who questions!" he calls for a kind of openness that is at once bodily and conscious. He addresses himself and seeks to reconstitute himself through a direct address to his own body. As if countering the psychoaffective dying-in-life that pervades the lived experience of the colonized, Fanon seeks to prompt the body into an open-ended inquiry. In the line directly preceding, he posits a new collectivity: "I want the world to recognize, with me, the open door of every consciousness" (232). He asks for recognition neither of his national identity nor his gender, but rather a collective act of recognition that would accord every consciousness its status as something infinitely open. And though he could not have anticipated what that universalizable recognition would mean for gender relations, it is nonetheless there as an incipient and unintended implication of his own words, words which perhaps carry more radical vision than he himself could do nearly a decade later when he wrote *The Wretched of the Earth*. "O my body"—this cry enacts a certain reflexivity, an address *to oneself* precisely as a body *not* crushed by its inessentiality, but conditioning a certain permanent and open question. This body, beseeched through address, is posited as an opening toward the world and toward a radically egalitarian collectivity. There is no God to whom he prays, but a body, one characterized precisely by what it does not yet know. This moment is doubtless repeated at the end of *The Wretched of the Earth*, despite the profound differences between these two texts. At the end of *Wretched*, Fanon does not know what new version of man will be invented once decolonization takes place. There is an openness toward the future that is far from the omnipotent claim, indeed, is emphatically unknowing and nonprescriptive about what will come.

Perhaps I seize upon this call to his own body to open again to a world and, more radically, to join with others in recognizing the "open door" of every consciousness precisely because it posits an alternative to the hyperresolute masculinism of anticolonial violence. Of course, *Black Skin, White Masks* was written nine years prior to *The Wretched of the Earth*, but perhaps they can be read together to consider in what this new invention of man or, indeed, this notion of humanity might consist. After all, the call to arms and the critique of pacifism and compromise demand that, for the moment, the police or the white Algerian or the government official *not* be understood as one whose consciousness is an "open door." Indeed, violence against the other *closes* the door of that consciousness, since according to the logic of violence "the open door" of the enemy's consciousness threatens to close the door of my own. According to the argument of *Wretched*, if I am living as the colonized, then to open the door of my own consciousness is only possible through the closing of the door of the other's. It is a life-or-death struggle. At the moment I do violence to an Other—one who oppresses me or who represents that oppression or who is complicitous with that oppression—I make room not only for my own self-invention but for a new notion of the human that will not be based on racial or colonial oppression and violence.

At the end of *Black Skin, White Masks*, Fanon addresses himself. This mode of address is not considered in the Sartrean preface, but it remains, perhaps, the most insurrectionary of his speech acts, allegorizing the emergent self-constituting powers of the colonized unconditioned by any historical or causal necessity. There he writes that only by recapturing and scrutinizing the self can the ideal conditions for a human world come to exist. "Why not," he writes, "the quite simple attempt to touch the other, to feel the other, to explain the other to myself?" (231). This sentence is cast in question form, and it seems to be that self-scrutiny implies this interrogatory relation to the Other as a matter of course. He makes this explicit in the next line when he writes, "Was my freedom not given to me then in order to build the world of the *You*?"(231). We do not know at this moment whether the "you" is the colonized or the colonizer, whether it is also a reaching, a relationality, that constitutes the intentional enthrallment of the "I" as it finds itself outside of itself, enmeshed in the world of others. Self-scrutiny is not merely an inward turn but a mode of address: *o you, o my body*. This is an appeal as much to his own corporeal life, the restoration of the body as the ground of agency, as it is to the other; it is an address, indeed, a touch, facilitated by the body, one that, for complex reasons, commits itself to regarding each and every consciousness as an open door. If the body opens him toward a "you," it opens him in such a way that the other, through bodily means, becomes capable of addressing a "you" as well. Implicit to both modes of address is the understanding of the body, through its touch, securing the open address not just of this tactile other but of every other body. In this sense, a recorporealization of humanism seems to take hold here that posits an alternative to violence or, paradoxically, the idea of the unfolded human toward which it strives (and which it must refute in order to realize in the end). *Over and against the view that there can be no self-creation without violence, Fanon here exemplifies the philosophical truth that there can be no invention of oneself without the "you" and that the "self" is constituted precisely in a mode of address that avows its constitutive sociality.*

When Sartre writes of *Wretched*, "What does Fanon care whether you read his work or not? It is to his brothers that he denounces our old tricks," he seems to be telling us that we may *not* read *Wretched* in light of the "you" that forms the ultimate address in *Black Skin, White Masks*. It is true that in the conclusion to *Wretched*, Fanon addresses "my comrades" and "my brothers." The "you" that closes the earlier work is now specified and restricted, but note that even in *Wretched*, he does *not* call on them to return to ethnic or national identity; no, he calls on them to create a new version of man, and so to inaugurate a universality that has never yet been established on this, admittedly wretched, earth. Indeed, what form this universal human may take is unknown, remains a question, and so the opening of the earlier work—the opening toward the "you" facilitated through the body—is finally echoed in the opening that closed the later one. Even in *Wretched*, there is this holding out, finally, for invention, for the new, for an opening that may depend upon a prior violence, but which also presupposes its resolution.

Fanon's address to the body to open and to question, to join in a struggle to recognize the openness of every other embodied consciousness—this struggle toward a new universality begins, perhaps, precisely when decolonization ends. This would mean that, philosophically, *Black Skin, White Masks* would have to follow *The Wretched of the Earth*. The effort to "touch" the "you" in *Black Skin, White Masks* would appear to be very different from the contact that constitutes violent negation. When Sartre refers to the "the infinite unity" of the "mutual needs" of all inhabitants of this earth, he does *not* appeal to everyone's capacity for violence, but, rather, to the reciprocal requirements that human embodiment implies: food, shelter, protection of life and liberty, means of recognition, conditions for work and political participation without which no human can emerge or be sustained. The human, in this sense, is both contingent and aspirational, dependent and not yet accomplished or realized.

I am reminded at this moment of that most extraordinary remark that Sartre makes in the 1975 interview with Michel Contat entitled "Self-Portrait at Seventy" where he refers to the prospect of "subjective life" being "offered up" and "given." In the preface to Fanon's *Wretched*, Sartre cannot address the colonized, does not understand it as his place. And yet, without such an address, how is a new politics of the human possible? He seems to know in this late interview that the future of the human is instituted through a certain mode of address that reorganizes gender, recalling Fanon, his address to himself and to the "you."

> We yield our bodies to everyone, even beyond the realm of sexual relations: by looking, by touching. You yield your body to me, I yield mine to you: we exist for the other, as body. But we do not exist in the same way as consciousness, as ideas, even though ideas are modifications of the body. If we truly wished to exist for the other, to exist as body, as body that can continually be laid bare—even if this never actually happens—our ideas would appear to others as coming from the body. Words are formed by a tongue in the mouth. All ideas would appear in this way, even the most vague, the most fleeting, the least tangible. There would no longer be the hiddenness, the secrecy in certain centuries that was identified with the honor of men and women, and which seems very foolish to me. (*Life/Situations*, 11–12)

Although Sartre holds out for an impossible transparency, for him such an impossible ideal maintains the ideality and infinite potentiality of desire itself. Of course, "the honor of men and women" holds them in distinct relations, articulates and maintains that difference, but it does more. If emasculation is the sign of dehumanization, then the masculine is the presumptive norm of humanization. That differential norm can only dehumanize in turn, so if, in these strange final confessions, Fanon and Sartre both concede that there is a touch and form of yielding that establishes a relation to a "you," then it would seem that in the place of a struggle over which masculine community will finally prevail, we find a pronoun that is open-ended precisely on the question of gender. It was Arendt who suggested that the question, "who are you?" is at the basis of participatory democracy.[8] On this basis, Adriana Cavarero, the Italian feminist philosopher calls for a rehabilitation of the "you" at the core of politics.[9]

The "you" may well take the place of "man" in the quest for a human beyond the constituted horizon of humanism. If there is a relation between this "you" whom I seek to know, whose gender cannot be determined, whose nationality cannot be presumed, and who compels me to relinquish violence, then this mode of address articulates a wish not just for a nonviolent future for the human, but for a new conception of the human where some manner of touch other than violence is the precondition of that making.

Notes

1. Jean-Paul Sartre, *The Wretched of the Earth*, trans. Constance Farrington (New York: Grove, 1963); Frantz Fanon *Damnés de la terre* (Paris, Éditions Maspero, 1961). The 1991 Gallimard edition omits the Sartrean preface. And the new English version, translated by Richard Philcox, includes commentary by both Jean-Paul Sartre and Homi Bhabha (2004). Citations are to the original Grove Press edition except where explicitly noted. All citations to Homi Bhabha are to the new edition.
2. For a further elaboration of this position, see my *Giving an Account of Oneself* (New York: Fordham University Press, 2005).
3. See Abdul JanMohamed, *The Death-Bound Subject: Richard Wright's Archaelogy of Death* (Durham, N.C.: Duke University Press, 1995).
4. See Walter Benjamin on the divine violence that obliterates the traces of guilt.
5. Sartre does not name Camus explicitly, but he is clearly referring to, among others, "Le socialisme des potences" and "Le pari de notre generation" that appeared in *Demain* in 1957 and that have been translated by Justin O'Brien and republished in Albert Camus, *Resistance, Rebellion, and Death* (New York: Random House, 1995).
6. Ronald Santoni, *Sartre on Violence: Curiously Ambivalent* (University Park: Pennylsvania State University Press, 2003), 67–74.
7. Rey Chow, *Primitive Passions: Visuality, Sexuality, Ethnography and Contemporary Chinese Cinema* (New York: Columbia University Press, 1995).
8. Hannah Arendt, *The Human Condition* (Chicago: University of Chicago Press, 1958), 183.

9. "The 'you' comes before the *we*, before the plural *you* and before the *they*. Symptomatically, the 'you' is a term that is not at home in modern and contemporary developments of ethics and politics. The 'you' is ignored by individualistic doctrines, which are too preoccupied with praising the rights of the *I*, and the 'you' is masked by a Kantian form of ethics that is only capable of staging an *I* that addresses itself as a familiar 'you'. Neither does the 'you' find a home in the schools of thought to which individualism is opposed—these schools reveal themselves for the most part to be affected by a moralistic vice, which, in order to avoid falling into the decadence of the *I*, avoids the contiguity of the *you*, and privileges collective, plural pronouns. Indeed, many revolutionary movements (which range from traditional communism to the feminism of sisterhood) seem to share a curious linguistic code based on the intrinsic morality of pronouns. The *we* is always positive, the *plural you* is a possible ally, the *they* has the face of an antagonist, the *I* is unseemly, and the *you* is, of course, superfluous." Adriana Caverero, *Relating Narratives: Story-Telling and Selfhood*, trans. Paul Kottman, (London: Routledge, 2000), 90–91.

Contributors

Paige Arthur is the Deputy Director of the Research Unit at the International Center for Transitional Justice, an international organization that assists countries pursuing accountability for past mass atrocity or systemic human rights abuse. She holds a PhD in History from the University of California, Berkeley (2004), and is a specialist on the intellectual politics of European decolonization and of its aftermath. Formerly, she was an editor of the journal *Ethics and International Affairs*, published by the Carnegie Council on Ethics and International Affairs.

Robert Bernasconi has been the Moss Professor of Philosophy at the University of Memphis since 1998. In addition to publishing over 150 essays, he is the author of *The Question of Language in Heidegger's History of Being* (Humanities, 1985), *Heidegger in Question* (Humanities, 1993), and *How to Read Sartre* (Granta, 2006, and Norton, 2007). He is also the editor or coeditor of nine volumes, several addressing the subject of race and racism, including *Race* (Blackwell, 2001), and with Kristie Dotson, *Race, Miscegenation, and Hybridity* (Thoemmes Continuum, 2005).

Judith Butler is the Maxine Elliot Professor in the Departments of Rhetoric and Comparative Literature at the University of California, Berkeley. She is the author or co-author of thirteen monographs, including the internationally influential *Gender Trouble: Feminism and the Subversion of Identity* (Routledge, 1990) and *Bodies That Matter: On the Discursive Limits of "Sex"* (Routledge, 1993). Most recently she has published *Giving an Account of Oneself* (Fordham, 2005) and, with Gayatri Chakravorty Spivak, *Who Sings the Nation-State?: Language, Politics, Belonging* (Seagull 2007). These works have established her as one of the leading critical voices in American academe, particularly in feminist and queer theory, political philosophy, and ethics.

Christian Delacampagne has taught philosophy and literature at several U.S. universities, most recently at Johns Hopkins. He is the author of some forty books. He has also published numerous articles and chapters in edited volumes on Jean Paul Sartre's existentialism and political theories, including most recently "Jean-Paul Sartre" in *The Columbia History of Twentieth-Century French Thought*, edited by Lawrence D. Kritzman (Columbia University Press, 2006) and "Sartre and His Century" in *La Règle du jeu* in January 2005, as well as in *Les Temps modernes* and *Cités*.

Lewis R. Gordon is the Laura H. Carnell Professor of Philosophy, Religion, and Judaic Studies; Director of the Institute for the Study of Race and Social Thought and the Center for Afro-Jewish Studies at Temple University; and President of the Caribbean Philosophical Association. He has edited or coedited three books, including most recently *Not Only the Master's Tools* (Paradigm, 2006). He has also written seven monographs, including *Bad Faith and Antiblack Racism* (Humanity, 1995), *Fanon and the Crisis of European Man* (Routledge, 1995), and most recently *An Introduction to Africana Philosophy* (Cambridge University Press, 2008) and with Jane Anna Gordon, *Of Divine Warning: Reading Disaster in the Modern Age* (Paradigm, 2008).

Jonathan Judaken is an Associate Professor of Modern European intellectual and cultural history and Director of the Marcus W. Orr Center for the Humanities at University of Memphis. Along with twenty articles published in academic journals, he is the author of *Jean-Paul Sartre and the Jewish Question: Anti-antisemitism and the Politics of the French Intellectual* (Nebraska, "Texts and Contexts" series, 2006) and editor of *Naming Race, Naming Racisms* (Routledge, 2008). He is Co-President of the North American Sartre Society

George Ciccariello-Maher is currently a PhD candidate in political theory at the University of California, Berkeley. His work has appeared in *Journal of Black Studies*, *The Commoner*, *Radical Philosophy Review*, *Monthly Review*, *Listening: Journal of Religion and Culture*, and *qui parle*, as well as a number of edited volumes, and he has translated books by Enrique Dussel and Immanuel Wallerstein. He also contributes regularly to *Counterpunch* and *MRZine*.

Steve Martinot is a retired lecturer from San Francisco State University, currently an independent scholar. His books include *The Rule of Racialization* (Temple, 2002), a critique of the interconnection of class structures and white supremacy in the United States; and *Forms in the Abyss: A Philosophical Bridge between Sartre and Derrida* (Temple, 2006). He also translated and introduced Albert Memmi's *Racism* (University of Minnesota Press).

Mabogo P. More is Professor Emeritus of Philosophy and currently a Senior Research fellow in the department of philosophy at the University of KwaZulu-Natal, South Africa. A leading scholar of existentialism and African(a) philosophy, Professor More was instrumental in bringing the work of Jean-Paul Sartre into dialogue with Steve Bantu Biko, one of the noted luminaries of the anti-Apartheid movement and South African political thought. He has published extensively on social and political philosophy in journals such as *Southern African Journal of Philosophy*, *African Journal of Political Science*, *Theoria*, *Dialogue and Universalism*, *Alternation*, as well as contributing chapters to various books.

Richard H. Watts is Associate Professor of French and Executive Director of the Center for International Studies at Tulane University. Along with numerous articles on postcolonial discourses in the francophone world, he is the author of *Packaging Post/Coloniality: The Manufacture of Literary Identities in the Francophone World* (Lexington, 2004).

Index

Action Française, 25, 47
Adorno, Theodor, 101
affirmative action, 8, 11, 60, 74, 116
alienation, 2, 29, 38, 50, 70, 140, 163, 170, 184, 190
Alleg, Henri, 37
allographic, 15, 194, 201, 203–204, 207
Anthologie de la nouvelle poésie nègre et malgache de langue française, 8, 16–17, 31, 63, 195, 197, 200–201
anti-Americanism, 55
Antisemite and Jew, 1, 8, 25, 27–28, 32, 33, 35, 40, 55, 63, 64, 88, 101–102, 105, 109, 113, 116, 118, 120, 121, 159, 163, 199, 200, 208
antisemitism, 2, 4, 6, 9, 10, 12, 13, 15, 24–29, 30, 31, 34, 38–39, 45, 55, 64, 101–109, 113–120, 157, 159, 173, 175, 199, 234
apartheid, 8, 15, 43–45, 173–187
Arendt, Hannah, 105–106, 230
Aristotle, 174
Aron, Raymond, 3, 5, 17, 19, 103, 106
Aronson, Ronald, 176, 181, 188–189
authenticity, 35, 40, 174

bad faith, 6, 9, 25–30, 37, 57, 59, 60, 63, 65, 69, 73, 141–142, 157–159, 163–167, 175–176, 178, 180, 183–184, 186
Beauvoir, Simone de, 2, 3, 18, 162, 168, 169, 207

Being and Nothingness, 4, 8, 25–27, 31, 38, 117, 130, 134–135, 137, 144, 158, 163, 165–166, 177
"Being Jewish," 119–120
Bergson, Henri, 3
Bernasconi, Robert, 141–142
Bhabba, Homi, 198, 217–218, 221, 223
bidonville, 82–83, 84–85
Biko, Steve, 15, 163, 170, 173–187
Birt, Robert, 163
Black Consciousness Movement, 4, 15, 29, 31–32, 55, 61, 63, 87, 88, 116, 124, 137, 142, 159, 163, 164, 173, 182, 184, 188, 194–201, 206
"Black Orpheus," 33, 75, 140, 148, 161, 162, 164, 165, 193, 228–229
Black Skin, White Masks, 160–161, 167
blues, 25, 107
Blum, Léon, 88, 95, 193
Bourdieu, Pierre, 205
Britton, Celia, 3

Cahiers pour une morale. See *Notebooks for an Ethics*
Cartier-Bresson, Henri, 4
Césaire, Aimé, 1, 4, 14, 19, 129–130, 144–149, 162, 165, 193, 197–198, 207
Chamoiseau, Patrick, 194–195, 203–204
"Childhood of a Leader," 3–4, 19, 25, 27, 47

civil rights, 10, 55, 56, 58, 72, 74, 76
colonialism, 1, 2, 4, 5, 8, 10, 13, 23–24, 29, 31, 33–34, 38, 40–42, 61, 63, 77–92, 122, 129–149, 160, 173, 175, 177–178, 182–184, 196–197, 201, 213, 215, 216–219, 222, 224
Colonialism and Neocolonialism, 1, 8, 182
"Colonialism is a System," 5, 35–36, 52, 83, 182
Colonizer and the Colonized, The, 5, 7, 35, 36, 113, 141, 178, 216
colorblindness, 8, 11, 58, 74, 116, 124, 163
Congo, 6, 9, 41, 45
consciousness, 3, 7, 8, 24, 26, 30, 32, 62, 63, 65, 67, 85, 87, 117, 120, 135, 137, 159, 163, 166, 174, 175, 187, 227, 229
Corbin, Henri, 202, 204
Critique of Dialectical reason, 7–9, 38, 61, 83, 120, 136, 141–142, 160

Damas, Léon-Gotran, 162, 193, 195
Davis, Angela, 15, 163
"De l'evasion." See "On Escape"
dehumanization, 9, 10, 12, 16, 160, 213, 230
Derrida, Jacques, 171, 182
dialectic, 7–9, 15, 25, 29, 33, 35, 38, 61, 64, 66, 87, 90, 101, 117, 122, 123, 126, 130, 136–139, 141–142, 159–160, 162, 165, 169, 199–200, 213, 216, 221, 223
dialectical history, 9, 38
Diawara, Manthia, 164
Die Schuldfrage. See *Question of German Guilt, The*
Diop, Alioune, 4
discrimination, 1, 9, 15, 23, 36, 44, 58, 60, 74, 79, 95, 100, 105, 116, 124
Du Bois, W. E. B., 11, 32, 51, 55, 75, 167

Emotions, The, 175
Enlightenment, 8, 14, 28, 101, 106, 113, 115–116, 118, 123, 133
essentialism, 9, 33–34, 137, 148, 164

ethnocentrism, 116
"Être juif." See "Being Jewish"
"Existentialism is a Humanism," 6, 29, 114

Family Idiot, The, 159
Fanon, Frantz, 1, 5, 7, 8, 12, 14, 15, 16, 33, 39–40, 42, 64, 75, 113, 120, 126, 129–130, 134–144, 147–149, 160–166, 177, 185, 199, 210–202, 211–230.
Finkielkraut, Alain, 14, 115–116, 118–119, 200
Flynn, Thomas, 82
Foucault, Michel, 14, 83, 129–149, 164–165
"France and a Matter of Racism." See "The New Racism"
Franco-Algerian War, 5, 23, 35, 36, 38, 39, 77, 80, 81, 83, 84, 86, 87, 148, 153, 157, 160, 175, 178, 180
Francophone literature, 2, 11, 15, 17, 32, 193–206
freedom, 4, 6, 7, 9, 12, 14, 25–29, 34–35, 38, 42, 46, 65, 75, 82, 88–89, 91–92, 102–103, 114–118, 124–125, 130–131, 137, 157–158, 160–163, 173–177, 187, 217, 228
"From One China to Another," 34
Front National, 79, 81, 93

Gauche Proletarienne, 79, 83, 86
gauchiste, 6, 13, 78–80, 83–86, 89–90
gaze, 1, 8, 9, 12, 14, 25–27, 29–30, 35, 40, 64, 120–121, 129, 134–140, 142–144, 149–197
Genette, Gérard, 194
Glissant, Edouard, 15, 193–209
globalization, 6, 8, 23–24, 42, 45, 86, 92, 217
Goldberg, David Theo, 163
Gordon, Lewis, 186–187
groups-in-fusion, 9, 163

Halimi, Gisèle, 86–87
Hardy, Paul, 196
Haymes, Stephen, 164
Hazoumé, Paul, 196

Hegel, Georg Wilhelm Friedrich, 31, 50, 61, 66, 113, 136, 138, 143, 180, 199, 200, 215
Heidegger, Martin, 3, 18, 132, 171, 175
Henry, Paget, 163
Hollier, Denis, 15, 199–200
Horkheimer, Max, 101
humanism, 6, 12, 14, 16, 20, 28–29, 34, 87, 116, 129–149, 164, 178, 211, 217, 218, 219, 222, 224, 228, 230
Hurricane Katrina, 8, 44, 206
Husserl, Edmund, 3, 18, 125

immigration, 2, 6, 8, 13, 15, 24, 44, 79–85, 90–92
institutionalized oppression, 29–30
intellectuals, 4, 5, 10, 14, 15, 75, 79, 82, 83, 89, 90, 101, 129, 131–132, 135, 137, 139, 141–149
interior colonialism, 6, 43–44, 80, 86, 93
Isaac, Jules, 104–108

J'Accuse, 78
Jaspers, Karl, 10, 37, 101, 174, 176–177, 179, 181, 188
Jay, Martin, 38, 135
jazz, 15, 160, 167
Jeanson, Francis, 5, 153, 161
Jews, 9, 17, 27–28, 31–32, 43, 88, 103–105, 107, 110, 117–118, 120–121, 123–124, 136, 159–160, 180, 189, 199
Jim Crow, 10, 55, 60, 72
Jones, William, 162–163
Judaism, 27–28, 64, 102–106, 109, 115, 117–120

Kandé, Sylvie, 203, 204
Kant, Emmanuel, 3, 113, 231

"L'Enfance d'un chef." See "Childhood of a Leader"
L'être et le néant. See *Being and Nothingness*
La Cause du peuple, 77–78, 82, 86
La Putain respecteuse. See *The Respectful Prostitute*
Lamming, George, 164
Lazare, Bernard, 104

Le Bris, Michel, 77, 86, 88–89
Le Dantec, Jean-Pierre, 77, 86, 88, 90
Les damnées de la terre. See *Wretched of the Earth, The*
"Les Pays capitalistes et leurs colonies intérieures," 44
Les Temps modernes, 5
Levinas, Emmanuel, 3, 14, 25, 113–127, 171
Lévy, Benny, 115
Lévy, Bernard-Henri, 173
liberalism, 13, 36, 118–119, 163, 174, 187, 216
liberation, 5, 6, 15, 40, 42, 78, 80, 86, 89, 92, 118, 148–149, 157, 163, 164, 167, 183–187
Locke, John, 113
Lumumba, Patrice, 8, 39–42, 201

Mamdani, Mahmoud, 183, 185
Manganyi, Noel, 163, 173, 187
Martin, Henri, 5
Marxism, 2, 6–7, 9, 14, 35, 38, 40, 82, 89, 91, 102, 165, 189, 223
Mazrui, Ali, 186
Mbeki, Thabo, 45, 186
Memmi, Albert, 1, 5, 7, 8, 35–36, 43, 52, 113, 141, 152, 178, 187, 189, 216, 235
metastability, 162, 166
Minute, 77–84, 91
Myrdal, Gunnar, 30, 50

Nausea, 3, 18–19, 160
Nazi, 3–4, 10, 38, 55, 113, 119, 146, 174
Negritude, 4, 8, 12, 15, 19, 31–33, 38, 75, 116, 137, 148, 151, 161–162, 194–204
Neocolonialism, 8, 41, 42, 82
"New Racism, The," 20, 23, 60, 83
Nietzsche, Friedrich, 117, 143, 161, 167, 171, 218
Notebooks for an Ethics, 29, 30, 50, 55, 58, 159
Nuremberg, 55, 106, 178

"On Escape," 119
Ordre Nouveau, 79
Organisation Armée Secrète, 5, 157

paratextual, 196–197, 201, 203–204, 206
Parkes, James, 104
Parti Communiste Français, 4
Parti Socialiste, 80, 85, 90
Poliakov, Léon, 106–107
"Political Thought of Patrice Lumumba, The," 39, 40–42
Poster, Mark, 131–134
poststructuralism. *See* structuralism
practico-inert, 9, 38–39, 136, 141
praxis, 1, 9, 38, 39, 49, 68, 122, 141
"Preface" to *Wretched of the Earth*, 5, 15, 39, 40, 138, 139, 142, 161, 177, 211–230
prejudice, 2, 11, 41, 50, 52, 63, 103, 139
Présence Africaine, 4, 29, 160

Question of German Guilt, The, 37, 101, 174, 188
Question, The, 37

"Reflections on the Philosophy of Hitlerism," 118–119
regionalism, 13, 79, 86, 89, 91
Respectful Prostitute, The, 12, 13, 29, 55–76
responsibility, 6, 8–10, 14–15, 25, 27–29, 37, 39, 48, 78, 110, 114, 122, 124, 150, 162, 167, 174, 186
riots, November 2005, 8, 23–24

Santoni, Ronald, 175, 224
Saussure, Léopold de, 115
Scharfman, Ronnie, 197, 199
Search for a Method, 7
Senghor, Léopold, 1, 4, 7, 8, 31, 50, 75, 126, 137, 148, 162, 193, 195–197, 201–202, 207
seriality, 9, 38, 65, 68–70, 121–122, 141, 163
Sharp, Granville, 113
Simon, Marcel, 104, 107
singular universal, 80, 87, 92
situation, 7, 9, 14, 25, 26–27, 29, 31, 35–36, 42, 65, 117, 130–134, 137–139, 140, 143–144, 174, 177, 199

socialism, 13, 75, 87, 90, 95, 118, 187, 230
sociogeny, 140–141, 148, 165
South Africa, 8, 10, 15, 43, 45, 53, 161, 163, 173–187
stereotype, 9, 11, 12, 33–34, 48, 115
structuralism, 1, 9, 17, 164
Suleiman, Susan, 199–200

torture, 5, 8, 10–11, 36–37, 42, 59, 72–74, 145, 175, 180, 182, 189, 217
totalization, 14, 38, 129–134, 137, 139, 140–146
Tout, 78
transcendence, 3, 26, 31, 122, 135, 184–5
Transcendence of the Ego, The, 3
Truth and Reconciliation Commission, 8, 15, 181–185
Turner, Richard, 173

Union française, 196
United States, 29, 30, 34, 38, 44, 45, 47, 55, 62, 71–73, 99, 101, 102, 105, 108, 157, 160, 161

Verwoerd, Wilhelm, 179, 183–184
Vichy, 4, 19, 100, 109
violence, 9, 11–12, 16, 23, 26, 30, 36–42, 45, 56, 62, 67, 68–73, 76, 89, 94, 122, 136, 138–139, 141–142, 145, 158, 160, 176, 183, 187, 189, 211–230

white supremacy, 12, 33, 55, 56, 59, 61, 63, 66, 67, 73, 75, 162, 163
whiteness, 13, 32, 56–73, 162, 164, 189, 197
Wretched of the Earth, The, 5, 12, 15, 39–40, 113, 138–139, 160, 161, 162, 177, 202, 211–229
Wright, Richard, 1, 51, 142, 161–162, 169–170

Yacine, Kateb, 202
Yancy, George, 164

Zack, Naomi, 164
Žižek, Slavoj, 44

www.ingramcontent.com/pod-product-compliance
Lightning Source LLC
Chambersburg PA
CBHW020648230426
43665CB00008B/354